YOUR FIRST
£100,000
— ESTATE —
AGENCY

CHRIS WEBB

OWNER OF THE ESTATE AGENT
CONSULTANCY

Dedication

This book is dedicated to my amazing fiancée, Bronte. This book, like many other aspects of my life, simply wouldn't be complete without you by my side.

Welcome to **"Your first £100,000 estate agency"**. In this book, we're going to take you on a journey from first setting out in the world of property, right the way through to earning £100,000 worth of commission within a single year. Sound impossible? Follow the steps in this book and you'll be on the right path to bringing this awesome figure into your business on an annual basis. We'll work through the core areas of owning and running an estate agency business and highlight time and money traps that many estate agency owners fall into.

Let's start off by looking at what the number one job of an estate agent is. Feel free to play along at home with this one. Some of your answers to this question might be, 'to sell properties?' You also might have said to 'deliver an amazing customer experience from start to finish.' Or how about to 'become the go-to agent in your town?' These are all valid answers. But ultimately, there is one job that stands ahead of all others and is the primary responsibility of any estate agent at any time in their business, and that is to list properties and to take properties onto the market.

Think about it. If you deliver an amazing customer experience from start to finish, but you haven't got any properties to sell, you're going to struggle to show said amazing customer experience. Want to sell lots of properties and make a huge income for your business? Great! But if you don't have any properties to sell, you're going to come up short time and time again. Want to be the go-to agent in your town? Let's see how popular you are with zero houses to sell! This highlights why the top priority of an estate agent is to get properties on the market. It is the key that not only opens the door to providing a fantastic service for your customers, but to huge earning possibilities, too.

We're going to focus in and look at how to not only successfully set up your business, but we're also going to break down the overall business goal into bite-sized chunks, too. Transforming what seem like huge, daunting tasks into easy-to-follow objectives in the day-to-day running of your business.

Setting yourself up for success

Warning – this section is about business planning. Now, please don't fall asleep on me. I promise we'll keep this light-hearted. I assure you there is no 'pop-out' excel spreadsheet in this book for you to complete, though that would be pretty cool! Instead, we are going to break down our £100,000 goal into bite-size chunks. Sure, £100,000 sounds cool, but it's an ambitious aim for day one.

So, let's break it down a bit further. You want to bring in £100,000 of commission into your business, that's the goal. But let's focus on the path to get there. Firstly, I'm going to make some assumptions in my maths below – I don't know where you live, I don't know your average house price and I don't know the average estate agent fee in your town (don't worry, we'll talk about that later). Instead, I'll look at national averages in the United Kingdom. Some of you will look at those figures and think 'well, that's a bit cheap' and others will exclaim 'how much?!' but overall, like Goldilocks, we'll find something that is just right for most.

The average house price in the United Kingdom is around £290,000 in 2023. The average estate agency fee in the United Kingdom is around 1.2% of the selling price (+ VAT on top). This means the average commission for a sale in the United Kingdom is around £3,500. The next question is how many houses do I need to sell to get to £100,000? The answer – just over 29 houses over a year. Which equals between two and three properties a month.

Suddenly, this whole £100,000 figure doesn't seem so scary. But wait, we can break it down even further.

Let's be pessimistic and aim for three completions per month in your estate agency business (this actually works out at £126,000 per year, but makes a far, far less catchy book title!). To have this many properties go through, we would need to sell four homes per month. This gives us a bit of wiggle room should a property fall through after it's been sold.

If we wanted to sell four properties a month, we should aim to bring around eight properties onto the market in any given month. Again, we should be aiming to have above 50% sold at any time but this again should give us some space to breathe if we have issues down the line. Finally, to get eight properties onto the market, we will need to book around 16 market appraisals into the business over the period of a month.

This is what we need to focus on. The question is no longer 'how do I get my business up to a revenue of £100,000?' but rather, 'How do I get 16 market appraisals into my business on a monthly basis?'

This is exactly the right mindset to have with your estate agency business and a theme that will run throughout this book.

A question for you. If you're reading this book, chances are you work for yourself in your own business or you plan to in the not-too-distant future. With this in mind, are you the boss of your company, or are you the employee in your company?

Have a think about it for a moment…

So, which is it for you? Most people choose 'boss'. It sounds cooler, right? 'I'm the boss!' Not many people want to hold their hand up and say they're an employee when this question is asked. However, the reality is that within your business, you are both these people.

Let's investigate further. It's the start of the month and you need to decide what marketing campaign you are going to deploy over the coming weeks. Who is that a job for? The boss, right? Ok, so now who is going to go out and deploy that marketing campaign? The employee. What if it's raining outside and it's simply much nicer to stay inside, who is going to tell the employee to get off their chair and get outside to generate some more leads… the boss!

In most estate agent businesses, you will need to play both of these roles. In estate agency businesses I oversaw in the past, I would always host a morning meeting. To show you just how important this is, even when I am working on my own, I still hold a morning meeting – a morning meeting for just me to talk to myself. Now before you cart me away to the nice, padded room, hear me out. In these sessions I'll need to make high-level decisions about where to focus my time that particular day, but also once these choices have been made, I need someone to go out and action them. That's my inner employee/boss relationship in action.

If either of these positions outweigh the other in your mindset, one of two things will happen. One: you think you're the boss. You make lots of decisions on a daily basis, but nothing gets done – not good for your business, great ideas but very little action. Two: you get stuck in an employee mentality and your business has very little direction. You end up working twice as hard for the same result if you had just planned everything out a little more efficiently and focused a little more on working *on* the business than working *in* the business. You can see there needs to be balance between these two attitudes, one out of two just isn't going to cut it. You need to know when to plan, and when to give yourself a kick in the right direction to ensure these tasks are completed in line with the business goals.

Your sales funnel

Although this might sound like technical mumbo-jumbo from the get-go, it's actually not complicated to understand. And by understanding the sales funnel of your business, you can optimise it efficiently and look for effective ways to improve it – even just at a glance.

So, what is a sales funnel? And how does this work in an estate agency business? Let's say you are in a room full of 100 strangers. You don't know anyone here, but you have a stage and a megaphone. You want to find out who in that room is thinking of selling their home in the future.

You could just blast out 'who wants me to sell their home?' Five people shoot their hands up and wave at you. 'Cool, that was easy' you think. This is how most businesses think, in the here and now. It's great that you've got people who want to sell their home now and that'll keep you busy for a while, but what about the other 95% of people in the room? Surely some of those will think of selling their property in the coming months and years.

Let's look at a better way we could have handled that room full of 100 strangers. How about starting off by asking 'who has zero intention of ever selling their home?' These people are cold leads in your business; very low motivation and short of a divorce, death, or a child coming up, chances are they aren't moving any time soon. This will remove people who are very unlikely to sell any time soon.

Next, we might ask 'who wants to sell their home within the next year?' These are your warm leads. There will be a mix of people who want to sell now, and people who want to sell in the next 12 months, but at some point in the future, they are looking to sell.

The third question we might ask is 'who would like me to value their home for them?' These people are at the market appraisal stage in your sales funnel, motivated enough to not only say they want to move within the next 12 months, but also motivated to have you, a complete stranger, come to their property to tell them how much it's worth and if you think you can sell it.

Our final question might be 'who wants me to sell their home for them right now?' Surprisingly, the same five people are waving back at you from the last example.

You can see how our sales funnel formed with those strangers in the room. We started with 100 strangers, we then narrowed it down to people that wanted to sell in the next year, then people who wanted a market appraisal on their property, and then finally, people who wanted to sell their home now.

This is exactly how your sales funnel looks in your estate agency business. Here's a diagram below showing exactly that.

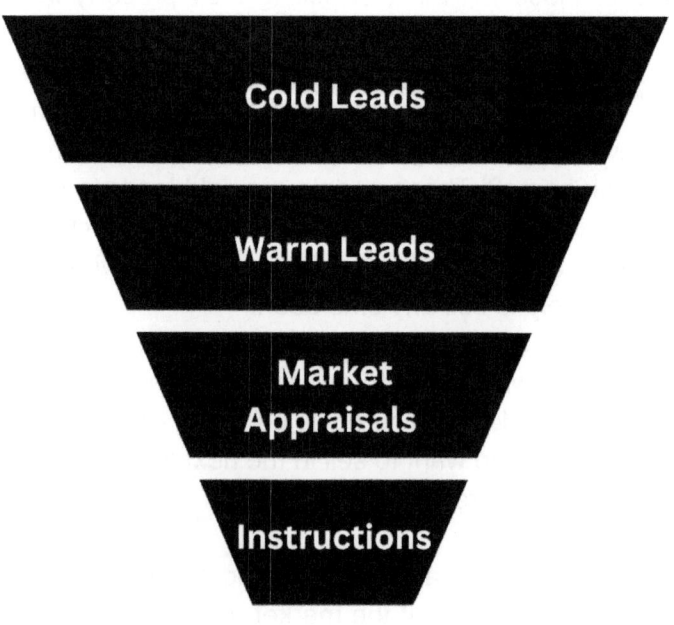

Now we know how a sales funnel looks in an estate agency business, we need to work out the 'flow' of leads going in and out of it. This is going to highlight a common mistake made by not only estate agencies, but also by many, many sales businesses around the world.

I'm going to get a tiny bit aggressive in this next bit, so I apologise in advance. Say someone is holding a gun to your head and the only way they will take it away from you is if you get a property onto the market from that room full of strangers.

Who would you speak to first? I'd imagine it would be one of the five people who so nicely waved their hand at you earlier that day, unless you have a total death wish. Good, you've survived a bit longer. Phew. Let's now say those five people have left the room, who would you go to next? To the people that asked you to value their property that day, right? Now, what if they all left the room, what next? You'd think you would speak firstly to the warm leads and finally to the cold leads, but what next? You've still got a gun to your head, and you've run out of people to talk to…not looking good!

Well, minus the gun, this happens in sales businesses everywhere. Sales professionals speak to the clients who are most likely to give them a sale first, then once these are exhausted, they speak to the next warmest, and the next, then the next, until finally they have no one left to talk or sell to.

This leads to boom-and-bust times. Because some months you'll be awash with leads as you work your way through all the warm ones. Then you run out of leads, panic and start frantically trying to find more people to sell to. This will reflect not only in the number of leads you have but will flow down into the number of sales and ultimately inconsistent incoming for your business, which is something that no one wants.

Instead, the way you should approach this issue is to be constantly looking to fill the top of the sales funnel. In the previous example, every time we found five people who wanted to sell their property, we should have instantly started looking to find the next 100 people to refill the top of our funnel all over again. Now imagine we are in the same room but as soon as the five motivated sellers waved at you, we kept the other motivated future clients and replaced the group of 100 with an even bigger room full of more people. Well, this is what you should aim to achieve in your business.

Let's put this into practice in an everyday estate agency setting. Whenever you remove a property from the bottom of the sales funnel, be it an instruction, a sale or a completion, our next job is to have a system and process in place to refill the top of our funnel with more people who might be looking to sell their home. These new people will then make their way through our sales funnel. Most won't be looking to sell, but some will, and the cycle starts all over again. This process of refilling our sales funnel ensures not only consistent leads for our business, but will ensure a far more consistent instruction rate, sales rate, and eventually consistent banking into your business. We'll look later in this book about how to achieve this result and how to refill your sales funnel consistently. Here's a diagram showing you how this should look in a correctly functioning estate agency business.

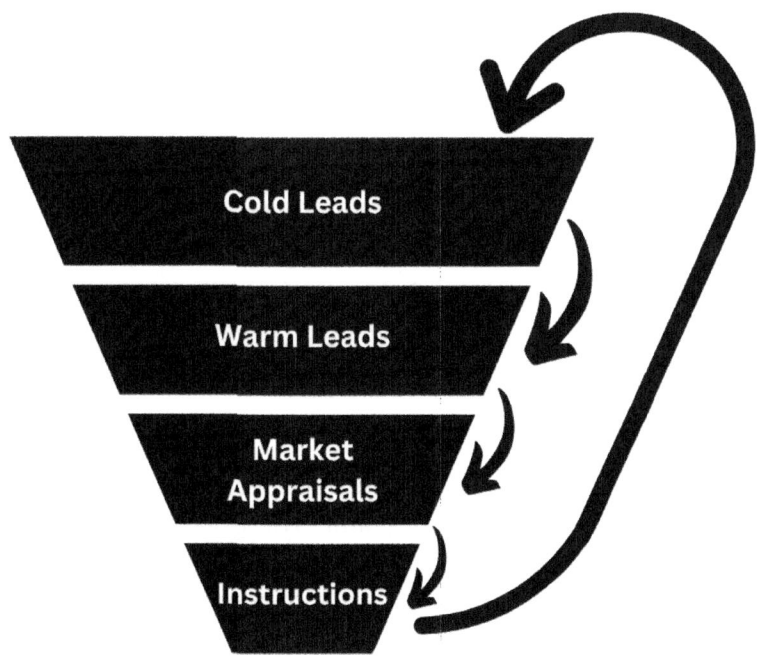

As you can see, it's a never-ending cycle. There is no start and there is no finish, just a loop of leads being taken out of our sales pipeline and new leads being put into the top.

With any sales funnel there are standard conversions from level to level and these will vary across industries, even from one estate agent to the next. The great news is that we can look at our sales funnel and highlight where our bottlenecks are. Then we can not only fix them but also perfect them.

Hypothetically, let's say it currently takes you 10 cold leads into the top of your businesses sales funnel to get a property onto the market. You might think that's pretty good, and it may well be... But what if we could improve the conversion rate from cold lead stage through to getting a property onto the market from ten down to eight with better sales conversations and marketing? If we are still generating the same number of leads, then for every 100 leads we will effectively get three instructions for free. Now that's something to brag about.

Let's explore this even further and imagine we're being instructed from market appraisal through to instruction at a better rate. It has gone from 50%, to 60%. Only a 10% improvement, you might be thinking. But scale this up further, over 100 market appraisal, that's an additional 10 properties coming onto the market with you. Even if you sell half of those, that will lead to tens of thousands of additional commissions, directly into your pocket.

You can see how optimising your sales funnel can have a massive impact on your business further down the line. The good news is that it won't take you long to have enough data to start marking informed choices for your business, probably only a couple of months. You'll see what is working well and where the potential pinch points are and put a plan in place to improve them.

If you find that your company is experiencing some months where it brings in more leads than others, or even worse, your banking is up and down, it's more than likely that you have a sales funnel issue that you need to fix to make the most of your business – and save yourself a lot of sleepless nights!

What are your USPs?

All estate agents are the same. If I had a pound for every time I've heard that expression, I'd be a very rich man. But this is the opinion of some, if not most of the British public, so we need to find ways to make our business stand out from the crowd and make us the obvious choice for any sellers in our area.

So, what even is a USP? It's a Unique Selling Point, otherwise known as 'what makes you different from the rest'. These come in all shapes and sizes; some might make a massive difference to homeowners whilst others might barely raise a shrug on mentioning them in conversation.

There are hundreds of USPs out there that you could choose from, and if you don't know what they are in your business, I suggest you learn what they are soon, because you're going to need them moving forward.

There is one USP in your business that you know more about than anyone else in the world. A USP that is so unique to you, that if you were going on Mastermind, not only would it be your chosen topic, but you'd wipe the floor with the competition every time. I am, of course, talking about YOU. There are around 7 billion people in the world but there is only one of you. There is no one else in the world with the same mind as you, skills, attitude or even the same body as you. Sure, some people will come close but there will only ever be one. If that doesn't make you feel special, then honestly, I don't know what will.

You will want to leverage this 'uniquest' of USP's to the maximum. This is especially important if you are working alone or in a small team, because by default, you are not only going to be the face of the business, but also the head of marketing, sales, complaints, and admin all rolled up into one human. You need to put yourself out there as not only the head of the business, but also its biggest cheerleader and supporter. Trust me, clients will usually go on the market with the estate agent that fits them personally. Sure, branding and marketing will get you through the door, but you, personally, will be the one they sign up to sell their home with, not your logo.

Now you've highlighted your USP's in your own business and if you aren't on that list, please go back and reread the last section a few more times. We're going to run a test for your business' USPs and I like to call it the 'so what' test. Let's pick a nice easy one to start with… Okay, we have professional photography done on all the properties we bring onto the market…

'So what?'

Erm… 'so your property will look nice?!' Wrong answer, junior.

Why should a seller care that they have professional photography of their home? Is it going to make any difference to their lives or property selling experience? Well, yes, it is, but you were confusing features and benefits. See, the feature in this situation is professional photography, now we just need to know the benefit. Did you know that Rightmove showed that the average property which has professional photography on it achieves 2% more than properties that don't? Interesting, right? So, let's try that process again, now we can say to the homeowner, because we are going to use professional photography on the marketing of your property, studies show that we will achieve £10,000 more than if we didn't. This is your 'so what'.

Did you say £10,000 more!? Okay now the seller is interested in having professional photography, and with those other agents who don't use this marketing method, the seller can see their potential £10,000 floating away into the distance.

So, you see in the above example we have made our USP relevant to the homeowner, they now see why professional photography is important in the selling of their property and this will pass the 'so what' test. Let's try one more and see if you can make this USP pass the 'so what' test.

'We appear on all the major portals' you might say… okay that's good, but so what?

Why would a potential seller care that you appear on all the major portals? I'll tell you why, more portals mean more exposure, more exposure means more enquiries, which means more viewings, which means statistically, more offers, meaning a better chance of getting more money for your property and finding the perfect buyer who can fit in with your timescale. Phew. So, more portals equals potentially more money and potentially a better buyer.

Do not, I repeat do not, fall into a trap which is referred to as 'showing up and throwing up'. This is where you spend your time with the potential seller just listing USPs that show no benefit for them and just create an endless list of '…and we have this'. You are far better off picking three to five USPs and explaining why these matter to the seller rather than the whole kitchen sink with no explanation as to why this would in any way benefit them. From my experience, most sellers want certain boxes to be ticked before they instruct any agent to sell their home. These are usually concerns they have or sale aspects that they care about and will ultimately determine whether they have had a good experience or a bad one. And these concerns are maximising financial returns when a homeowner sells their property, which is a posh way of saying 'getting as much money as possible for the property'. You'll need to have USPs on hand that show the seller that you'll be getting them as much money as possible. Don't be fooled by sellers who seem to not care about how much they will sell their property for. Trust me, they all care and want this box to be ticked whether they show it or not.

The next is timescale, how long are you going to take to sell their property and how long before they can wave goodbye to this house-moving malarky and get into their nice new property? Again, you'll need USPs at the ready to show how you can get them moving quickly and efficiently.

Finally, customer service or customer experience is important so you'll want USPs that demonstrate that you can and will do what you have promised. This might be from reviews, testimonials or even just a 5-star ranking on Google from previous clients.

Most potential sellers you meet with will want the three options above ticked in some way, for some it might all be about the money and customer service is low down their radar. For others, money is less important because they just want to move quickly. Your skill is going to be understanding what is important to the seller and picking the USPs out of your arsenal that suit that valuation and their current needs.

Mystery shopping

You're soon going to be the new kid in town with your Estate Agency business. You'll want to know what the other agents are up to in your area and how their offering differs from your own. After all, is a USP all that unique if everyone else does it?

Well, it's time to get your investigation hat on and see what everyone else is doing. An easy place to start is other agents' own websites: how do they present the properties that they are currently selling? Is their website even any good or are you getting flashbacks to 2001? Once you've done this you can then move onto their social media accounts: what do they do on here? How active are they? How often do they post and what's the overall theme of the account? At this stage you should have a pretty good idea about what other agents in your town are about. Now the real fun begins – mystery shopping.

Let me caveat this first, if you have been an estate agent in your local town for the last 20 years, don't all of a sudden start doing the rounds of the other local estate agents asking for property details and a valuation on your home. They'll know who you are, and you'll get a completely different customer experience than a random member of the public would get, making the whole thing a waste of time. On the other hand, if you are not known to the local estate agents, then by all means go round to a few either alone or with your partner and register looking for a property to buy. You can even book a market appraisal on your own property and experience the other agents first hand in your living room. You can see how they pitch their services, which USP they have as their 'go-to' and what their customer journey looks like. If you are well known in your local town, ask a friend or a family member to do just this on your behalf. Afterwards, they can tell you how it went – good bits and bad bits – and they can pass over any marketing collateral they received on the market appraisal appointment for you to look at, so you understand how their business works.

Two bits of information outside of the overall customer experience that you'll want to either find out yourself or get your nominated friend to find out for you is, firstly how much the local agent charges for selling a property. This information will come in useful on other valuations you go to later down the line when you might be up against that agent. The other is how long they 'tie-in' potential sellers to go onto the market with them. This is the amount of time that a seller is committing to stay with that agent, at a minimum. This tie-in varies from zero-week contracts right through to 26 weeks, which is six months to you and me.

Once we've got all this information, we'll have a greater understanding of what the standard is for estate agencies in our local area. Certain parts of the other agents' sales process may have made you cringe and think to yourself 'well, I'm definitely not going to include that in my sales pitch' whilst other parts might have you thinking 'that's quite clever, I'll use that in my own business.' Either way, having this knowledge is only going to help you when you inevitably come up against these local agents in the future.

While you're waiting

When you first set up an estate agency business there's a fair amount of paperwork involved. And even once that is done, you still need to wait for business cards, leaflets and even For Sale boards to be printed. This is going to leave us with some time on our hands whilst we are navigating the exciting world of Companies House and the joys of the HMRC website. So, what should we be doing with ourselves over this time?

Well, we should be putting ourselves in the best possible position to launch our business in the coming weeks and months. This will mean getting as much groundwork done for our estate agency as we possibly can, so that once the starting gun goes off, we're not thinking about what we should be doing next, because we know what we need to do.

They say that we are only six degrees of separation away from anyone in the world at any time. That means that if you went through six different people in the world who all know each other in some way, you would be able to be connected to anyone on the planet. With this next job we are going to use this to our advantage. The first job is to record a video of yourself saying something like the below, and if you don't feel very imaginative, just read out the below in front of the camera. And yes, you need to be able to see yourself in this video, no hiding!

'Hello. I hope you are well. You may have seen online that I'm just about to launch my own estate agency business in *insert your area here*. It would be amazing if you knew anyone that was looking to sell, buy, or rent out their property in that area and it would really help me out. If you do know anyone, I would be so grateful if you could connect me with them. Thank you so much in advance, see you soon.'

Notice how the above video isn't bespoke, it doesn't say 'Hello Julie, haven't seen you since June last year' it's just a generic message which most people will click with. In an ideal world everyone would get a personal message, but we are trying to balance time and scale with this exercise.

In a similar direction, you could simply write a nice message out to all your contacts saying pretty much the same thing, but from personal experience people connect more with seeing a video of you and this will increase your reply rate. This is something that we want to happen, because more replies equals more chance of someone referring over a friend or someone they know that are looking to sell in your area.

Now jump onto your phone. Your job is to get this out to as many, if not all your contacts as soon as you can. A nice, easy way to do this is with 'broadcast lists' on WhatsApp. It allows you to send one message to multiple people in a few clicks. For the receiver, it just seems like you have sent one message to them and isn't part of a huge mail-out process, which it most definitely is! Select everyone who you want to receive the video (which should be everyone in your phone), upload the video to the chat and press send. There you have it; lots of your contacts have just been messaged in 30 seconds or less.

Once you have ticked off this job and all your contacts have received this video from you, jump on to your biggest social media platform and use this same video on any contacts that you haven't sent it over to already. Annoyingly, with some social media platforms, they don't allow you to 'bulk' send in the same way WhatsApp does. With the video recorded though, it will take you around 30 seconds to send the message to each contact on the platform. You can even do it whilst you're watching Netflix in the evening, which definitely counts as multitasking – win-win! Work your way through all your social media platforms and contacts until every single one has had a message from you. From personal experience if you are ever on the fence about sending the message out, just do it. What's the worst that can happen? You've currently got zero instructions, so you can't get much less than that! After you've completed this exercise correctly, every contact you have on your phone or social media should have had a video from you saying exactly what you are doing with your business and exactly how they can help you out. At this point, you may have read that last section and thought 'I don't want to message everyone that knows me about my business, what if this estate agency lark doesn't work out, I'll look stupid to my friends and family'. Trust me when I say this is completely the wrong attitude. I have dealt with this many, many times in the past and it almost becomes a self-fulfilling prophecy for your business. You don't tell anyone what you are doing because you are worried that you are going to fail, and guess what, you end up failing because you don't tell anyone about your business. Who would have seen that one coming? So, bite the bullet and press send. After all, what are friends for if you can't ask them to help you out in your time of need?

The importance of a core area

Our next job, before launching, is working out a core area to focus our marketing on. To do this we will need to take one step back to then take a huge leap forward.

We need to talk about marketing touchpoints. These are marketing interactions that you have with any business or any brand. It might be a leaflet through your door or it might be an advert on TV. Either way it's a small impression made by any business that with enough exposure, makes you connect a certain brand with what they are selling.

To show this in action, I recently took a rare trip to the cinema. It was a long three-hour film, so I thought the sensible plan was to book a screening of the film earlier than I normally would go. This meant that by the time the film finished it would be around 7 pm, a time when most people go out to get some food. In the build-up to the film there was not one, not two, not three, but four adverts for McDonalds. Clearly, they wanted to get their marketing touchpoints across so when the cinemagoers left the screening nice and hungry their next thought would be to go to the nearest McDonalds to eat. You might think that McDonalds is a multi-billion-dollar company who are well established, why would they need to pay for four adverts in one build up for a film? It's because they know the more marketing touchpoints they can get in front of potential hungry customers, the better the chance of them going to one of their restaurants. Studies show that at least 11 marketing touchpoints are needed for clients to feel like they know and trust a brand, and your estate agency business is no different from this.

Now imagine that for your estate agency business, you have selected an area to target which has 100,000 people living in it currently. You might think to yourself, 'so many houses to sell!' and you are right, there are a large number of properties to sell in that area. BUT as we have shown we will need to get a huge number of marketing touchpoints in front of these 100,000 people before they will even consider calling your estate agency business.

If we wanted to get up to 11 touchpoints with these potential clients, that's going to be 11 multiplied by 100,000 or 1.1 million marketing touchpoints. Ouch, that sounds expensive. You'd be right to think this, you could easily spend tens of thousands of pounds per month to get anywhere near that number. If that's in your budget, then great, but I'd imagine for most readers of this book, we'd be looking for something more modest. To do this more effectively, we will want to select a core patch for our estate agency business to operate in. This will be around 5,000 households per member of staff. For example, if there is one of you, 5,000 it is. Two means 10,000 and so on. The reason we have this number in place is because it allows us to have multiple touchpoints within our core area that can add up over time until you are seen as the local authority in your core patch. Effectively, you are becoming a big fish in a small pond.

So, the big question is, where do we pick for our core patch? Well, it depends on where you see your estate agency in the local market to start off with. If you see yourself at the super high end, it makes sense to target areas with that calibre of properties. Or, if you see yourself as a slightly more working-class estate agent, you will want to target areas that reflect this. As a general rule for most estate agency businesses that aren't at the extremes of pricing, you will want to target an area with solid family homes which come on the market regularly and sell quickly. This might be anything from smaller bungalows right through to detached family homes.

We can use statistics to assist us in our choices as well. We'll want an area with a strong percentage of stock coming on the market but also then going under offer as well. A good place to start with this is on the major property portals. Take a section of your town that is potentially in the running and see how many properties are currently listed for sale there and how many are under offer. Then turn this into a percentage. If one area has 100 properties up for sale and 50 are under offer, then 50% are selling. This percentage isn't a bad line in the sand for your own areas, but the higher the percentage, the better. Once you've run this task over the potential areas you are considering, you should have a good idea about where you want to target. As a side note, the 5,000-household figure can be made up of smaller areas, such as two 2,500 areas, but for the sake of time travelling and brand awareness I'd try and get these as geographically close together as possible if you can.

You might be thinking, when should I expand my 5,000-household radius? The answer depends not only on your geography but also your business goals as a whole. Let's say you're happy being a one-person band and you don't have goals to hire staff to join you. You might have 5,000 households as your core marketplace for the next 20 years should it produce enough business for you to earn the living you want. However, if you are looking to grow and expand your business beyond this area, I would usually look for around 10 properties either on the market or sold in your core patch, on average, before you think about moving into a wider area. We want to be set with these sorts of figures in place because what we don't want to do is to take our foot off the gas in one area, only to move to another patch where no one has heard of you before. You'll just end up with two patches that aren't doing very well. At least before you had one good area that was bringing your market appraisal.

Now we're at the stage where everyone you know is aware that you are launching an estate agency business soon and we've selected a core area that you are going to focus your marketing efforts in. The next step from here is to look at what marketing avenues are at our disposal and which ones are going to give us the biggest bang for our buck.

Marketing in your estate agency

Whether you know it or not, you are about to start a marketing company. Not only will you be marketing properties for sale, but you'll also be marketing your business and even marketing yourself as the trusted local property expert.

When launching anything it requires more energy to get started than it does once you are up to speed. To look at a literal example of this, think of a space rocket first trying to get off the launchpad. It will use a huge amount of fuel just to get the first foot away from the ground, but as it gets higher, faster, and its velocity increases, it can ease off the power and still maintain its pace. Your business is no different from this. It's going to take more effort to get your business off the launchpad first, than it will when you're a mile up looking down at the earth cruising along at 17,000 miles per hour.

We know already that we are going to need to get a large amount of marketing out initially to start making an impact in the local property market. You'll want to be pushing towards those multiple marketing touchpoints as soon as you possibly can. Because the sooner you get to those numbers, the sooner your business phone will start ringing. Marketing your estate agency business will fall under two main categories, one being 'done for you' and the other being 'done by you'. 'Done for you' marketing is any marketing which is deployed by a third party. The only input you'll usually have will be paying the invoice at the end of the month. An example of this might be something like Google Ads which requires a certain amount of prior knowledge to produce results, and no one is expecting you to master the intricacies of pay per click optimisation. In this example, your input in this timewise is minimal but you will be paying a bill at the end of the month.

On the other end of the spectrum, you have 'done by you' marketing, this marketing is generally cheaper to deploy but requires effort on your part.

An example of this would be delivering leaflets. They are not expensive to produce but the hard bit is delivering the leaflets for multiple hours at a time without losing the will to live. Some marketing, however, can potentially fall under both of these avenues. For example, we mentioned that leaflet dropping is a 'done by you' marketing because it's you who is out delivering these first hand. But we could look at outsourcing this to a local distribution company to do for you, converting this into a 'done for you' piece of marketing. The only change being that now you don't need to deliver the leaflets yourself, but it is going to cost you more every month.

In the ideal estate agency business, there should be a balance between these two marketing avenues. Though some businesses with a higher marketing budget in place may decide to push the line away from 'done by you' marketing and get almost all their marketing done by third parties. Whilst on the other side of the coin, estate agency businesses who don't have a massive budget for marketing might choose to do most of the marketing themselves to start off with and then look to outsource more and more as their business grows and builds a potential pipeline of future income. Otherwise known as properties for sale and under offer.

No matter which direction or shade of grey you decide to take your business in, one of the most important aspects is that you have a regular marketing budget in place. For some, this might be £500 per month whilst others might have £5,000. You should set this aside and expect to spend it. Most benchmarking metrics in the estate agency world show that for every £1 of revenue into your business, you should look to spend 10 pence of that on marketing. This means that if you are looking to bring in £100,000 in a year, your marketing spend over that year should be in the ballpark of £10,000. I should point out that this is just an average, some businesses will easily spend more than that, whilst others who put the leg work in themselves will spend far less, it's just an average after all.

To truly succeed in today's market, your estate agency business should also have a strong balance of online and 'real world' marketing. Gone are the days when you can't be online and not having a presence here is no longer a viable option. If you purely focus online, not only are you in a very noisy and competitive marketplace, but you will also find that the cost for eyeballs (maybe not even the right ones) can add up very quickly. On the flipside, if you are purely a 'real world' marketer you are going to miss out on a huge marketplace. Also, most people when they look to interact with a company, will first of all check them out online, having your most recent post online from 2006 when you first set up your profile just isn't going to fly and will certainly put most customers off.

We now know how important marketing is for our business. We have a core area which we know we are going to target, and we have a marketing budget which we have set aside to invest into our business every month. The next question is, 'what on earth am I going to be spending my marketing budget on?'

In this next section we are going to look at main advertising routes that are available to you. To start off with, this is not an exhaustive list, there is an almost endless number of advertising routes out there from postcards in the post office through sponsoring petrol pumps. Advertising companies will quite happily take your money and put your logo pretty much anywhere these days.

What we'll go through here are the main, and probably the best options available to you. And if I were launching my estate agency business tomorrow, I'd be picking from this list to get my first listings. All marketing works in some way, we just want to focus on the ones that work *really* well. Once we know what the options are we'll work through the most efficient way of deploying these in your business.

Leaflet distribution

Let's begin with a classic. Leaflets. I know, yawn, right? These come in all shapes and sizes, check your post-box most days and you'll find a good assortment of them. And what do you do with them most of the time? 10 second glance and then into the bin. This is going to be true for 99.99% of all the leaflets you deliver. This is why they are all about numbers. In fact, you'll look at getting around one market appraisal booked for every 1,000 you deliver and from a man who has delivered lots and lots (and lots) of leaflets in his time, the average person delivers around 100 per hour. So that's 10 hours leafleting for one market appraisal. I hope you've got a good audio book to listen to and a solid pair of shoes lined up. Now we need to look at what we want to say on our leaflets.

This message will evolve over time, your tagline on day one will be a distant memory by the time you get to year two. When you first start, I'd suggest a simple and clear message, which is based around launching your business in their local area. And if you yourself are local in that area, even better to make a big deal out of that. My advice would be lots of photos and not much text, the mistake that lots of small businesses make is that they want to get across so much information that they just add line after line of selling points and information about them that no one is going to read. Keep it short, sweet, and obvious who you are and what you want. Avoid 'showing up and throwing up' just in written format, this time.

A picture says a thousand words, so use them. If you are the face of the business, get your face on there! Remember the lifespan of your leaflets is going to be sub 10 seconds so get across the main points: I'm an estate agent, I need properties, call me on this number.

As we mentioned, this leaflet message is going to evolve over time into a message that converts with a better ratio. No more 10-hour walks for you, hopefully…

As our business grows so should our marketing message. Let's fast-forward a few weeks and say we have now listed our first house onto the market, this achievement is now our new bulk leaflet. Instead of we 'want' houses to sell we can now change this to we 'have' houses to sell. This shows the public that you are active in the area now and your hypothetical homes to sell have now turned into a reality.

In an ideal business you should never need to take a step backwards into the initial marketing message you were using. What I mean by that is that you are bringing enough properties onto the market, selling and completing on them so often that 'we've just sold your neighbours home' is now your new favourite marketing message. Along with a nice photo of the home you've just sold, as well. Never again do you need to just aimlessly pitch for 'we need houses to sell please'.

Letters, letters, letters.

Staying in 'the real world', the next area we should look at is sending letters out to try and get properties on the market with your agency. The first question is, who should we be looking to target with these letters? You would aim to write to people who are on the market in your area. This could also include anyone who has recently reduced their asking price and even people who have just come off the market. One of the most common gripes I hear from estate agents up and down the country is that they don't get in front of enough motivated clients on a daily basis. You have to imagine that any homeowner who is currently on the market with another agent has not only had at least one estate around their property to value it, they have then signed up with them and then gone through all necessary compliance checks. Even once they have done this, they have then had the agent around their home to take photos, and even then, invited some strangers into their property to view with the estate agent in the hopes of selling it. To go through all those stages, it's fair to say they must have a fairly solid motivation in place, otherwise they simply wouldn't have bothered to start with.

Statistically, the most likely time for someone trying to sell their home to switch from agent number one over to agent number two is three weeks after they have adjusted the price of their property. But if you wait until this point, then chances are you are going to be too late to the party, as the potential new client has more than likely already made their mind up on who they are going to go onto the market with next. This means we need to be on the 'radar' for all homeowners who are currently on the market. What we mean by this is, do the local homeowners even know who you are? If they were going to switch from their current estate agent, are you even in the running? Or would they simply go to the phone book, and flick down the list of agents to see who catches their eye?

Letters come in all shapes and messages, though they will generally fall around the message of 'it seems things aren't working out with your current agent so why not try us out instead?' I've very much paraphrased there, but if you boil most letters down, that is the gist of the messages sent out. The other avenue to explore, which is totally underused in my opinion, is the onward search for the homeowner. These letters focus on where the homeowner wants to move to and offers help and assistance in trying to find their next home. This can be a breath of fresh air for some homeowners as almost all letters they receive from other agents will follow the classic 'come to us instead' message.

If you'd like some free letter templates, scan the QR code below where we have multiple tried and tested letter templates that you can download for free and use as much as you'd like.

Targeting withdrawn properties

Targeting homeowners who have taken their properties off the market can be an excellent way of securing listings. Studies show that if someone takes their property off the market this year, there's a 30% chance they are going to list again to try and sell in the following 12 months. This stat makes withdrawn-from-the-market properties a potential gold mine for your business.

You must remember, if someone were looking to downsize because they struggled with the stairs, just because they didn't sell their property last time doesn't mean that their knees have suddenly got any better. Or the fact that someone couldn't secure that larger four-bedroom family home last year doesn't mitigate the fact that they still have three children in a three-bedroom home. The motivation to move is still there, it just didn't work out last time.

The big question though, is how do we target these homeowners who were once on the market? The short answer is direct letters, the slightly longer answer depends on if you have a buyer for that property or not.

Let's look at a worst-case scenario and say that you don't have a buyer for the property that has been withdrawn from the market. In this instance you would just use a general withdrawn letter, this letter will effectively just say, 'you were on the market last year, it didn't work, but why don't you try again?' As you might imagine with such a broad message it can be slightly 'hit and hope'. From experience, around every 100 of these letters you get in front of homeowners will result in one phone call, which is better than none, but it's not exactly setting the world ablaze, I think you'll agree.

A better converting method than this letter can be adopted but you need to have a buyer looking for that type of property in that area. Let's say you have a buyer who is looking for a property in a certain development within your core area, this is good news! We can use this person to vastly improve the conversion of our withdrawn letters going out. What we would then do is to print off all the properties that used to be on the market in this development. You can do this by simply looking at websites such as Rightmove Plus and filter by 'achieved properties over the last couple of years'. Once you find a property you think fits the criteria for your buyer, size, location etc, print this off and show it to your potential buyer. They'll look over the selection you have offered to them and choose the ones they would like to view.

Your next job from here is to send the *specific* withdrawn letter out to these properties which has an added benefit from the *general* withdrawn letter. As with this letter, not only can we include the fact that we know they used to be on the market but now we have a buyer who has seen the old details for their property and has even said they want to have a look around the property. Now, if the homeowner has any thought of potentially selling their property again soon, they are going to jump at this opportunity. From my experience doing this, around one in ten letters will get a response back from the homeowner. That's 10 times the level of just sending out the general untargeted withdrawn letters. Sure, it's more work upfront but the results speak for themselves.

Deploying letters can become expensive and time consuming. After all, you're going to need to know which house is on the market for the postman to deliver to the right property. One solution for this is outsourcing this time-consuming task. There are multiple companies out there who can automate this for you, which not only takes less time, but also can be more cost effective than doing it yourself – stamps certainly aren't getting cheaper. Later in this book we'll look at a way of doing this yourself and combining it with other jobs to not only save money, but also to be more efficient.

If you'd like to have access to both of these letter templates so that you can use them in your estate agency business, simply scan the QR code below to be able to download them.

Are you a VIP?

Keeping on the letter theme here, the next method we'll focus on is VIP letters. Also known as sniper letters. Don't be confused – these are one and the same thing, it just depends on where you work and what companies call them. For the sake of this book, we'll call them VIP letters.

So, what is a VIP letter? And where am I finding these VIPs? Is Simon Cowell looking to buy a house through us all of a sudden? Sadly not, though I'd imagine he's a very hard client to please. VIP letters are bulk marketing letters that go out to a particular area that we have someone looking in. Let's imagine you are speaking to someone who wants to buy a property in your local area and even better than that, within your core patch. They might say something like 'I'd love to buy a family home near the school, but they never come on the market', a lightbulb should turn on in your head at this point. This is potentially a whole marketing campaign from one throwaway comment.

'So, you want to buy a family home near the school? What if I could find you a property that isn't on that market but that suits your needs, would that be of interest to you?' As soon as we've got a 'yes' to this, we've got the green light to deliver our VIP letters to all the properties around the school that might fit the criteria for your buyer. The next stage would be to complete the VIP letter template which you can find with the following QR code, where you can download this and customise it for your potential buyer.

To summarise the letter, it might say something like, 'I have Mrs Jones who is looking for a good-sized family home to live in within half a mile of Winchester primary school. She lives locally and can be flexible with timescales for the right property.' In an ideal world, you want to tell a story with this letter and paint a picture of the buyer and why they are looking to move. This could include how long they have lived in the local area or how many children they have, for example.

Notice how the text is written, I've not gone into exact detail or precisely specified what Mrs Jones wants to buy. I could have said, 'the property must be three bedrooms, must have a large driveway, must have a south facing garden and can't be more expensive than £400,000' but how many properties do you think would tick all of these boxes and whose homeowner is actually thinking about selling? The reality is, next to zero. This is a technique I call being specifically unspecific. Most homeowners will read the initial text and think to themselves, 'I live in a family home and I'm within half a mile of the school'. Therefore, we give ourselves more chances of getting a phone call off the back of this letter. Will the property be perfect for Mrs Jones? Maybe, maybe not. But once we are through the front door, we can assess that. And either it is, in which case we have a viewer for the property already, or it isn't right for Mrs Jones, in that case it's a fairly simple conversation stating that actually their home is too big or too expensive for Mrs Jones, but there are lots of buyers out there who would love to buy a home like theirs.

Notice how we explained that this property wasn't right for Mrs Jones with positive reasons? We didn't say this house is too small or too cheap for our potential buyer. Trust me, you'll make yourself a lot more popular by doing it this way.

For this homeowner to give us a call off of our letter, there must be some sort of motivation to sell, whether that is short-term or long-term. Now we are now firmly on their radar as a potential agent for them in the future.

Can you think of any other marketing we could utilise for Mrs Jones looking near the school? How about looking at withdrawn properties that used to be on the market and seeing if they'd like a one-off viewing? As you can see, just one conversation with Mrs Jones has unlocked not only 500 letters going out around the school, but also specific withdrawn letters going out to properties she might want to view.

Do you remember what the number one job of an estate agent is? To get properties on the market, and what's better than one property on the market? That's right, two. For this reason, wherever possible, we should use these proactive marketing techniques on clients in situations where once they find a property to buy, we'll be in line to take their own property on the market as well. Double commission incoming.

In any letter you send out, it can be really powerful to include a 'P.S.' This could be as simple as 'P.S. If you don't think this suits you but would suit a friend, please let them know!' Another tip is to include a QR code. This can either link to your website or could even go to the online details for a recently sold property you are promoting. Anything that makes it easier for clients to get in touch with you or that sends them to your website is a good thing!

Knock, knock, don't run

What's the best way of finding clients who are looking to buy in the local area? Simple, knock on the doors of people who are currently on the market. These sellers are motivated to sell their properties and will also be moving somewhere unless they fancy being homeless for a while, which I somewhat doubt. Not only is this the most direct way of contacting motivated sellers, it's also the cheapest, verging on free, as well.

Firstly, let's look at the overall goal for a door knock. It isn't to be invited inside the property to give a valuation then and there. If you think that's your goal for this exercise, you are going to feel very disappointed and deflated very quickly. The real goal with door knocking is to get the homeowner's name, contact details and address. The good news is that if you're standing on their driveway, outside their home, then you already know the latter. That's one out of three in the bag already, nice work.

Now for a bit of role play. Imagine you own a home and you have recently put your property up for sale. At work on Monday, a co-worker asks you 'Hey, how's the house sale going?', you might say something like, 'good thank you, early days, but the estate agent seems to think it will sell soon enough'. Fast forward three months and you still haven't sold your home. Imagine how much you would look forward to that same coworker asking how your house sale was going? I doubt it's going to be your favourite topic of conversation at the water cooler, and in fact, you're probably a little embarrassed that your home hasn't sold, so you try to avoid the topic altogether. If a colleague asks you how your sale is going, for the sake of office politics, you may well have to put on a bit of a fake smile and assure them that 'it'll sell when it sells.' Even if you're not exactly over the moon to be discussing it, keen to move the chat onto something else as soon as you can.

Now imagine how thrilled this seller is going to be when you, who is presumably a complete stranger to them, comes trotting up their driveway to inform them that they are indeed on the market, and that they should have sold already. Also, that their estate agent is doing a terrible job at marketing their home and they made a bad choice by instructing them in the first place. You're probably not going to make yourself too many friends or future clients with that approach.

Instead, we want to focus on the positive part of their moving journey, the bit the owners actually want to talk about. This being where they want to move to in the future and achieving their actual overall goal. For most homeowners though, selling their property isn't actually their goal. It's getting into their next home. If there was a big magic button that said 'put me in my new house now, please' I'm sure most movers would push that button pretty darn quick. Selling the home they currently live in is just a speed bump on their house moving journey that they need to overcome to facilitate everything else.

With this in mind, let's talk to them about their goal, where they want to get to and why they are looking to move. Have a five-minute chat about how lovely it will be when they move to a larger home in the local area near to the woods. They'll want to talk to you about this far more than why their boring old house hasn't sold over the last three months. One of the key questions you will want to ask is 'have you found a property to buy yet?', if the answer is 'no', or 'we had one but we missed out on it' (basically anything but 'yes'), a lightbulb moment should happen for you.

This is a core candidate for VIP letters and specific withdrawn letters if they are in your core area. Should they be looking out of your local area, and you are part of a national network, you can offer to speak to the local agent who covers that area and see if they can put them on a VIP client list, so they get calls first about new properties. Now that sounds pretty cool and something most homeowners will jump at.

Occasionally some homeowners will say 'well, that all sounds a bit pointless until I sell this property'. Awesome, we can now chat about how their house sale is going. And what's even better is that they brought it up, not you. Two key questions you'll want to ask are: how many offers have you had? And, what has the feedback been from viewings? The reason why these two questions are good to ask, is because if they haven't sold yet, the answer to the first question is probably 'zero offers' and usually, with most estate agencies, the answer to question two will be 'I don't know, I don't hear back from my agent'. Thank you very much Mr or Mrs homeowner, you have just started digging your current estate agent's grave for me to kindly nudge them into.

If the answer to our initial question is 'yes', they have found a property, I have always found that chatting to the homeowner about their feelings and emotions around the current situation is a good way to go. Use phrases like; 'it must be frustrating sitting on the market whilst the property you want to buy is still available'. You can then use the questions about offers and feedback from their current agent to see how the sale is going and move forward from there.

If we do find ourselves on a doorstep, talking to a seller who is looking to buy in the local area, how much work do you think their current estate agent has put in to try and help them find their next home? I'll give you a clue, it'll be zero. This is where you can show your worth and blow their current agent out of the water. 'That's great that you're looking to stay locally, would you be interested in seeing if I could find some off-market properties for you?' If they answer yes to this (and most do), you can then think around setting up a VIP letter to go out for them, and a withdrawn property search.

The number one rule of doing this for a homeowner who is on the market is: make sure you tell them what you are doing! If you're going to do a VIP leaflet-drop for them, send them a video of you whilst you're out and about, telling them exactly what you're doing. If you've carried out the initial part of the specific withdrawn process and you've just delivered the letters, let them know you've done this. I assure you, the more you can communicate what you are doing for them for free, the more likely they are going to turn to you to help them to sell their own property.

We can also engage this exact process when you do market appraisals of properties. You'll hear expressions such as 'as soon as I find a property to buy, I'll go onto the market' or 'there's no point going onto the market yet, all the bungalows are sold'. This again should be a shining beacon to understand that if you can try and find them their next home, you stand a far better chance of being instructed over an agent who simply pesters them about their selling their property, hoping for their next bit of commission to come through.

There is little to no downside of having these proactive processes in place. Let's look at the options that could happen. Option one, we deliver 500 VIP letters and we target 10 withdrawn properties with the specific withdrawn letter and we don't hear back from a single one. Nada. Nothing. In this worst-case scenario, the seller who asked us to do this thinks we are awesome for even doing it and is far more likely to instruct us down the line. What's more is we've done some excellent marketing out in our core area. Option two, we hear back from one property, we carry out a one-off viewing, and they love it. Potential double deal, here we come. Option three, we hear back from one property, we carry out the one-off viewing, but the one-off viewer doesn't like it. Well, we are now in communication with someone brand new that clearly wants to sell their home and our seller thinks we are great for doing it, even though it didn't work out the way we hoped it might. Option four, we get multiple replies from properties, and we have some that are suitable and some that aren't for our one-off viewer. Well, they can't buy them all, so this is now a gold mine for future listings for you and your business.

As you can see, there is very little downside to going through this process with someone who is looking to buy in your local area, and absolutely zero downside should they have a property to sell locally.

Door knocking itself, like any piece of marketing, is a numbers game. Knock on one door and no one's home and you could shrug your shoulders, walk away and say 'door-knocking doesn't work for me.' You might be right about that one moment on that one home, but it's all about numbers. Knock on 100 doors over the space of a week, and usually around half of the owners will be at home, so that's 50 conversations with motivated sellers who are currently on the market. How long do you think it'll take before you find one who wants to change agents?

It's purely a numbers game, I promise you. You don't need to be the best salesperson because sheer quantity of number and tenacity will make up for any missing skillset. But if you learn over time what works and what doesn't work, you'll have quality and quantity on your side. This will be dynamite for your business and the best part is, it's amazingly cost effective.

Supporting local events

You may have picked up on a careful choice of wording for this chapter title. It could have easily been called 'sponsoring local events' but implies handing over money to a local event in exchange for placing your logo on some small piece of marketing that chances are, no one is going to see or care about.

Instead, we want to be 'supporting' local events. You might be asking yourself 'How can we do this if we are not financially giving them anything?' Like most events these days, publicity and exposure is key to the success of the event. It could be the best occasion ever organised, but if no one knows it exists or attends it then it's all a waste of time. This is where we come in. As an estate agent, you have access to boards that can go outside properties, and you more than likely also have a business relationship with someone who can erect and collect these boards, making the whole process even easier.

What we are going to look to achieve here, is the presence of our boards promoting a local upcoming event. We should aim for a month's worth of exposure out of each event. So, if an event is at the start of March, we should attempt to have the boards up for the whole of February until the event takes place.

To initiate this process, we should email all local schools, charities, nurseries, basically anyone that hosts events in your business' local area. We would highlight that we are looking to support the community as a whole and thus support local events to do this. What we are willing to do is to have slips produced to go onto our boards that highlight details of the event. We will then organise the boards to be erected locally.

This is all provided completely free of charge for the event itself, but the event organisers will need to provide our business with a list of addresses that are happy to have one of these promotion boards up in their front garden, advertising the upcoming promotion.

Once we know the number of boards we are able to get up, we should then get this number of slips printed to go on the ones we already have. I'd suggest you set a minimum number of addresses provided by the event organisers, a minimum of 20 to make this exercise worthwhile. You can also produce social media posts on this topic to further link your online presence to the local community.

As you might imagine, there are two big parts to making this a success. Firstly, you need to make sure you organise this well in advance, as we want to get a month of advertising for these promotional boards. You can't really do this last minute and make it work. Lots of businesses support the same events year on year, so make sure you have reminders in your calendar. Secondly, you need to be aware of your costs for going through this process. You'll need to take into account the cost for potentially printing more boards, ordering slips and getting the boards collected and erected before you go ahead. Only if both these areas align for your business should you consider moving ahead.

Once you are happy that this is a viable marketing avenue for your business to explore, it can produce amazing results. You can go from having literally zero board presence in a local area to having 30 boards up overnight, and for a whole month as well.

So you pay per click?

We're now going to shift from the real world to the online world and the main marketing options we can use. The key word here being 'main', because as with advertising in real life, on the internet there is no shortage of companies who will happily take your money and put it into 'the next big thing'. Sometimes these new shiny bits of marketing are brilliant and open the door to lots of leads for your business, but more often than not, they don't, and you regret not sticking with something that has been tried and tested thoroughly already.

Let's start with one of the easiest ways to get results quickly, Pay-per-click, also known as Google Ads due to Google being the biggest player in this space. First things first, what on earth is pay-per-click advertising?

For most of the population of the world, if you want to find something out quickly and efficiently, you pull your smartphone or laptop out, head over to your favourite internet browser and type in an internet search engine. You might search for 'Chinese takeaways near me' and a few milliseconds later, a search page will appear with a selection of local Chinese restaurants nearby to choose from. Not only this, but it will show you a star rating for these restaurants and some details about what sort of services they offer.

As you might imagine, the higher you appear on the search results, the better, in this example. I doubt anyone is queuing up to order from the Chinese restaurant on page eight in your local area.

Pay-per-click is a shortcut to appearing at the top of these search results. You are paying Google and other search engines to be at the top of the page and therefore more likely to be clicked on by the general public. This is not to be confused with organic ranking on Google which we will talk about shortly. Organic ranking is where you are seen as highly relevant on that topic by Google on your own merit, and they then place you higher up the results page. Pay-per-click is simply a shortcut to this status.

For some of the population, searching for an estate agent to sell their home will be no different than searching for a Chinese takeaway. Remember what we said earlier in the book, that some people think all estate agents are the same? They'll think about selling their home, head over to Google and type in a huge selection of searches all pointing towards selling their property. Some of these might include 'estate agents near me' 'who's the best estate agent in my town?' or 'how much is my house worth?' As you might imagine, there are almost an infinite number of questions and search terms available to the public. The job of your pay-per-click account is to connect these key search terms to a potential client of your business and lead them to your website with details there for them to click on and action.

As the name suggests, you only pay the search engine a fee when someone clicks on your advert. But what you will need to do is set a daily budget that the platform knows it can spend. It'll then assign this spend over the month. Certain keywords are more expensive than others and certain geographies are more expensive than others. I'm sure that if you want to be top of the search results in Mayfair, you will be spending considerably more than a business looking to be top of the ranking on the Isle of Wight. This is simply because Google runs a bidding system and whoever pays the most gets the top spot. Therefore, in areas with more funds to spend, the search engines will happily sit back and watch the local businesses throw money to be at the top.

Does all this sound very complicated? That's because it is. I've seen many estate agency businesses over the years try to do this themselves with a range of results, but the massive majority fail miserably at it and end up outsourcing it to a professional company. Therefore, I strongly suggest you skip out the 'let's give it a go' stage and go straight to getting a professional company to manage this for you.

The question you're thinking now is, 'Okay, how much do I spend on this per month then?'. Well, as the examples above demonstrated, it is going to vary depending on where your business operates, so let's look at an average which will be around the right sort of ballpark for most businesses. Although there is no maximum to spend, there certainly is a minimum – below £150 per month isn't worth spending, you're probably better off spending that elsewhere if that's the budget. Mainly because of the low-level keywords you'll be able to afford. You'll simply be outbid on everything that is worth having. For most businesses, £300-£500 is the right sort of ballpark. Obviously, you can spend more than this if you like, but this should be enough to get some traction off the back of it and start getting a return on your investment.

Another key point here is that one area's key search terms will be completely different from other places around the United Kingdom and even the world. I can't imagine many people who want to move to Slough searching for 'how much does a sea view add to my property value'. Whereas for somewhere like Bournemouth, this could be a common search term. This means that not only will our pay-per-click provider need to look at local changes in search terms, but also review over time what is working well in your area and what isn't. They'll then need to adjust your campaign accordingly to get the best bang for your buck in the future. I'd suggest you nudge them to review this after a couple of months of having your campaign live, if they haven't done it already.

You are what Google says you are

We've now looked at how you can shortcut your way to the top of the page on search engines spending money. What we are going to look at now, is how you can organically appear higher up the rankings on search engines like Google for free.

Let's first start off by looking at what platforms like Google want to do. That is, to show potential customers strong local businesses who are active online and have a good reputation. This means that your goal, put very simply, is to make Google see that not only are you an active business online, but also that clients are interacting with you, using your services, and having a good experience.

To start off with, before you can do any of this, you'll want to set up a Google Business Profile (which used to be called Google My Business). To do this, simply head over to Google and search for 'set up Google Business Profile' and follow the steps provided. Although this process online is fairly quick and shouldn't take you more than 30 minutes to get everything going, sometimes Google will want to verify that you are a real person and operating in the area where you say you are. They'll do this by posting you a four-digit code for you to enter online and as you might imagine, this can take a few days to come through. So be aware, this stage might come up, and your 30-minute job suddenly turns into a few days through no fault of your own.

When you are setting up your profile, you'll want to include as much information about your business as possible, including your website details, opening hours, operating areas, contact phone numbers, email addresses and so on. You should be looking at filling as many of these options as you possibly can, as in Google's eyes this is a good thing to do.

You'll now have a fairly blank-looking Google Business Profile set up for your estate agency, this is a good start, but we need to start adding extra layers to your account to make it as great as it can be and so not only does it look good in the eyes of the public, but from the search engine's point of view, it ticks enough boxes that it wants to show it to the searching public.

Let's start with the obvious one – reviews. Although these are very important, most search engines actually see these as secondary to having an active profile which we'll discuss shortly. Nonetheless, nothing declares 'I'm awesome at my job' like a tonne of 5-star reviews saying exactly that. The general public also likes to use companies that other people are using, so if you have lots of reviews, this means that other people have chosen to use you before and had a great experience. It means that new customers are far more likely to consider using your business to sell their home when they see this.

What you want to do is to get a selection of great reviews for your business as soon as you possibly can. Not only will this give you the social proof we have spoken about already and show the search engines that you are doing a great job, but it also protects you from a worst-case scenario. That would be your first review coming in and it being a one-star review. In an estate agency, you deal with a lot of people, and you can't get it right every time. But your heart should always be in the right place. Occasionally you might get the odd less-than-5-star review which you need to look at and learn from moving forward. If the first review you ever get is one-star, this can take a long time to dilute down with better reviews until it's less of an issue. What's best to do is get a good selection of reviews in place already so if you were unlucky and received a bad review, it would be absorbed by the better reviews around it, making it less of a big deal to your business.

I have seen multiple businesses I have worked alongside get an initial bad first review, even when they haven't launched yet. This is usually a confused customer who thinks you are someone else, or another estate agent trying to take you down a few pegs. Nice, right? Protect yourself by getting at least ten five-star reviews as soon as you possibly can. You should be asking everyone for a review. If you have previous clients that you have helped historically, a great way to do this is to record a video of yourself asking for exactly this, make it as easy for them to add a review, so include the link that Google gives you to get reviews added to your page. Like with most elements of this book, this is going to be a numbers game. Message five people and the most you'll get is five reviews, although probably more like two or three will actually do it. So, aim high with those messages you send, and you'll be amazed who will happily give you a 5-star review if you make it easy enough.

Don't be fooled though – this job isn't done, quite the opposite. You'll want your business to be getting regular five-star reviews as often as it can. Most of the time all you need to do is ask, though more important than that, remember to ask! Certainly, one for your inner boss to stay on top of and your inner employee to action regularly.

Okay, so we have now ticked one for the boxes on Google; we give a good customer experience and the customers we have dealt with are saying how great we are. The next box to tick is showing Google that we are active online and regularly update our page and our content. I know what you're thinking, this sounds like a big job. I promise you it isn't and will take you about three minutes a week, seriously...three.

There are two sections we'll want to look at for this, one area is the photo section, and the other is your updates section. Both of which are easily kept up to date. In both these sections, at least once a week you will want to upload at least one photograph and update for your business. This could be a photo of a house you have just brought onto the market, it could be a photo of you out and about leaflet dropping, or just a photo of your new For Sale boards arriving today. Uploading these images into these two sections at least once a week will show Google that you are not only getting great reviews, but you are regularly active on their site. I'd suggest adding a reminder in your diary to do this as it can be easily forgotten. I update my account every Monday with any photos or content I have produced that week, I'd suggest you do the same on a day that works for you.

Improving our organic search engine results is only going to help your business. It's going to assist any pay-per-click advertising you have in place as well. By simply investing a few minutes each week you can potentially save yourself a lot of time, effort, and money in the future.

Facebook adverts

The next area of advertising we are going to focus on is social media adverts, primarily Facebook and Instagram. Social media has grown massively over the last 20 years, to the point where over 60% of the world's population has a social media account. That's just short of 5 billion people at the point of writing this book. 5 billion, with a B! That's a lot of potential customers when you consider that in our business plan, we needed to complete three properties per month.

Social media is going to be massive for your business, so much so that it is going to get its own chapter in this book. We're going to go through exactly how to grow your following online and grow your business off the back of it. The section below is just about paid online advertising via social media, which can shortcut your business to being in front of thousands of potential sellers without first growing your own organic following which can be a longer, more drawn-out process.

It's no secret that social media companies hold a huge amount of information on the users on their platform. From simple information such as name, sex and age, right the way through to knowing that you like collecting model cars or you have a soft spot for cats. All this information goes into making a personal profile for you and highlights which products might be of interest to you. Suddenly you go from just browsing photos of cats on social media to being asked to donate to a local cat charity or come to their launch of a new cat care centre. This isn't by luck, you've been identified by the social media's algorithm as someone who would be interested in this sort of content and adverts have been placed in front of you with this in mind.

Similar to the previous section on pay-per-click advertising, you can create and use social media adverts in your business without using a professional to do so. If you are active on social media yourself, you'll know that every now and again the platform you are on will say to you 'fancy giving this post a boost?' or 'would you like this post to be seen by a wider audience?'. This is the social media platform inviting you to spend some of your hard-earned money on social media adverts.

In my personal experience, I find the main difference between doing this exercise yourself and outsourcing it, is not only the time saved to produce the content but also the results that it delivers. On the surface, the initial outputs look the same. You might boost a post yourself and get in front of 10,000 people. This is a great number, you might think. But is it the right people?

I certainly wouldn't want my money wasted by showing my advert to 10,000 people who have zero interest in selling their home. I'd rather my advert was shown to less people but got a better overall result. Remember your goal here isn't for views, that's purely vanity. It's for booking market appraisals. That is the ultimate measure from this, and every other marketing exercise we go through.

Facebook ads have had a setback though (or a step forward depending on your viewpoint). Over the last year, the topic of housing has become a 'special ad category'. This has been put in place for multiple industries and areas that are seen by Meta (who own Facebook) as being high-risk for fraud. This means that it has become harder and harder to specifically target homeowners who might be looking to sell in your town.

In my personal experience, this means that overtime this has reduced the quality of leads that you would receive off the back of this advertising method. This translates into you getting more and more low-quality leads before you get to any really juicy ones for you to contact. It's for this reason that if I was going to choose one main route for my online marketing budget to be spent on, I'd be more inclined to look at spending a budget on pay-per-click ads rather than social media ads because you simply get more bang for your buck from this these days.

You're on the mailing list

When it comes to online marketing, there is one method which stands head and shoulders above the rest. It's instant, it's free, and in my experience, it converts better than any other online option out there.

Email first came out in 1971, and from this first communication it has grown massively to where we are today with some 5 billion of the world's population having an email address. No wonder you couldn't get just 'your name'@ your chosen email provider!

You can use email to create a newsletter which will inform potential customers of a huge range of topics such as: what your business has coming up, success stories, reviews, videos, even some light-hearted moments. There are so many topics for you to cover with your potential customers that will lift the lid on your business and show the public exactly what you are about. After all, people buy from people.

Email can provide excellent touchpoints with future clients of your business free-of-charge on a regular basis. I would suggest sending out at least one email per month to your mailing list, covering a wide range of topics, some of which we mentioned earlier on. You need to be your biggest cheerleader on this; sold a house for over the asking price? Add it to the newsletter. Got a 5-star review? Add it to the newsletter. Helping out at a local charity this weekend? Add it to the newsletter.

As you can see, this newsletter will cover a wide range of topics rather than simply the listing and selling of homes that month. I'd suggest you create this newsletter with a number of small articles which also include at least one photo per article. If the reader isn't interested in your article about local house prices, they might be interested in the opening of your new office coming up soon. Your potential clients probably don't have time to read a 10,000 word essay about helping a local charity, but they will look at a photo of you helping out at the weekend, with a few lines of text highlighting exactly what you are doing and why it is important to you and your business. It's important to keep these articles short, sweet and complete with images to make them as engaging as you possibly can.

The big question now is, how do we get these email addresses to start with? Sadly, there is no super clever way of getting future clients' details in bulk, but we will discuss shortly how you can easily get contact details for local homeowners in your area. What we want to have in the forefront of our mind is when we do come into contact with anyone in the general public who might be interested in selling their property either now or ever, we should be looking at adding them onto this mailing list.

You should be thinking about anyone who views a property with you, anyone you have been out to value, anyone whose door you've knocked on or anyone you might previously have had contact with before you launched your business. Email will be a brilliant way for you to keep your name in the forefront of the mind of someone who might be looking to sell a property, whether it be now or in the future.

The next question is, how do we send these emails out? Well, you have a couple of options for this. Most CRM systems have a bulk email function built into them which you can use for exactly this job. If you don't have this built into your CRM, there are service providers such as Mailchimp who do exactly this and have email templates you can use to make your emails really pop out of the screen. They will, of course, charge you for this service but the costs are seldom huge.

The final option, and as a worst-case scenario, is you can just do this from your usual business email account. However, this should really be a last resort because remember that this email represents your business, so if it looks awful, so does your business... regardless of how great the content is inside. Another key point which I urge you to double and triple check is if you are going to send out mass newsletters from your business email account, ensure all addresses are entered as a Bcc option so that no one can see everyone else's email address. This would be a breach of GDPR rules, and you would need to contact the ICO to report this mistake – something I'm sure you're keen to avoid!

Setting the bar low

What is a lead in an estate agency business after all? I'd see this as someone who is looking to sell their property either now or in the future interacting with your business in some way.

With this in mind, we will want to set our bar of entry as low as we possibly can in our estate agency business. Let me explain by what I mean by this. Most marketing in estate agency business revolves around one core message and that is 'would you like us to come around and value your home?' If you rewrite that in about 100 different ways you effectively have most estate agency marketing businesses wrapped up in under a minute.

What we are asking in this question if we expand it slightly more is:

'Would you like me, a complete stranger, who you've never met, come into your home, have a look at where you eat, sleep and shower, and then tell you how much I think it might be worth should you look to sell it? All of this after you've tidied up for a few hours of course.'

When you phrase it that way, it isn't really that surprising that people aren't exactly jumping for joy to invite an estate agent round to value their home. But what if there was a better way?

What we would look to do is set a lower bar of entry for local homeowners to interact with our business, without the immediate need for them to get the hoover out of the cupboard and start to panic. After all, having a valuation is a big commitment for most, usually by this stage people have either decided to move or not and might have even found a home to move to already.

In my experience, the moving process takes most people around a year to achieve, the first six months I like to call 'the window-shopping stage'. This is the hypothetical mover's stage. At this early stage, these people will check out the property portals on a nightly basis, drive around the area they might want to live in and check out the local schools. It's nothing concrete, just a lot of 'it would be nice if' conversations and looking online. After this hypothetical stage, things kick up a gear if this motivation is right, they might start viewing properties, having valuations and so on. You might be thinking, 'Great, let's get some marketing material in front of them as soon as we possibly can, they've just got serious.' And this is true, suddenly they've gone from maybe moving to definitely moving. Chances are though, they have looked at local estate agents already and probably decided at least on who will value their property and potentially who the front runner is before they've even picked up the phone.

The question is, how do we engage with these people as early as we possibly can, ideally when they are still in the early hypothetical stage? The answer is by giving value to them. Giving value sounds very much like a nice modern term, one that no one really knows the meaning of, so I'll break it down to how I see value and how you can offer it.

Giving value is helping people. That's it.

So how can you help people? Well, you could give out free advice on all stages of the home moving process to make their journey easier and make them feel better informed. You can produce literature for them to read that is going to help them have a smoother sale and purchase. You can recommend the top things to do in your area. You can highlight the top places to live. You could talk about the top places to have dinner in your town. The list goes on and on and on.

Make something cool and helpful and give it away.

You probably think that this sounds like a really time consuming exercise, I assure you, as a person who gives away a lot, it doesn't have to be. Let's pick a nice example. Currently, as I'm writing this book, it's mid-

October. The nights are getting darker and soon it'll be winter. So, what's coming up soon? Fireworks night. Who likes fireworks? Kids (and me).

I would say that in less than 10 minutes, I could go onto Google and find out where the fireworks displays are in my town this year. I could then turn this into a pretty looking PDF with my logo showing where and when all the fireworks are in the coming weeks. Head onto the nearest community Facebook group saying, 'we've created a free fireworks guide showing where the local fireworks are so your kids don't miss them, like this post to get the guide.' I bet you'll get likes in minutes asking you for this guide. If you're feeling super clever, you could even rebrand it and post it on local animal care groups, so they know when to keep their animals inside during the displays. Once the public starts to like your post to get the guide, simply ask them via direct message on the social media platform and ask for their email address so you can send it over to them. As if by magic, you now have a growing mailing list of locals in the town who may want to sell their home in the future, no emergency hoovering required by them.

Another easy example to produce at this time of year might be a 'get your home ready to sell in the new year' guide. As it gets toward the end of the year, lots of homeowners will want to get their property ready to sell for next year. This guide could be full of tips and advice on how to best present your property when you look to sell it in the new year, you could then repurpose this guide throughout the year as your 'Easter guide, summer guide and autumn guide' with some slight design and seasonal alterations.

At this point you're probably thinking, 'I don't have time to write a guide like this', I assure you, you do. Head over to your nearest piece of AI software and type in 'what jobs should I look to do around the home before selling my property'. This will produce a bullet point list for you, I know this because I've just done it.

Sure, the list produced won't be 100% tailored for your market, it'll have some bullet points which won't be applicable, but it'll be the initial 80% that you can just tweak to make your own. All in all, this should take you 30 minutes to an hour to produce. Once it's produced, rinse and repeat the process from before! Suddenly our barrier to entry into our sales funnel has dropped from having a complete stranger around our property, right down to simply one tap to 'like' a post.

Another way to give value to the local public is with tips and advice that you give out on your social media pages about moving home. Now this is a near limitless subject to cover, and you are very fortunate that you are working in one of the topics which the United Kingdom loves talking about the most, and that is housing. You can talk about everything from how long it takes to sell on average, tips about how to get your property presented correctly, what you need to have in place to go onto the market. Honestly the list is long. So long, in fact, that when one my clients said a few weeks ago, 'I've stopped posting on social media and I've run out of things to talk about', this frustrated me so much that I spent the next 30 minutes writing a list of over 100 topics to talk about online to give value to the listeners and watchers. If you'd like a copy of this list, you can get it simply by scanning the following QR code.

As you can see, by following the steps above and adding value to local residents and movers, it gives us a way to not only build a good local reputation for giving value but also to build your local network of homeowners at the same time. It's a solid win-win for your business.

Marketing overview

As you can see from the sections we have just covered, there is a huge amount of marketing materials you can deploy in your estate agency business. And we now know that when we first start, we are going to have to add extra fuel to our marketing rocket to get it off the ground to begin with.

Just to show you how important marketing is in your business and therefore how seriously you should take it, I have a question for you.

Who do you think would win in a penalty shootout between you and Cristiano Ronaldo, debatably one of the greatest footballers in the world?

I know what you're thinking, this is going to be an absolute whitewash, right? Well, maybe in a fair fight then yes, you would absolutely lose (sorry to burst your bubble there) but what about if Cristiano only had five shots at goal but you had 100. Who do you think would win? I'd be willing to bet you would stand a pretty good chance of winning the penalty shootout. Even though you are less fit, less talented, less gifted at football and let's face it, probably less good looking than Cristano. But despite all of that, you've just beat him in a penalty shootout. Why? Because you had 100 shots at goal, and he only had 5.

What this should demonstrate to you is that having a brilliant lead generation machine in your business can cover up a lot of shortcomings elsewhere in your estate agency. You could be the best estate agent in the world and only have one market appraisal in your diary all month. The most you're going to bring to the market is one, maybe two properties if you're really good. Whereas a very average estate agent with 30 market appraisals in their diary for the month is going to trip over an instruction almost by default every couple of days.

Put the numbers in your favour and put a huge percentage of your time and effort into generating new leads into your business. This is your number one focus when you first launch a business and should consume about 80%+ of your time at work. Even when you have been up and running in your business for several years, I would still suggest at least 90 minutes of lead generation on a daily basis. That's right, even when you're busy selling and listing properties at the level you want to, I would still heavily suggest you spend 90 minutes on lead generation per day until the day you finally hang up your laser measurer.

One of the most important jobs for you to do is to record where any market appraisals in your business have come from. Without this data, you are purely pitching in the dark about what is working and what isn't working for you. When first launching an estate agency business, you need to hedge your bets and have as many options open for people to see and react to whether that is online or physical. Though over time you will want to look at which marketing routes are giving you the most traction and double down on them, as this will save you investing money in marketing that doesn't work so well and allow you to spend more on marketing you know works.

This recording process, if done correctly, is seldom a clear-cut answer. We've spoken already about the number of marketing touchpoints before someone is likely to contact our business. What if most touchpoints were from social media engagement with the client but they called off the back of the leaflet they got through the door today, where do we credit the win there? Ultimately, it was both marketing avenues working together. This is where we want our business to be – omnipresent marketing. That means that we are everywhere all at once. Check your mail, we're there. Log onto Facebook account, we're there. Drive to the shops, our board is there. This is where people will start saying to you, 'I see you everywhere I go!' and the answer to that is 'good!'. This is exactly what you should be looking to achieve.

Your social media

I'll start with a story in this chapter and hopefully it will demonstrate not only the importance of social media, but also how important it is to have an up to date, good-looking and value-offering profile.

Some five years ago, I was a spritely 30 something-year-old and I decided to start on the journey to find a new partner. So, I did what everyone does these days. I downloaded Tinder. No more going to bars for me. Sitting on the sofa swiping left or right, I could just about do, though.

Me being me, before I even downloaded the app, I started researching what were the dos and don'ts throughout this process. After all, you wouldn't want to put yourself out there, get absolutely no matches, be left feeling stupid and still single! I watched YouTube channels, read blogs, and looked at posts online. I was reading all about how to get my profile as amazing as it could be. Until finally I saw a stat which had me worried. It stated that if you connected your personal Instagram account with your Tinder account, you were far more likely to have someone swipe right on you (which is good) than if you didn't have an account.

This was apparently because people on the site were dubious about matching with someone with little or no social media presence. It was seen as a negative attribute to have no social media at all. You could potentially be seen as an online catfish, basically someone pretending to be someone else. You don't need to be one of the Kardashians on social media, but you need to have something going on there. I shamefully logged into my dusty personal Instagram account to see the last time I posted on there – three years ago… oh dear, that's not good news. Now, not only did I need to find a selection of photos for my Tinder account, but I also had to find some new photos entirely to post on my Instagram. This was turning into a full-time job very quickly. The following week, I set about uploading one photo of me with friends every day. Then finally after a week, I connected my Instagram with my Tinder account and put myself out there for the world, or at least anyone in a five-mile radius to see. A few dates later and I finally matched with a beautiful woman called Bronte who I have now been with for over five years, and we are set to get married in the not-too-distant future. Thank you, new photos on Instagram.

As you can see from this slightly mushy story, the world has changed. Having no social media presence whatsoever is seen as a negative factor and something to worry about. 'What have they got to hide?' people might be thinking. This is no different for your business, if you aren't posting on social media on a regular basis, it is seen as a detractor from your business. The public wants to go onto your business page and see a fun and successful business with stuff going on both in the property sphere but also in the local community as well.

Let's start off with what are probably the two biggest buzz words in the property industry right now. Personal brand.

What on earth is a personal brand and why should I want to create one?

Do you ever have one of those situations where you walk down the high street and you might pass hundreds of other people out shopping, when you see one face in the distance and think, 'I know that guy!' Amazing, isn't it? Out of those hundreds of people you can recognise that one particular face that you have met at some point in your past.

Humans have been around for some 300,000 years and over this time we have needed to recognise who we know and who we don't know, because if you got this wrong, it could lead to fatal consequences. Because of this, the human brain takes this all very seriously as you might imagine, even today. Your brain, though completely amazing in many ways, still cannot tell the difference between real life connection and visual connection though, which we can exploit in our business. Let me explain what I mean by this. Think of a celebrity death that may have upset you.

I'll pick a big one that got me. It was when the Queen of England died. After this event, millions of people lined the streets for the Queen's funeral and there wasn't a dry eye in the country. What percentage of the country do you think had actually ever met the Queen? You'd imagine less than one percent, yet the whole country was upset at her passing. This is because the public had grown up with and come to love the Queen being around them, not physically, but on the TV, radio, even on the corner of their mail. People felt genuine loss and sadness for someone they had never met because they had connected with her through the media.

This feeling is now commonplace in the world, people talk about celebrities as if they know them personally because they are able to immerse themselves in their world through what they post and what is written about them. This is what personal branding is all about, getting across who you are as an individual, what you look like, what you sound like, your sense of humour and so on before they ever interact with you in real life. It can make it so people feel they know you and can relate to you before you have ever actually set eyes on each other.

Imagine how transformational it would be for your business if before ever interacting with any of your clients, they already thought you were a great hard working, knowledgeable and honest person. Surely the instruction would be yours to lose. This is the true value of a personal brand.

As we mentioned earlier in this book, studies show that it takes around 11 interactions with someone before you feel you like and even trust them. If you post on your social media once a month, it'll take some 11 months before this tipping point is reached. This is far too long as I'm sure you'd love to build a personal connection with your audience far quicker than within a year. Also, with this sort of spread-out approach, by the time interaction number two comes around, chances are that they have forgotten all about touch point number one and the process starts all over again. For this reason, we should be looking at posting on social media at least three times per week every week consistently.

We now know how often we should be posting on social media, the next question is what sites we should be posting on. This is going to be mainly dictated by not necessarily which social media sites you prefer, but by which sites your buying public prefers, as this is where their eyeballs are going to be.

Let's start with the biggest, and that is Facebook. Love it or hate it, it has the most users by some distance, so this is a non-negotiable. Some two billion users are on the platform on a daily basis. The site also tends to have a slightly older demographic which will no doubt align itself with the sort of clients you deal with daily.

Next up from here is Instagram, it's no slouch with 500 million daily users. This social media platform, which is owned by Meta, has a bigger focus on photos and now video content. It's easy to connect with local businesses here and most people you encounter will have an active account.

Moving down the pecking order slightly for your ideal demographic, you also have Twitter (now called X) and its newest competitor Threads. They have a slightly different dynamic to them, but still have millions of users using their platforms every day.

Next up is TikTok, a video sharing app with 50 million users logging on every day. This site is mainly used by the younger generations who may well be looking to buy a home in the near future.

And finally on this list is YouTube, which isn't technically a social media platform, it's a video content platform. But it's very important to be on here and to post on a regular basis. The reason it's so important to post on here is because YouTube is owned by Google. We've spoken about how you will want your business to rank as highly on Google as you can, and by having an active YouTube channel you will get pushed up the rankings at double time. For this reason, it's an easy win.

At this point, you're probably thinking that next we are going to pick one or two of the above and focus on those. You'd be wrong. We are going to be posting content on them all. Now we're going to zoom in on what you should be posting on your company's social media accounts each week. I'd like to be very clear here, the part that takes the most time with social media is producing the content to start off with. Once you have the content recorded, sharing this message across other platforms takes a few minutes to do.

Timing your posts is crucial to ensure that your content is seen by as much as the public as possible. I personally post on LinkedIn a lot, and any posts that are published outside of working hours, never do well. This is because people go on LinkedIn whilst they are at work, outside of this time its user base drops away, meaning the posts get less exposure.

Different social media platforms have different peaks and troughs of activity during the week. If you'd like to know at what time of day is best to post on platforms, you can get a handy guide by scanning the QR code.

So, what should we be talking about? There are so many topics that I could put here that I could write another book in its own right. As we covered earlier, the name of the game is adding value to the people that follow you. There's a well-known marketing technique, which is called the jab, jab, jab, hook technique. Broken down, the 'jabbing' part means to add value, and the 'punching' part (the hook), means asking for the business.

So basically, we are saying give value, give value, and then some more, and then ask for some business. This can work very well but in the noisy world of online marketing and social media where everyone seems to want something from you, it can wear thin very quickly. Instead, what I would recommend is just 'jab'. Jab away and offer value to the people who might be future customers, this could be local market information, local guides, local selling statistics and so on. You've got the social media topics guide from earlier chapters, take a look at this if you haven't already. It'll show you just how many topics you have to talk about. I promise you that if you're giving out enough value, people will not only follow you, but they will tell their friends to follow you as well.

The job of your social media for the first six months of your business is not to get instructions for you. That's right, you are very unlikely to get any instruction off the back of your social media for the first six months of uploading online. Instead, your social media accounts combined with your Google Business page is going to act as a validator for you personally and as an estate agent in the local area. This means that when someone receives a leaflet from you, a high percentage of interested customers will either look at your business on Google and/or look at your business on their favourite social media platform. This is another reason why we need to be on the most popular platforms. Fail either of these tests and your phone is never going to ring off the back of all your hard work.

It's completely fair to expect that for the first six months of your business, on your social media account you are going to be pretty much talking to yourself 9 times out of 10. Sure, your friends and family might comment on the post about how nice the house you've just sold is, but it probably won't go much further than this. Not yet anyway. You will need to commit to posting on your social media account three times a week, no matter what the results are. We all like quick wins in life and we'd all love to post online and get hundreds of likes, messages, and shares within a minute but that's simply not realistic in the short term. Instead, we need to realise that even the posts that do badly are stepping stones to where we want to be in the future. Try as much as you can to ignore the result and focus on the journey. This seems near enough impossible to do but, please try nevertheless. You'll feel better for it, I promise you.

With all this in mind, what exactly should we be posting on social media three times a week? Let's start off with a worst-case scenario. You've just launched your shiny new estate agency business, so you can't come straight out of the box saying how you've just listed 20 houses for sale. Unless you have, in which case, congrats. Instead, during this launch period, I would first make a big song and dance about your business, who you are and what you are about. After all, launching a business is a big deal. It requires hard work and effort to make it a success.

After this, I would focus on what you are doing in your business at the moment. I assure you people are interested. This shouldn't be a minute-by-minute breakdown of your 9-5, instead just pick one job you are doing that day and tell a story about it. It might be, you have a buyer looking in a certain area or that someone asked you a question about your estate agency the other day and you thought you'd record a video answer for the public's benefit, too. People are interested in you as a person, and what you are up to. This all links back to the personal brand we spoke about earlier. We want them to know what you are personally about before they even pick up the phone.

When it comes to posting content online, video is king, followed by photos, and finally (someway in the distance) by text alone. You should be aiming to upload mostly video content onto your social media account. The reason why we should be leaning mostly towards video is because it allows us to get across the most information in the shortest amount of time. Not only can people see what you look like, but they can also hear your tone of voice, understand your mannerisms and connect with you emotionally, far quicker than if they just read some text from you or simply from a photo of you. Not only this, but social media platforms are pushing more and more towards video content. Remember Instagram five years ago? Not a video (or reel) in sight, now this is the medium they push the most.

It's for these reasons that video content that features you in it is a must in your business. If at this stage you notice a slight feeling of dread at the thought of recording a video, you're not alone. Everyone when they see themselves on video thinks they either look awful, sound awful or a magic combination of both. To be blunt, you need to get over this, and quickly. The first three-minute video I ever recorded took me two hours to record. Yes, two hours for a three-minute video. Nowadays, I'd be annoyed if this took me four minutes to get right. The more you feature in video content, the less it affects you, I promise. You become less concerned about how you look and sound to the point where it simply doesn't bother you anymore, but you must get through the initial stage first of all.

When recording video, there is, of course, a technical element to it. I'm going to assume you have a smartphone and it's got a pretty decent camera on it. Technically, this is all we need to get started and post our first video. It really is as easy as that. Over time, though, you will want your video production quality to improve. Again, I can speak from personal experience here. When I first started posting video content, I used the front facing camera only, although it's a lower resolution camera, I could see myself in the screen below which I found helped to ensure I was entirely in the shot. I had no microphone in place outside of the phone and nothing to stabilise the camera whilst I moved around.

After watching my first videos back, it was clear that the sound quality could have been better, so I invested in a clip-on lapel microphone. Once I started using the microphone, I then focused my attention more on the actual resolution of the video content and started using not only the bigger rear camera on my phone, but also invested in a gimbal to ensure my videos became smoother. After only a few weeks of recording, I'd gone from videos which at the time, I thought were pretty good (but now, on reflection – not that great) to videos that could hold their own. If you find being subjective to your own content hard to do, ask a friend or a loved one to watch one of your videos and give feedback on what they liked and didn't like. Just make sure you have a good enough relationship that they'll be honest and not just polite.

Even if you ignore all of the tweaks and adjustments to your video production, I assure you that 90% of video content is just doing it. Even if you don't have a microphone, a gimbal, tripod or anything fancy in any way, shape, or form, when you start posting video content, you'll start getting traction. That final 10% is simply the fine tuning at the end.

Now you've gone onto your favourite social media site and you've set up a page for your new business. You've uploaded your logo, added a cool-looking banner at the top and updated all your contact information, including websites, and you're all good to go. We're looking good so far, right? Until you look at the number of followers you have on your account – zero. Okay maybe not quite so cool, well not yet anyway.

The first thing you'll want to do is make your first post live. No one is rubbing their hands together to join a blank social media page. I'd recommend your first social media post be a video of you talking about who you are and what you are doing with your business. Keep it short and sweet, no one other than your mum is going to listen to a five-minute ramble about how you have 'always wanted to do this.' Instead, focus on the main points: who you are, what you have started and why, and what your goal is. I suggest you make this a positive message based on what the public will want as well, i.e. 'to deliver an exceptional customer experience' or 'to help people find their dream property', so that you are instantly on the same page as your public. Remember to be short and to the point, no waffle.

This is your first ever post on your social media account, it isn't going to 'go viral'. It's your baseline to make everything better from here, so please don't spend too much time trying to get this 100% perfect because you felt you 'blinked too many times in the last video.'

It'll never be perfect, just get it done and learn from both the good bits and the bad bits. I assure you, everyone with social media looks back and says, 'What on earth was I thinking?'

Now, let's look at how you are going to get your first followers on social media. To start, let's look at some low hanging fruit and work our way up from there. Your family and friends will love to see what you are up to with your new business and will follow you as soon as you send them the link. You can even do this on the same broadcast list we set up earlier in this book, asking for anyone they knew who was looking to sell in your area. I'd also suggest doubling up on this, and post this also on your personal social media page so that everyone can follow your new business by clicking on this link. If at this stage you think, 'Hmm, I'm not sure if I want to spam my online friends like that', have a word with your inner boss and come back to me in five minutes. It's cool, I'll wait. If you have done this correctly and your friends and family are following you, you already have some fantastic cheerleaders for your business. People that are going to like and comment on almost everything you post; this is a great start.

Next up, we are going to target some people that don't know you. Head to the search box in the corner of your social media platform and type in the name of your city, town or village. In my example I might type 'Winchester'. If you are able to filter 'My pages' as well, do so (Facebook allows you to do this). You will then be presented with a long list of all the pages which include the name of your local town.

This will include the local council, community centres, bowling clubs, knitting clubs, honestly the list will go on and on. Follow all of these, with two exceptions, maybe three depending on where you live. The two types of pages that I wouldn't follow would include anything about politics, and anything to do with religion, as they both split public opinion and you don't want to lose any potential clients because you are blue, and they are red. The third and final thing I would avoid, and you may have guessed it, is football teams. I'd stay well clear of this mainly for the same reason as religion and politics; it divides opinion and therefore cuts up your potential marketplace – something we do not want to do.

Local businesses will follow you back. They are always looking for online support on their posts, blogs and local messages as well.

If you are part of a bigger estate agent group offering, this next step is for you. Let's say you are part of an estate agency franchise model and they have 100 offices throughout the United Kingdom. Well, I'll give you one guess on what we're going to do next! Head to the search box and type in the name of the estate agency group, search for 'pages' and follow all. Again, these fellow estate agents will follow you in a flash as they know exactly what you're going through and will be keen to support you.

Despite all of this, doing the steps above isn't guaranteed to result in some quick wins because some people aren't as reactive on their social media as others. Don't be surprised if after a day or so, only a small percentage have followed you. They'll start dripping in over the coming days and weeks, building your following over time.

As you can see, we are heading further away from people you know. We've started off with friends and family, then moved to work colleagues and then businesses in the town or city you operate in. The next chapter of this, now that we have a solid following in place, is looking to grow your online presence. This falls into two camps. One comes under organic growth and that would be to constantly post great content that people take value from. So much value, that when people in the local area go on your profile, it's a page that they feel they simply must follow. Now this is really good but is a bit of a long-term play. If we can skip a few chapters to boost our social media presence, we should, as it gets us close to our goal.

What kind of people have an interest in property in your area? What social media pages would they follow? Well, I imagine they would follow estate agents in your town, great. These other agents are probably a chapter or two ahead of us as they have been on social media as a business longer than us. Pull up their social media pages, go to their followers and get connected. These followers are more than likely local people who have an interest in property, so wouldn't they want to follow you as a new estate agency business? This is the second camp, boosting our follower count by leveraging other similar social media accounts around us.

I would like to put a warning in here: do not go too crazy on the clicking. Almost all social media platforms have something called 'shadow banning'. This is in place to protect users from spam and people generally being annoying online. It's a formula that I'm sure is very long and very complicated which effectively means that if you step outside the boundaries of everyday, normal use on the platform, your profile will be blacklisted for a certain period of time and your exposure will drop down dramatically.

I can speak from experience here, as I was blacklisted from LinkedIn some time ago. I even emailed customer support and they confirmed it to be true. My impression per post that I was putting up on the site dropped off a cliff from being in the thousands per post, to being between 10 and 20 people, not 10,000 or 20,000, literally 10 lonely people. As you can imagine, it was a serious kick in the nuts for my social media. As I slowed down over the next couple of weeks my account went back to normal, and I was allowed out of social media prison.

This is what happens if you break the rules too much on social media. If you are adding people in bulk, please don't do 200 in an hour – that's not normal in the eyes of social media. Instead, add 20-30 per day throughout the day and you're far less likely to be arrested by the social media police and put in shadow ban prison.

Posting content and adding other people goes some way into building your social media presence. The other part that is going to help you grow and be on the radar is to like and comment on posts in the local community regularly. Ideally ones that are getting a lot of traction, as you'll just organically be in front of more eyeballs by doing this. To be clear, I am in no way telling you to sit on social media all day liking and scrolling, you're not 13 after all. Instead, put time aside every day to like and comment on posts in the local community. Personally, I do this for three different social media platforms all within 30 minutes by spending 10 minutes on each, liking and commenting on the most popular posts which fortunately due to the way most social media sites work, are almost always at the top of your feed. Once you have done this, back away from social media. You create content now, you don't consume it, like the other 99% of the world.

You'll want to join all the local community groups of all smaller villages and developments you might cover, although once inside these groups you will find that most of the group is focused on complaining about the bins not being collected on time. Occasionally someone will post that they are looking to buy a home in the area (Ding!… we can help them) or that someone is looking to sell (Ding, ding! We can definitely help here). We'll also look later in this book on how to use these local groups to help promote not only our listings, but also our success stories as well.

Dealing with comments

Once you start listing properties online your followers are going to begin commenting on them. It's important not only for the way your business looks, but also for getting more exposure on your posts, to reply back to all comments, both positive and negative. You'll always want to have an upbeat and positive tone in these communications as a rule of thumb. You'll also find that sometimes your followers will tag their friends and family on certain properties. This is awesome and exactly what we want to see. Not only would we want to connect with this friend, but also, I'd be looking to follow this with a message to see if they wanted more details on the property and potentially view it down the line.

Picture the scene, you've worked hard putting a set of property details together and you can't wait to get it online for the world to see. You upload the property on your social media accounts, you take a look five minutes later and there is one comment. '£300,000 for that shoebox? You've got to be kidding me!' You can almost feel your heart sink in your chest as your excitement makes way for a mix of anger, dread and bemusement at the situation you have found yourself in. So, what do you do? Firmly put your keyboard in CAPS LOCK mode and tell them they don't know what they are talking about? Stick your head in the sand and hope they will just go away? We're going to do neither of these, sorry to disappoint. The first thing we are going to do is take a breath. Is this annoying? Yes. Is it a personal attack on you? Certainly not. Is it the end of the world? Not for a second. And it should be treated as much.

Mark Twain once said, 'Never argue with an idiot. They will drag you down to their level and beat you with experience.' This is true of negative online comments, if you argue back, you'll just get pulled into some painful online argument which is just draining for everyone involved. Instead, just close off the conversation with a short and sweet reply and try to keep it positive. After all, you are representing your business here. A simple 'thanks for your thoughts on the matter' will suffice. This approach doesn't give the commenter any room to come back, after all, you've said thank you!

The crazy thing is that with the way social media works, the more comments you get on a post, the more it will spread. So, the fact that this person has commented a slightly annoying comment on your post actually means it will go out to more people. Thank you very much.

Call to action

What do we do next? When producing social media content, we should always have a clear message about what the end user needs to do next to progress to the next stage of the process. This might include clicking a link, liking a post, or sharing this post with a friend. These are all calls to action (CTA) on our social media page and they're crucial to the success or failure of anything we post.

We spoke earlier in the book about having the lowest level of entry into our sales funnel. Well, this is no different. Imagine you post on social media about a property you have just listed with a call to action which said 'once you've looked at this post and decided you like the look of this home, go to Google, search for our estate agency business details, be on hold for a few moments, have a chat with someone from our team for 10 minutes where they'll ask you loads of questions and then you can view this property within a week'. How many people would be interested in that? Not many, I'd be willing to bet.

For this reason, we need to make the barrier to entry as low as it can possibly be, so we must paint this clearly to the public with a call to action on all our posts. A few examples might be 'DM us here to book your viewing', 'Like this post if you'd like to live here one day', 'Click this link for more information', these are all easy tasks that are put in front of our social media viewers, telling them what to do next. Without these, they'll either just guess what they should do next, or not bother at all. Neither of which are good for our business. Also, we'll be encouraging people to do what we want them to do, which is interact with the post by liking, sharing, commenting, and so on. This will boost engagement and will mean our post goes to a larger audience.

I mentioned earlier about how you should also have a YouTube channel in place for your business. As you produce video content for your main social media accounts, I would also be posting this on YouTube on a regular basis. YouTube now supports and promotes both short-form (called shorts) and long-form videos on its site, so the length of your video doesn't really matter, it should still be posted online. You've done the hard bit already by creating the content, putting it up on another site is just a few more clicks and time spent waiting for it to upload, something that for most videos, is done in minutes. A couple of key elements to really pay attention to when you are uploading videos on YouTube. First of all, the thumbnail. It needs to be eye-catching. If at this point, you're scratching your head slightly and wondering how this should look, go online and see which video thumbnail designs catch your eye and take creative inspiration from them. Remember, this is just a starting point for your video content, you can improve them as you move forward.

The other area you should pay extra attention to is the video's description on YouTube. As we covered earlier, YouTube is now owned by Google, which means that when you search for something on Google's search engine, it is very likely to recommend a YouTube video, should it be relevant to the search. You'll want to get keywords into your video description that the algorithm can index and use. A few examples which should feature in pretty much every upload description would be your town or village name, your business name, property, homes, estate agent and so on. This means that if someone were to go onto Google and type in 'best homes in Winchester' or even 'estate agents in Winchester', one of your videos might come up.

The way to think about this content you are producing is as digital assets for your business. They won't sleep, they won't eat, they won't die. If someone wants to go on their phone at 3 am one day and watch your videos, they'll be there to happily oblige on your behalf. You'll also be amazed by the lifespan of not only your video content, but also your social media content in general. Not a day goes by without a like coming through for a post I put up at least a couple of months ago and had completely forgotten about. These are all little helpers there for the rest of your career.

In this section, we are going to have a bit of a quickfire round of aspects of social media you should and shouldn't do. After all, we want to get you up that learning curve as quickly as we possibly can. These are lessons that I've learnt the hard way, so you don't have to!

Let's start with the technical aspect of video. Always shoot higher than your eyeline, no one wants to look at the underside of your chin! This angle also makes you look better as well which is great! Always try to have your eyes on the camera, and not the screen, no one wants you to be looking off to one side. This can take a bit of practice but eventually you'll just talk to the lens. The public will watch a video with poor picture quality but won't watch a video with low sound quality. So, if in doubt, buy a clip-on microphone from day one. This will also cut out a lot of wind noise which might not feel that bad when recording but will sound like a hurricane when you listen back to it.

Moving back now to social media as a whole. Always look at which of your posts do well and which ones don't and learn from them. All your posts should always have at least a photo and ideally a video that goes up with them, therefore your posts should never ever just be text. Not only will the public skim past these very quickly, but the algorithm will also punish you for not adding some media to the post. You should also be looking to include hashtags in your posts but where possible, include them in the actual text. As a short example of this, your text could read; 'Are you looking for a #home in #Winchester to buy?' as you can see, this comes across more organically than just listing #home #Winchester at the bottom of your text. To achieve this and to fit in all the keywords you want to, sometimes it's worth starting with the keywords you want to get in, and then work these backwards into the description you want to produce. Don't go crazy with the hashtags though, the days of adding 50 hashtags are well and truly over, three to five per post is ample for most platforms.

As you can see from this section being one of the biggest in the book, social media will play a key role in your business and its progress going forward. The good news is that even if you are a complete novice at social media now, it really doesn't take long to learn what works and what doesn't. I remember when I first started posting after not being on social media for around 10 years, I felt hugely out of touch. But after posting for a couple of weeks I found a natural flow with what worked and what didn't. Just remember to always look at what you are doing now and think, 'How can I make this even better?'. That might be higher quality video, posting more often or even just saying less in a video. You have to start at some point in order to improve, so it might as well be today.

Please keep in mind that for the first six months, you are largely going to be talking to yourself with no real obvious signs that your social media efforts are working. But a lot of the public who receive other forms of marketing from you will be checking you out on social media and will want to see not only an active profile, but also one that is operating in their area, too. It is perfectly natural to look at everyone else's social media pages and think 'Why have they got so many followers and likes?'. Trust me, they were once in exactly your position, thinking exactly the same about someone else. Don't compare your chapter one with their chapter twenty. You need to stick to it. No one goes to the gym for just three days and walks out looking like Arnold Schwarzenegger. This doesn't mean that exercise doesn't work, you've just not done it long enough to see any results – apart from the red face, obviously, which is delivered usually in the first 30 seconds of exercise.

Stacking your jobs

When you first start running your business, your time is crucial. Therefore, you want to be as efficient as you can be with any task you take on. As we highlighted in the first chapter of this book, the number one job of an estate agent at any one time is to get properties on the market. In this section, we are going to look at how to deploy your 'done by you' marketing in the most efficient way, ensuring that whoever we target is going to receive the piece of marketing collateral that is most likely to convert them to a market appraisal in our business.

The first element that we need to understand is that not all marketing is created equally. Some will just convert better than others and result in more traction with the public depending on the message. For example, a bespoke and specific letter to a homeowner who used to be on the market telling them we have a buyer who wants to view their home is going to convert better than a generic leaflet going out to the same person which just says, 'Do you want to sell your property?'. It's just the way it is.

What we'll want to do is deploy the piece of marketing material in our core area to each property that is going to give us the biggest bang for our buck. For properties that have previously never been on the market, this might just be a generic leaflet through the post. For a property that is on the market currently, the most effective marketing you can do is most likely knocking on their door and asking them where they are looking to move to.

Here is a marketing conversion funnel below which should give you an overall idea of the ratio from the number of marketing units you need to deploy, to gaining a market appraisal. These will vary from business to business but will give you an outline to work from.

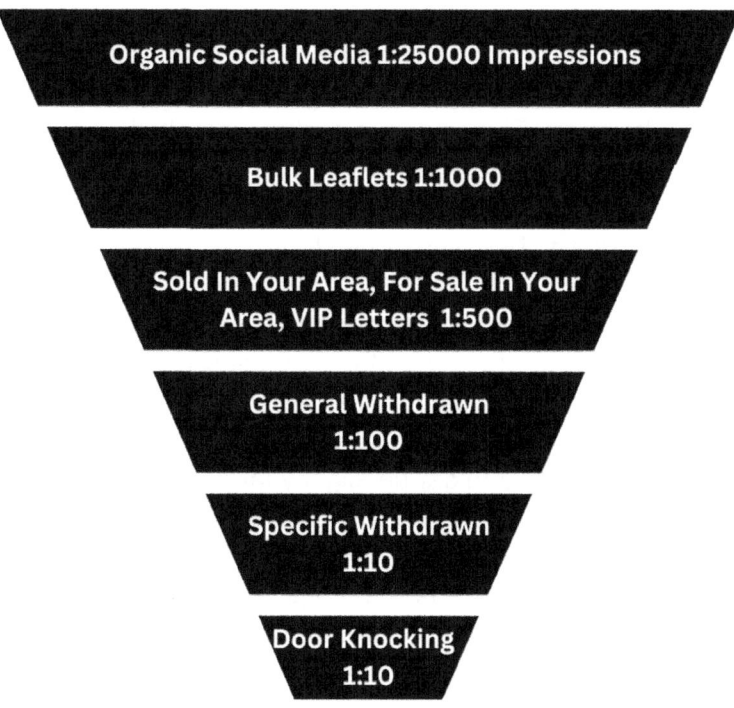

Now imagine our nasty gunman is back from our earlier chapter, and again he is telling you that you need to get a market appraisal soon or there's going to be trouble. Where would you start on the funnel above?

I would very much hope that you picked as low down the funnel as you possibly could. If someone was holding a gun to my head to get a market appraisal, my next thought certainly wouldn't be, 'what social media post can I think of to get me inside a property super quick?' As with a conversion of 25,000 impressions to one market appraisal, I'd be in trouble pretty sharply. Instead, I would hope that we'd focus on door-knocking and specific withdrawn letters to start with and once this was exhausted, we would work our way up this list onto the marketing which is less likely to turn into a market appraisal. This should keep not only us, but more importantly, the gunman happy.

You might now be thinking to yourself, 'Ok, I'll just go out door-knocking and dropping letters off through people's doors who have been on the market already.' Seriously, this wouldn't be a terrible place to start, but there is a better way. This is with a technique called process stacking where we 'stack' multiple jobs we are looking to do into one action, rather than doing them one by one. Think of it like being on a treadmill whilst listening to a podcast. Two birds, one stone.

To start off with, take your main core area and divide it up into smaller sections. For the sake of easy maths, I'm going to divide mine into five times 1000-household areas for the remainder of this book. These smaller subsections don't need to be exactly the same size, some might be slightly smaller, some might be slightly larger. But where possible, if they are approximately the same size, that would be ideal for our future diary structure. The reason we are going to divide your area up into smaller subsections is because you are an estate agent, not a taxi service, so we want to minimise the amount of time you are out driving on a daily basis because this is time where you just aren't bringing leads into the business... even if you do have a branded car. Instead, what we will want to do is be in one area for the day and complete as many tasks as we possibly can whilst we're there, before moving onto the next area to do the same all over again. This will translate into, whilst we are in one subsection of our core patch, knocking on everyone's door that is on the market. Also dropping off any specific withdrawn letters we have for that area, delivering any general withdrawn letters to a property we don't have a buyer lined up for, and this could even include a bulk VIP leaflet drop in that area if we have a buyer, or just general leafleting if we don't.

The goal of this process is that by the time you leave this 1000-household area at the end of the day, everyone living in that initial area should have the highest-converting piece of marketing (the lowest down the funnel that matches with them) delivered to their property.

This means that I could knock on any front door in that area and say, 'Have you heard of Joe Bloggs estate agents?' and some homeowners will say they had you knock on their door earlier to talk to them as they're currently on the market. Whilst others will have received a letter from you acknowledging that they used to be on the market and asking if they want to try and sell again. They'll have received this letter if they have been withdrawn from the market some time ago and you don't have a potential buyer lined up for them. For others, they might have simply received one of your bulk leaflets if they aren't on the market, or haven't been up for sale at all, you haven't sold in their area, and you've got no buyer looking in their area. This is a worst-case scenario as far as your marketing distribution goes as this has the lowest conversion rate outside of social media.

As you might imagine, this is going to take some preparation to get this process flowing smoothly on a daily basis, and you'd be right. We'll cover diary preparation later in this book, but ultimately, you would look to have all of the above prepared and ready to go by the end of the day before, in preparation for the following day.

To do this there are some quick wins to try first. Namely, have we listed, sold or completed any properties in this area already? If the answer is yes, these marketing materials are going to form the bulk of your drop the next day.

If you haven't sold any properties in the local area, do you have any buyers looking to buy in that area who would benefit from a VIP letter drop? If the answer to this question is yes, this will make up the bulk of your delivery instead.

Finally, If the answer to both the above questions is no, then our generic bulk leaflet is what is going to make up most of our deliveries in our chosen area.

Next, let's find the details of anyone currently on the market and up for sale. Again, we are doing this by area, not by length of time on the market. I don't mind if someone has been on the market for two weeks, two years, or two minutes, we're going to have a chat with them on their doorstep regardless and assess if we want to take it any further. Whilst we are doing this search, we can also highlight properties that have been taken off the market and not sold over the last couple of years. Remember, just because it didn't work out the first time doesn't mean they won't be open to trying again.

There are multiple ways to carry out this search and we're going to look at it from a worst-case scenario. There are a lot of property data providers out there who will be able to give you the full address of properties that are currently up for sale and withdrawn over a selected time period, but you have to pay for these. So, we'll look at how you do this the free way. You can always save yourself a bit of time down the line and pay for a provider to find the data for you, if you wish to.

To do this, we'll first need to have our login details for Rightmove Plus, which is the paid for section of Rightmove reserved only for property professionals. In this part of the site, you can look at properties that Rightmove not only have on the market currently, both for sale and sold, but also you can look back and see other properties that were on the market and didn't sell.

Once you are logged in, head over to the best price guide. Think of this as a normal Rightmove search but on steroids. Enter a postcode in the centre of your 1000-household area which you have selected to target the next day. Set a radius around this area which you feel covers all of your target area. You'll also want to adjust the date for the searches you are looking to do, because remember, we are also looking for withdrawn properties for the last couple of years. With this in mind, set the date parameters back a few years from today's date. You can obviously adjust this should you want to look at more recent or older properties. Then submit the form to show the properties that match these criteria.

There are going to be two stages of properties we are going to look to highlight with this process. The first being on the market and available currently, these are easy to spot as they have a nice green banner telling you exactly that. The other will be withdrawn properties which will be shown as greyed-out, archived properties. We will want to focus on the properties in this sector that don't have an SSTC label next to them. This generally means that they were on the market but didn't sell for one reason or another. What you also want to look at is the difference between the listed date and the date the property last registered with the land registry. If, for example, the property was last up for sale in March 2023 but last went through the land registry in 1999 for £200,000, we can be fairly certain this property didn't sell. Be aware though, the land registry can take three months to update. So, if you see a property without a sold price shown in the last three months, this could mean it just hasn't registered yet. In this situation, I'd always lean to the 'if you don't ask, you don't get' angle. So, if you're ever on the fence, select that property to get a letter. I'd rather we received a phone call saying 'actually I've sold' rather than not sending a letter out and missing out on the perfect potential seller.

Once you've gone through this report and selected every property which is either on the market currently or has been withdrawn over the last couple of years, most of your research is done. Phew! Follow this process through and what you'll end up with is a list of properties which are either up for sale or withdrawn from the market in your 1,000-household area. Not only this, but the report will generate a map for you showing you which streets these properties are on. This effectively is going to become our guide for delivery the next day.

Now we have the information from the Rightmove report, we will know that whilst we are out in our 1000-household area tomorrow we will be knocking on the door of X number of properties that are on the market and delivering letters to X number of properties that used to be on the market but are currently showing as withdrawn.

This means that we know what marketing collateral we will be needing to deliver tomorrow. With this in mind, we should look to print off any collateral that we need for this at this stage, if you haven't done so already. For the withdrawn properties, you can simply print off the withdrawn letter. Chances are that you won't have the property's full address unless you are paying for this service, so you can simply print them in bulk. For the properties that are currently on the market, there is roughly a 50/50 chance they won't be at home when you knock on the front door. So, you're going to want to have something to leave behind to make sure knocking on their door wasn't a waste of time. For these cases, I'd suggest leaving a letter asking if you can help them find their next home. This is a different message from every other estate agent who will be sending letters out giving 101 reasons why their property hasn't sold and why they should swap over.

If you would like the letter template for when a homeowner isn't at the property once you have knocked on the door, simply scan the QR code below.

We should now be in a position where we know what our bulk delivery for the following day is going to be. For example, as we mentioned earlier, if we have sold a property in the area we are in, it might be to deliver sold-in-your-area leaflets. If we have a buyer looking in that area, it might be VIP letters. And as a worst-case scenario, it will be a bulk leaflet asking for a market appraisal.

A final thing I will add is that on the outside of all these envelopes, I would state that this has been 'delivered by hand'. Trust me, this small add-on will increase your chances of getting a phone call from any letter you send out.

Now we know how to stack our deliveries to get them as efficiently deployed as we possibly can. But we need to look at the diary structure of your business and how to make this as efficient as we possibly can.

Perfect your diary structure

When you first launch an estate agency business, your diary structure is crucial to your success. Focus on the wrong aspects of your business initially and you'll find not only a lack of leads coming into your business, but also frustration and confusion about what you should be doing day-to-day to get the phone ringing. You will also find that the moment you first launch any business is when there is the most flexibility to get your diary structure completely wrong.

Let's say I dropped you into a fully functional estate agency business. You have eight market appraisals lined up for the coming week, you have 20 viewings to carry out and lots of calls to deal with around this. How wrong can you go? Well, as long as you do all the appointments, viewings and phone calls, you don't have a huge amount of time for anything else. Your diary has effectively built itself by having to fit everything into your 9-5 structure. If someone else called in and asked you to carry out a market appraisal, you'd probably pull a slightly pained face, but you'd find a slot to fit it somewhere that week, I'm sure.

In this example, your diary structure becomes more efficient because it has to. Whereas when you first launch, if you don't have preset jobs and tasks in, you have the possibility of just floating through the day, acting busy but not actually achieving anything. This is not what we want. For these reasons, we're going to fill your diary with tasks and jobs that you will need to focus on for the allotted period of time.

'Appointments in your diary give your power' - *Tom Panos*

This is a very well-known phrase in the property world because not only is it very true, it's also important for your business. In my mind, this works in two ways – let me explain. Imagine you are looking to buy some food from one of two food stands in front of you. One has a long queue with people waiting to order their food, whilst the other has a person out the front trying their hardest to drag people in towards their stand, but with zero line outside.

Which one of these food stands do you think has better food? The one with the queue, surely? All those people can't be wrong, can they? Now, imagine you phone an estate agent and they're free all the time to value your property. Name a time and they'll be free. How well do you think their estate agency business is doing? Not very, you'd be thinking. This means that even when we are quiet, we need to give the public the perception that we are busy. Later in this section, we'll set a diary structure in place, so you appear busy all the time, even when you're not. Popular and always having something happening.

The other way that having appointments in your diary gives you power, is because it gives you the ability to say no. Imagine you've been running your estate agency business for six months and no matter what you do, you can't get a property on the market. Now imagine someone coming forward and saying, 'Okay, you can take my property onto the market BUT I want to put it on for £100,000 more than you valued it for. And, that decent fee you suggested, well I only want to pay 50% of that'. You might be tempted to take that property onto the market. After all, it could be your first listing in six months, and it could be this or nothing. Though if we had a huge number of upcoming valuations and instruction appointments in our diary and also had a stocklist of 20 properties up for sale and sold already, I'd imagine and very much hope that you'd give this seller the following ultimatum: either we come on at the price and the fee that I suggested or I'm simply not interested, thank you very much.

As you can see, having these appointments in our diary has given us the power to say no to this seller, as we have more than enough going on without having to lower ourselves to bringing this property onto the market. This means not only a better standard of stock for sale but also better fees. In the past, I've not listed properties purely because the seller gave me the impression that they would be a pain in the backside to deal with, and I had more than enough sellers who weren't, so I happily passed on the opportunity.

When looking to set out the structure of your diary, the first place to start with in my experience, is listing all the jobs and tasks that you need to get into your diary on a weekly basis, I mean all of them. Below I'll put a list of the most common ones, but you might have some additional tasks that you will want to add in to create your structure. You should end up in a position where if it isn't in your work diary, it simply doesn't exist. For example, if you need to be away from the office for an hour every two weeks to go to a Zumba class, that's fine. But it needs to be in your diary.

One of the most important parts of your day as we covered in earlier chapters, is having a daily morning meeting in your business. In this meeting you will recap what tasks you carried out the day before, what went well, and what didn't. You are also going to look at what you have in your diary for the coming day and look for business opportunities there that you can capitalise on. You'll also make sure you have everything in place for the coming week to ensure you can fulfil your job to your full potential. And yes, if you operate on your own, you should still spend five minutes each day going through this process.

Next, we'll look at probably the least exciting topic in your business and that is administration time. Every business has admin, you can't escape it and estate agencies are no exception. In the same way that you can't escape it, admin never ends. You can always redo a spreadsheet or put your paperwork in a different order. Admin truly never ends. Please remember this, you'll never be done.

Luckily, in the estate agency world, there is very little admin to do on a daily basis. As regulation in the property world gets tighter and tighter, this may change. But at the moment, it is a very admin-light industry. For this reason, we need to make sure that our admin time not only has a start time, but more importantly an end time each day. I'd always suggest that this is one of the first things you should do when you get to your desk in the morning. I'd also give yourself a maximum of 30 minutes admin time per day, that's it. If it's urgent enough, you'll fit it into that time, if it isn't, then it'll simply roll over onto the next day. This start-and-stop time gives you permission to put your excel spreadsheet down after 30 minutes and move onto the next task.

The next section in your day will be hitting the phones and getting feedback from the previous day's viewings, chasing any market appraisals that are due for chasing that day, and dealing with any subsequent offers that might come in around this time. If your business is brand new, you might miss this stage completely, but when you do start having people to chase up, feedback to obtain, I suggest you put this in as the second job you do each day. One of the core reasons it's in so early in the day is because you will have sellers who had viewings the day before and will want to hear from you, eager to know how the viewing went. Also, if you do have an offer to put forward, this gives you a good amount of time that day to get all the information you need to accurately submit that offer. Which is something we'll cover in more detail in later chapters.

On the average day, this should take around 30 minutes again, but if you have no houses for sale then it might be zero. And if you hosted 40 viewings the previous day, then this will take you significantly longer!

We know already from the previous chapters that we should be looking to put some time aside at the end of each day to prepare for the next. We'll want to have time aside where we can plan and produce any marketing material and print any letters that we might need. This will also give us time to prepare where we're going to go and which properties we're going to target, so when it comes to the following day, we can head out the door without having to organise anything else.

This should take no more than 30 minutes to do. If you are printing off lots of your marketing materials in bulk, it may even take a lot less. In fact, researching and highlighting which properties you can target for door-knocking and withdrawn letters should take you no longer than 15 minutes, once you know how to do it. One of the reasons that this is done at the end of the day before and not in the morning for the day ahead is that, as I'm sure, you'll be keen to finish work and spend time with your loved ones. Therefore, this should motivate you to get this job done swiftly. Also, you can come to work the next day with a structure and what you need to achieve this laid out for you.

There are going to be certain jobs that you only need to do once a week (at least) and one of those is updating and adding content to your Google Business page as mentioned in earlier chapters. This is a very important job to keep you ranking higher on search engines in your local area. You'll also want to spend 15 minutes a week planning your social media for the coming week. One of the biggest mistakes I see estate agents make is they get out of the office to do something social media-worthy but then completely forget to record any content about it. Then they realise about two days later when they don't have anything to upload. These 15 minutes are to stop exactly that. Spend 15 minutes looking at your diary for the week ahead and highlight where you're going to be and what opportunities for recording a video you might have coming up. Starting viewings on Saturday? Great, record a video whilst you're there. Got a new property coming onto the market on Wednesday? Super, record a video whilst you're on the appointment. If you are doing this correctly you should never need to make a one-off journey just to record a social media post because you will have already planned it in your diary and completed it whilst you were there the first time.

Another task that you will want to have in your diary once a week is vendor care. I'm not going to go into too much detail here as this is a massive topic and deserves a full chapter to do it justice. For this section though, you'll need to understand that it is crucial to speak to anyone who has their property on the market with you once a week at least. The easiest way to ensure this happens is to rule out a time slot in your diary to do this task. Opinions vary about when the best day or time to do this is, personally I've always scheduled this task for a Wednesday afternoon just after lunchtime. This is a section of your diary that you simply don't book over. It's free time where you set yourself the goal to speak to and update your sellers. After all, what's the point of working your backside off to get instructions onto your books if you aren't going to provide any communication to them resulting in them leaving you? If you have no properties to sell, then clearly you don't need to have this in your diary. But if you're working with lots of sellers, then you'll want to set aside more time to make sure they are all communicated with, or at least attempted, as you can't always guarantee someone will answer their phone.

As you can see from this diary structure layout, it is heavily weighted towards the beginning of the day being in the office and back again at the end of the day, when you're doing your preparation work for the coming day. This means that we have a huge amount of time during the bulk of the day to focus on growing our estate agency business. This core time is going to be focused on generating leads because without these we really are up the creek without a paddle.

Remember our 5000-household core patch we selected earlier in this book that we then subdivided into smaller areas? In our example we made them into five smaller 1000-household patches. Well, this process allows us to not only transport this into our diary in a more efficient way but also adds an element of achievement as you deliver them in your local area. You can tick off each patch as you complete it rather than having one larger area to target, which could feel endless. This means that we should be targeting each of our subareas before moving onto the next, and our diaries should reflect this.

For example, you might start your week in area one of your patch – your first 1000 households. you would stay in this area until you have finished it and after it has been completed, you would move onto area two, three, four and finally, area five. When this is finished, you will have effectively completed an entire lap of our core area and everyone in that area should have had the most effective piece of marketing delivered to them. Remember, the test here is that when you leave an area, you should be able to knock on any door in this patch and ask them about your estate agency. Some who answer the door will say they received a leaflet, others a withdrawn letter, whilst others will say 'why are you knocking on my door again today?' This means that everyone has had something from you. We are now ready to move onto the next sub area. You should be looking to complete a lap of your core area every three to four weeks. Any less than this and you have the capacity to include more households. If you are taking longer than this to do the lap, five weeks for example, you're probably leaving too much time between marketing being delivered and therefore too long a gap between marketing touchpoints, and you run the risk of the public forgetting about you from one delivery to the next.

The above diary structure is a really solid place to start, but as soon as you throw the general public into the mix it can feel like you are starting to herd cats on a weekly basis. It is important at this stage to remember that this is *your* diary, and you decide what is acceptable and what isn't. As a rule of thumb, when you start booking in market appraisals and viewings, you should wherever possible, push them towards preassigned slots that are designed for exactly that.

When speaking to the general public about when the best times of the day and week are for viewing properties, you usually get two different answers, one will state that weekends are the best time for them, whilst others will say something like evenings from 4 pm will be the best for them. Keeping this in mind, we should push viewings and market appraisals in these directions as statistically this is when most people are going to want to view a property. There's no point going against the tide as it'll just prove very hard work! This means that if anyone wants to view a property, or have their own property valued we should, where possible, book them in either towards the end of the day or at the weekend. This system isn't perfect, and you'll always get one person who insists they can't make that time but for 90% of the public, this should work. I have had countless conversations with viewers over the years where they have insisted they can only view on a certain day at a certain time, and when I've come back to them to inform them that 'that time/day doesn't work' they quickly changed their mind and magically became available. You just need to back yourself and have the strength and resolve to push them into a more efficient position for your business.

The trap that lots of estate agents fall into, especially when they first launch, is they just want to say yes. 'Can I view the property at 10.30 am on Wednesday?', 'Yes'. 'Can I view that house during my lunch break on Friday?', 'Yes'. Really the answer shouldn't be yes in these examples as they fall outside our allotted viewing times from 4 pm and at the weekend, we should at least be exploring other options before simply agreeing with what works best for the viewer on the first go.

Imagine you have three viewings on a single property in a day. You could potentially have one at 10 am, one at 1 pm and one at 4 pm. With travel time there and back, this might add up to over three hours of viewing time. Now imagine instead, if we had them all book in 30 minutes apart but on the same part of the day. One at 4 pm, one at 4.30 pm and one at 5 pm. Even if we add the travel time, we have more than likely saved an hour of wasted time which we can then use to generate more leads into our business. Now picture this happening every day of the week. Suddenly, you are wasting over five hours per week travelling to appointments which you simply don't have to do. Sure, you feel busy, but you're not being efficient at your job. This is where your employee/boss mindset should give you a prod and tell you exactly that.

Getting leads into your business

We should by now have a really solid idea of how we are going to get leads into our business. Spoiler alert, it's all a numbers game. The more marketing you can get in front of your potential local sellers, the more leads you are going to get and the more leads you are going to get equals more instructions for you to sell. Awesome. Estate agency is one of those wonderful industries where there is always more to do, so if you ever find yourself thinking about what to do next, lead generation is probably the answer.

To be 100% clear on the way our marketing should be deployed, it should be carried out on an area-by-area basis. What I mean by this is that if you are in one of your subsectors, you should be there until that area is finished and everyone who lives in that area has received the best converting piece of marketing material for their situation. The mistake that many estate agents make is they will think 'Today, I'm going to target every property that has been on the market for 16 weeks.' This action takes them on a very scenic driving route around their town for the following six hours, of which a very small percentage is spent actually delivering anything and 90% of it is spent trying to master the town's one way system in their car. You should aim to spend as little time driving around as possible, unless you have some sort of Uber gig on the side. You do not get paid to drive, but generating leads will pay out down the line. So, drive to one area, set up camp for the morning or day and just saturate the entire area, then move on to the next.

Now we are in a position where leads are going to start coming into your estate agency business, which is great. This is exactly what we have been working towards. But before we start getting too excited, there is something you need to understand. You are about to start dealing with the Great British public. Something which can be tough to judge and can be unpredictable at times. It stands to reason that we should have a good idea about what and who we are up against before that phone rings for the first time. After all, everyone is different and not everyone is just like you.

The last time you went on holiday did you try to speak some of the local lingo? I'd imagine, and slightly hope the answer to this question is yes. Even if it was just a 'please' or a 'thank you' whilst you were ordering your dinner. It demonstrates to the other person whose first language probably isn't English, that you are trying to understand them on their level even if you eventually break into 'Full English abroad' mode later on, complete with the loud talking and pointing! Well, back home in the United Kingdom, people are no different to this; we all speak and understand others' use of language and prompts in different ways. Some people you meet are blunt and to the point, whilst others will chat to you for 20 minutes before they even get to the question they came over to ask you. It doesn't mean they are trying their hardest to be rude or to bore you to tears, it's just their personal communication style that they use in their everyday lives.

A small disclaimer here, this is a huge topic in itself; people have written many, many books twice the length of this publication on this subject alone and I'm going to try my hardest to paraphrase it into one chapter. My goal is that by the end of this chapter, you'll have a good understanding of the basics. Enough so you can use it in your everyday life or at least be aware of its importance when you are meeting lots of people on a daily basis.

Studies have shown that as humans we generally fall into one of four categories. These are Q1, Q2, Q3 and Q4. You don't necessarily fall entirely into one of these boxes either. In fact, almost everyone has a percentage of their personality over multiple boxes, as we're all a bit too complicated to fit into just one, apparently. Let me explain what each of these 'Q' numbers mean. As a hint before we start, I personally find it easier to think of someone I know that falls into one of these sections quite nicely, it'll help you remember each of these in the long run.

105

Q1, also known as 'Drivers'. These people are to the point with very little padding around it. Why waste 100 words when you feel you can tell the same story in 10. A high Q1 score indicates a person who is assertive, dominant, and outspoken. They tend to be self-confident and enjoy being in control. They are often seen as competitive and driven. With these factors in place, people who fall into this category can come across as rude or blunt to others who may not understand their no-nonsense approach to conversation.

Q2, who are also known as 'Steadiness', far from drivers, these individuals tend to find themselves far more detail focused. They also tend to be more risk-averse than someone in Q1 territory. Additionally, they will value harmony in a work environment over conflict. They also make good team players and good listeners as well.

The next category, Q3, is known as the 'extroverted' personality type. This is exactly what you think it is. Think chatty, confident in social situations. They also are very expressive and can be more confident than other Qs as well. These people love to be in a social environment.

Finally, Q4, which I like to call 'Performers'. These are people who if you have done something, they have done the same thing, but plus one. Been on holiday this year? They've been twice. Brought a new kitchen and spent £20,000 on it, well guess what, they spent £22,000 on theirs and that was before they got the marble countertops in. Simply put, they're the highly motivated over-achievers of our society.

Now you have an understanding of each of the personality types, assign someone you know to each of them. Don't worry, I won't tell them which one you put them up against.

You can now see why there is such a huge possibility of people not getting along. Just imagine putting a driver in the room with an extroverted personality. After 10 minutes the driver would be insisting that the other person 'didn't shut up', whilst the extrovert might think that the driver was rude because they hardly spoke and when they did finally talk, it was very direct and to the point. This isn't a good outcome as they were both just being themselves and were unlikely to have intended to upset one another.

There is a third variable in this equation. Yes, you guessed it, it's you. To effectively manage the personality types you deal with on a daily basis, you are going to have to know what personality type you are to start off with. This will highlight which types of people you may potentially form either a strong relationship or more importantly, a clash down the line. So, pick one. Where do you stand? There's no right or wrong answer here. If you are struggling to picture where you might go, simply go online, you'll find a personality test that will take you about five minutes to complete and this will give you a good idea of where you sit.

Personally, I find myself sitting primarily in Q1 and Q3, this means that I'm pretty social and take to this fairly naturally, but also, I just want the facts of the situation. I can get put off quickly if someone is beating around the bush a bit too much. Just give me the answer, I don't need your life story to go alongside it. My future wife tells me this comes across as rude sometimes, but I don't mean it to, I just want to know now, without the scenic tour included.

Later in this book, we'll cover a key question you can ask someone when you are booking in a valuation on their property that will highlight to a good degree of accuracy which ones of these categories they fall into. You'll then know before you even meet them whether they are going to be blunt and to the point or whether they are going to spend an hour telling you how much their driveway cost to install. You can then adjust your language and even personality type to fit in with that person. That's right, you're going to adjust your personality to fit in with the way they communicate, pretty cool right? Prepare to accept your Golden Globe!

In your estate agency business, to start off with, you are going to find that you're chasing a lot of people to get their property onto the market. What I mean by this is, as soon as your website goes live, and you put one post up on social media, your phone isn't going to magically start ringing off the hook with market appraisal requests. You are going to need to proactively put yourself out there and in front of the public and motivated sellers as much as you can before they will start inviting you round to their home. In my experience, this process of you being the chaser happens until you get around 10 properties on your books, this could be five properties for sale and five properties under offer, for example. Once you get to this level, people will start booking you to value their home. Suddenly, the chaser becomes the chased. As you might imagine, being chased is a lot easier and far less hard work than chasing people around to get a listing. This means that our goal is to get 10 properties onto the market as quickly as we possibly can.

Think about it like starting out on a diet, you've got one of two options, you could either hit the diet hard and find yourself in good shape in a couple of months and then just maintain that weight moving forward. Or you could take the diet slowly and easily, some days watching what you eat, whilst other days not so much. This means that it will take you a lot more time and work to get to the same result that the first option got to in a couple of months. Maybe never even getting there at all, finding yourself yo-yo dieting over the coming years.

In reality, this is where some estate agents find themselves – never getting up to 10 listings onto the market. Sometimes they might have five, then seven, then two, then five again, and the pain goes on and on, never getting to the top of that hill. To be very clear, this is what we want to avoid. I want you to hit the marketing with a bang and get to 10 listings as fast as you possibly can.

How to best contact leads

At this stage, if we have done every step in this book correctly so far, leads should start flowing in. This is a good thing, as the more leads come in, the better our chances of getting an instruction. We're now going to look at how to best contact and communicate with any leads that come into your business. Because if you have a solid process in place for this, you will find that a higher percentage of these leads will then convert into market appraisals, giving us more possibilities of selling a greater number of properties.

The biggest killer of lead conversion into your business is going to be time. 'Distance makes the heart grow fonder' was not in any way referring to sales leads, I can tell you that right now. Studies show that quite simply, the quicker you contact a lead into your business the better your chance is that that lead will convert into a market appraisal. If I asked you what you did yesterday, for example, you may scratch your head, take a moment, and tell me all about your day. What if I asked you what you did on Wednesday last week? You may not have a clue, as too much time has passed between then and now. Now imagine that you contacted an estate agent last week on the back of a leaflet or advertisement you saw online. Chances are, by the time this returned call comes round a week later, you have completely forgotten which agent you had called, and why you even called them in particular in the first place. This is not good as we have paid for that advertising, so effectively paid for that lead.

In an ideal situation, all leads that come into your business should receive a call from you within 15 minutes of coming into your estate agency. This not only shows the customer your proactivity, but also, they are far more likely to actually remember why they specifically called you as they may even still be on your website or have your leaflet on their kitchen counter.

Not always is this going to be possible, after all, what if you were out valuing someone's property and a lead came through? You're not going to drop everything and tell the homeowners to 'hold fire' whilst you make this call to a lead that has just come through from their living room. In this situation, contacting the lead should be your very next job after you leave that appointment, meaning that they should have a call back within an hour or so of enquiring. As a very worst-case scenario and as a backstop for the business, by the time you leave to go home at the end of the day, you should have no outstanding leads that have not at least had an attempt at contact. Meaning that any leads that you find yourself with the next day have come through overnight, outside of your office hours, and haven't simply rolled over from the day before.

Now we know the timescale in which we are contacting leads, the next question is how are we actually going to touch base with them? There are so many communication channels these days that there is almost an endless array of options in front of us. We can text, facetime, record a video, email, the list goes on and on. However, all of these are secondary to the invention by Alexander Graham Bell. That's right, the good old reliable telephone. So why would we choose the phone over other slightly more modern communication methods?

In an ideal world, we'd love to see everyone face-to-face at this point, but this simply isn't going to be practical as you don't scale a business by running around all over town. The reason why we'd love to see everyone face-to face-is because if I'm talking to you in a room in-person, a massive 55% of our communication is actually nonverbal, which basically means body language. This means I could be shouting 'Hi, good to see you!' as much as I like, but if I'm swinging a meat cleaver at you, the friendly words don't really matter all that much. I think you'll agree.

38% of our communication is verbal. This doesn't even mean your choice of words either, all this means is the tone of voice you are communicating in with the other person. Again, any sentence can take on a completely different meaning depending on the tone given to it.

Finally, the words you use make up a measly 7% of all our communication from one person to another. It stands to reason that we want to include as much of the above as we possibly can in any conversation, as it allows less chance of miscommunication and people getting the wrong end of the stick. Have you ever fallen out with someone over text message before? Well, as you were communicating with them with only 7% of your potential effectiveness, no wonder some of the communication got a bit lost in translation somewhere in the remaining 93%. Although picking up the phone doesn't cover 100% of the above, it does cover a good amount. Not only can we hear the tone of voice of the other person, but we can also hear if they are rushed, if they're keen to hear from us, interested, not interested and so on – something that would be almost impossible to pick up on over typed messages. This is why the phone is your number one communication method for your business. Trust me, if you ever want to speak to someone about anything even remotely important, pick up the phone. It'll take you far less time than sending some super long email and there is a significantly reduced chance of anyone getting the wrong end of the stick.

We now know we want to be picking up the phone to leads as soon as we possibly can. But what do we do if someone doesn't answer the phone when we call them? We'll leave them a message, but not just any old message, a voicemail that they will actually want to return. Most voicemails go something like this:

'Hi Paul, I've just received your contact details with regard to selling your property, give me a call back and I'll get that booked in for you. Thanks, bye'

Doesn't exactly shout 'call me back', right? Poor old Paul probably died of boredom by the time he got to the end of that message. Let's make it so he feels like he wants to call us back as soon as he can.

'Hi Paul, I've just received your contact details with regard to potentially selling your property in *your area* and I was so excited to see that you live in *Pauls' Road* as I've got buyers looking for properties in that area at the moment. Please call me back as soon as you can so we can come round and see your lovely home.'

Suddenly Paul is thinking not only is this a proactive agent, but they are also excited to see my home and they even have buyers lined up already! Move over boring voicemail estate agents, I've got an agent on the phone who sounds like they have as good as sold my home already.

If Paul for whatever reason didn't return this initial call, I would phone him again either towards the end of the same day or the start of the next depending on what time his lead came in. What we don't want to do is phone him each day at 9 am as he might be busy then. Mix it up, one call in the morning, then one at 4 pm perhaps, when he might be able to answer his phone. If after two attempts at contact you still haven't heard back, the next stage is to change the medium we are using to contact them. We've tried to phone twice and that hasn't worked out for us, the next plan is messaging them but as you might imagine, not just any old message. Similar to the reason why we use the phone, with this message we send, we want to use as high a percentage of those communication elements as we possibly can. This means recording a video message, as not only will they hear you, ticking off words and tone, but also, they'll also be able to see you and your body language as well. Don't worry, this is easy. I promise you.

Take your phone out and record a video of yourself saying pretty much the same thing you said on our initial voicemail. Keep it positive and upbeat and look at the camera (not the screen). Think of this as a video voicemail, if you will. Once you've saved this video, add the client's name into your WhatsApp contacts and send it over to them. You'll see that it's been delivered and if they have opened the message. If they don't have WhatsApp, you can text them this video or you can use video sending software and send it via email, but WhatsApp would be my first option. Hopefully this is enough to prompt them to come back to you. If they have had two calls with voicemail and have received a video message, chances are they aren't that keen to speak to you right now. The important part of that last sentence is 'right now', though.

Personally, I would also double the amount of time I leave it when someone doesn't answer my call on a cold lead. After the initial contact attempts, I would advise up to six months as a maximum time gap. This means that after I have tried to contact a lead a couple of times in a few days, I would then leave them for a few more days. If they don't answer that call, I'll call them in a week. Don't answer that one, I'll call them in two weeks. If they don't answer, I'll call them again in a month. Don't answer that one, I'll call you in two months and so on. Until finally, as a worst-case scenario they will get a phone call from me every six months outside of our all-important email nurture campaign which we spoke about earlier in this book.

Now we've got the negative out of the way, let's focus on the glass-half-full side of this equation and that is that either our call gets returned, or our lead answers the phone the first time we call them. Firstly, we want to look at what we want to get from any phone call in our business. The true judge of any sales phone call is what you get from the call. I don't care if you both love the same football team, and you're best friends separated from each other at birth. A good call will have tangible results out of it that befits your business, not just the fact that you got on well with them and had a chat about the weather for 20 minutes.

So, let's look at some of the biggest ticket items you can get from any sales lead that comes into your business.

The number one job of an estate agent is?... You guessed it. Your number one priority should be whether or not this person has a property

I can sell or rent out in the local area. If they do, this could be worth thousands, if not tens of thousands of pounds to your business.

Next up is third-party income which we will go into in later chapters, but effectively can we refer this person to either a mortgage advisor or a solicitor to get a quote on a mortgage or conveyancing. This is going to be a regular income stream for your business and provide greater control over future deals, so you certainly want to ask about this with anyone you speak to.

Finally does this lead know anyone else who might be looking to sell their property in the future? After all, as I mentioned earlier, we're only six degrees of separation away from anyone in the world, and these guys might know someone else who is looking to sell in the local area.

The above should ultimately form a checklist in your head that you should be working through with clients as you're on the phone to them. Discover they don't have a property to sell at all? Okay, fine, now let's see if they're getting a mortgage. Okay, they're a cash buyer, let's see if we can get a quote for solicitors, then. Already have that lined up? Fine. 'Do you know anyone else that is looking to sell in the area by any chance? I've got lots of buyers looking at the moment.'

If you come off a phone call and you can honestly say that you got the most out of it that you possibly could, then that is a good phone call. Sometimes it might be all of the above (high fives all round), though sometimes it might just be a referral to your mortgage advisor, but you should always try and get as much as you can from people you come into contact with. Your business will thank you down the line, I promise.

When it comes to moving house, what is someone's goal? To sell their home? To get the best price possible? Not get stressed over moving? Well maybe all the above, but for most people the primary goal is to get into their next property.

Their goal in most situations is not to sell their home, this is simply part of the process in which the homeowner needs to take action to make their big goal come true. If all you focus on in your business is people trying to sell their home, then you are missing out on the big picture. As estate agents get paid to sell properties, I can easily understand why they feel that the selling part of moving is the most important and while it does make the rest possible, for someone looking to move home, it's getting into that next property that is most important. The selling part is just a step in the right direction. We can use this to not only grow our estate agency business further, but also to cement clients working with us as well.

Let's say we are in the process of booking a market appraisal for a homeowner who replied to one of our leaflets. During the call, we asked them where they are looking to move, and they mentioned that they're still staying local but looking for a larger property. At this stage, a big red lightbulb should go off inside of your head. If we can help find the right property for them to move into, not only will it be very likely that this seller will come onto the market with us but also, we can double the amount of commission we make, boosting one deal into two. And even if we can't find them the perfect next property but we try our best to achieve this, this seller will still think we went above and beyond what any other agent has tried to do for them because we have understood their goal and not just focused on the fact that we can sell their property for them.

Using this example, can you think of what we could do for this seller to help find them a bigger property locally? Personally, I would be thinking that I could get a VIP letter out in the area they would like to start with. Also, a specific withdrawn letter to properties they have highlighted for viewing that used to be on the market over the last few years. You could even make a social media video saying 'I'm out in *insert area here* today. I'm delivering some letters as I have Mrs Jones who is looking for a property in this lovely area. If you know anyone who's looking to sell, get them to give me a call'. You could also post this same video on social media groups that cover that area to boost exposure. The most important part of this exercise though, is that you let the potential future seller know exactly what you are doing and how hard you are working for them to find them their next home before they have even paid you a penny. Worst-case scenario is you've got some awesome marketing out in one of your core patches, anything else is a bonus.

On the other side of the coin, let's say the valuation you are booking in is looking to move out of your area and to elsewhere in the country. How can you help here? Well, if you're a one-person band without national coverage you might think you'd struggle, but you can offer to help negotiate the seller's onward purchase when they do find a property – which will be a massive relief for them. You can also offer to help highlight sold and withdrawn properties in the local area which may assist them when it comes to deciding on how much to offer for the property they find.

If you are part of national network of agents, I would definitely look at offering to speak to your local agent in the area the seller looking to move to ask them to give the seller a call to chat through any suitable properties they might have and keep them front of mind for any other properties that might match up in the future. It's super important that if you offer the other office to give them a call, that they follow through. Otherwise, you've broken a promise to your potential seller in the first 10 minutes – not exactly a solid foundation to build a relationship on.

Booking the perfect market appraisal

When it comes to booking a market appraisal into your business, there are certainly pieces of information you will want to find out not only about the property you are going to visit, but about the owner of that property as well. To start off with, you are going to need to know basic information about the individuals you are meeting at their homes. This will include names, phone numbers, address, care-of address, email addresses and so on. It's important to get as much information and contact details at this stage as you possibly can. Down the line, if you've got a seller that you simply can't get hold of, you are going to struggle and become very good friends with their voicemail, very quickly. Which is no good for anyone involved.

Now you have their basic information you are next going to want to find out more about their property. Remember earlier, I mentioned there was a really good question to ask that would highlight which personality type the seller had? Well, here it is:

'So that I can best prepare for our meeting. Can you please talk me around your home?'

Notice how this is a nice open question for the homeowner to start talking about their property. It's not 100 questions fired at the potential seller as that can feel like an interview, and honestly, it's just really hard work for you to simultaneously record everything they're saying and prepare for your next question.

This way, the homeowner can talk you through their property for a few minutes whilst you just jot down the information they are giving you. You can then ask them specific questions on anything they might have missed, such as the garden, parking, and any other topic you think you need more information on. Soon you'll have a really good idea of what the property you're going to value is like.

Spoiler alert, you can cheat slightly, here. If you know the postcode or address for the property, pop onto your favourite property portal or simply Google their address beforehand. You'll have a better idea of exactly where they are in their street which can make you seem more knowledgeable about that exact road than you would have been without it. You can add comments which will allude to this local knowledge as well as you book the appointment in.

As we highlighted just now, the way the potential seller answers this question about describing their home will also reveal their personality type. If you are on the phone for 45 minutes with the person on the other end of the phone going into endless details about every aspect of their home, chances are that you are dealing with a Q2. This means potentially putting more time aside for the market appraisal, and on the market appraisal itself, be prepared to go into details on everything you do and why. On the other hand, if you find that the owner gives a very brief description of their property to you, then chances are they are a Q1, therefore your market appraisal will be a quicker appointment with far more to-the-point conversation. Although this isn't conclusive, it'll give you a good understanding of how the market appraisal is going to look and the style of conversation you are likely needing to adopt during the appointment.

As we spoke about earlier in this book, ultimately, the goal of the homeowner isn't necessarily just to sell their property, so if you end the conversation having just discussed the property then you are missing the bigger picture overall. A large part of this conversation with the homeowner should be why they are looking to move and where they are looking to go. You can then potentially help them find their next home, not only helping them with their onward move, but also your business as it gives you ammo to go out and get more leads off the back of this.

You also have a great opportunity standing in front of you here, to refer your potential client over to third-party suppliers who can help the owner plan their forward move once they have all the potential costs in place. Where booking a market appraisal is one of the first jobs people look at doing when looking to move in the future, chances are they probably won't yet have anything in place with regard to this, leaving the door open for you to refer your chosen provider nice and early in the process.

The final job when it comes to booking in a market appraisal is confirming the time and date of the appointment. It's really important that this is the last thing you do. It all comes down to who wants what from the call. The person trying to get their own home valued just wants a time and date for you to turn up and value their property. You on the other hand want name, phone numbers, email addresses, information about the property, onward move details, the list goes on and on. As soon as you book in the appointment time and date, effectively the person booking has what they want out of the conversation and is far more likely to switch off for the rest of the conversation. By leaving this booking element until the very end you ensure maximum engagement from the person on the other end of the phone, and you ensure you get every bit of information you need before the call ends.

When booking in a market appraisal, it's important to make sure that all decision makers are at the appointment. Otherwise, you can find yourself doing the most amazing sales pitch to Mr Jones, when really Mrs Jones is the one you want to be talking to, as she'll potentially have the final say. In all reality, how much of your hour-long presentation do you think is going to make it over to Mrs Jones, 5%? If you're lucky. You'll probably only manage to communicate the price you valued the property for and the fee. This is not a good result as all our unique selling points are out the window, and at this stage we are basically just a name in a hat hoping to get drawn almost by blind luck. To avoid this, make sure that all homeowners are going to be in for your market appraisal to ensure that the main decision maker or makers are going to be there.
At this stage you might be thinking, 'I wish there was some kind of market appraisal booking form I could work my way through.' Well, I've got you

covered there. Here's a market appraisal booking form you can use in your business but with one important caveat. Please try and learn this form to the best of your ability. No one wants to book a market appraisal on their property with someone reading from a form. You don't need to know every line of it, just know the sections to get you going and the rest will follow. Again, do not read word-for-word whilst on the phone, people will be able to tell, and it'll make you look like you don't know what you are talking about. As before, scan the QR code below and you'll be directed to the form you can use.

Before the appointment

Now you might be thinking we're about to start looking at the preparation work for our upcoming market appraisal. But there is one more crucial step to do before we get to that stage.

We know already that your biggest USP in your business is you. That's right, that person looking back at you in the mirror. There is only ever one of you and ultimately whether you get instructed or not will be determined by whether or not the seller likes and trusts you as a property professional. Studies show that the more time you spend with someone, the more you will like and trust that person. As we covered earlier, this doesn't have to be exclusively real-life time, this can just be digital time. Think about the way people love their favourite celebrity despite never having met them.

We're going to lean into this element further and get some one-on-one time with our potential seller before our market appraisal appointment even takes place, with a pre-market appraisal confirmation letter. Not only does this mean we get to meet our sellers before we walk through their door in a few days' time, but we also get to see the outside of the property as well, giving us a greater understanding of the property we're going to value. This will help us out in our upcoming research.

The letter should be hand delivered to the property we're going to value, ideally on the same day we book the market appraisal, and as a worst-case scenario, the following day if the appointment is only booked into the diary at the very end of the day.

In its most basic form, this letter purely confirms the time and date for the appointment, but you can push this further and include details of properties you have sold nearby, or some other marketing content that is going to make a good impression before you even walk through the door. Primarily though it's there for you to meet the sellers at their property so that they can start getting to know you and start trusting and liking you before the appointment.

I can speak from experience on how well this works, as I personally sold a property of mine some years ago and booked in three estate agents to visit my home and value it first. The first two agents I spoke to on the phone didn't follow this process and just turned up for the market appraisal a few days later to carry out the appointment. But the third agent I booked into hand-delivered a confirmation letter to my home. Not only this, but a magazine full of the properties they had sold along with an A3 fold-out brochure full of photos of cards and flowers they had received from happy clients. I'll give you one guess who went on to sell the property. They were a step ahead before the other agents had even walked in the door.

There are a few golden rules when it comes to hand-delivering this letter. Number one is that it needs to be hand-delivered. I know, the clue was in the name, right? This means you need to write this on the outside of the envelope to make the hand-delivered element clear if the owner is not in. The next rule is that you need to knock on the front door to deliver it, no ditching it through the letterbox and running. Finally, you need to be aware that for 10% of these that you deliver, the homeowner is going to say, 'Actually I'm free for an hour now if you fancy coming in?'. Do not say yes to this, you've done zero research at this point and will be out of your depth very quickly.

Instead, just explain to the owner how you would love to come in right now but sadly you are SO busy with other appointments that the date you have booked in for the appointment already is your next free date. Now they know not only are you providing a great service but you're busy, too, which means popular in their eyes.

If you'd like a template of this letter, simply scan the following QR code and you'll then be able to use a pre prepared template of this letter

Market appraisal research

Before we move into this section all about how to research the value of a property, I feel it's necessary to answer this important question, 'What is a property worth? Some people might say that it's whatever an estate agent values a property for, some might even say it's worth what the seller thinks they are going to get for it. Well, sadly, these are both incorrect answers. Ultimately, a property is worth what someone is willing to pay for it, that's it. It's simply supply and demand.

If you put a house on the market for £250,000 and you find people tripping over themselves to pay more, it certainly seems to be worth more than that figure in the current market. If you put a property on the market for £250,000 and it feels like you almost can't give it away, then chances are the price is simply too high for the current market. I have been an estate agent for 20 years and I cannot tell you how much a property is going to sell for. The example above could sell for £248,000, it could sell for £251,564 honestly, I have no idea. What is important to do is to get the property onto the market at a price that will generate interest, viewings and ultimately offers on the property for the owners to consider. Because without these aspects, the property has little or no chance of selling.

The reason behind this air of mystery is because the value of a property is subjective. For one person, it might be the bargain of the century, whilst for others it could almost be insulting to ask for that much money for a home in that street. You need to take a view on the current market sentiment and ultimately settle on a price that is low enough to generate interest but high enough that you have some happy sellers at the end. At the end of the day, the market dictates the price of any property, not you, and especially not the seller.

When it comes to selling property, you will find that there is one thing that will either sell a property instantly or leave it hanging around on the market for years at a time. That is the price of the property. You could be the most amazing estate agent in the world with the best property details, photos, and VR tours, but if the house is listed for 20% over what the market thinks it should be, the only thing visiting the property will be tumbleweed. On the other hand, you could have simply the worst estate agent in the world with one photo of a property that they took from a car window that they simply threw online. But if the property is listed at 20% below market value, they will be beating the viewings and subsequent offers off with a stick. Price is always the biggest factor in selling a property. Always.

Let's start looking at how we would put a marketing price on the property we are due to value. I'm going to lay out my personal method for doing this, but techniques will vary from one estate agent to the next. I'll also set the bar very low with regard to technology used as there are a huge number of platforms out there to assist in this process, but at an additional cost. I'll presume you don't have access to any of these, but if you do, that'll be a bonus and will make your life easier.

One of the questions you will have asked when booking in the market appraisal is 'How long have you lived in your current property?' Although this sounds like a nice question to ask, the real reason we want to know this is because if they have bought the property over the last 20 years or so then we can easily look online to see how much they paid for the property when they purchased it – a great place to start for working out today's value, I think you'll agree. To find this information, simply head over to Rightmove, enter the postcode for the property under 'Sold house prices' and look for the property you are going to value. If your property appears on here, that's great, but even if it doesn't, print off this report as it will show you every sold price for the street you are going to. Next up, head over to your Rightmove Plus account. From here, you can go onto 'Best price guide'. This gives you more information than the normal site and insights into not only the for sale and sold properties but also withdrawn properties as well. From here, enter the postcode for the street you are going to value, keep the rest of the options as they are, but take the date back so it covers the last 20 years. This report, similar to the sold prices in your road report, will show you all the properties that have been on the market in this street for the last 20 years. Not only the ones that have sold but also the ones that have more importantly been withdrawn from the market as well. This will give us a good idea about what has been happening in this particular road over the last 20 years of the property market. Print this report off along with the sold house prices from earlier, as these are going to come with us on our valuation.

So far, we have looked at historical data for the street, we've looked at how much properties have sold for, and also, we have looked at which properties have been on the market historically and have either sold or not sold. This is a good place to start, but it doesn't show us the here and now of the property market in the area. To do this, head back over to your best price guide report and start a new report. Again, enter the properties postcodes and set a radius around it. I'd suggest half a mile to start off with, but we may adjust this depending on the number of results that come back to us when we run the report in a moment. Next, select the right style of home you are going out to see. You might select 'house' and 'three bedrooms' as an example. Effectively, what we are doing here is a search that's very similar to someone who is looking for this size and style of property in this area so we can see how our potential new listing sizes up in comparison. Finally head down to the date section at the bottom. Automatically, this date will cover the last three months of the property market, which is fine as a place to start with. Run the report and see what comes up.

What I'll do next is give you the goal we are looking to achieve here and then we can work backwards from there. What we are looking to get from this report is two or three properties that we feel are worth more than the property we're going to value. We are also looking to have two or three properties that are below where we expect the price to be. Finally, we're looking to highlight three to four properties which we feel are about right compared to the property we are going to value.

In the example we mentioned just now, for a three-bedroom house, our upper properties might be a couple of four-bedroom properties and our lower end might be a selection of two-bedroom homes, and the majority of our comparable properties being other three-bedroom homes that are similar in size and location.

Now we know the goal, we can fine tune our search results to ensure we get the best possible comparables for our upcoming market appraisal. The two areas we can adjust to allow us to get our best results are, the radius around the property and also how far back in time we go for the results. For example, if you ran the report with a half a mile radius and went back three months and no properties came up at all, you could either make the radius larger, bringing in geographically wider results into your report, or you could go back further in time than the three months, again bringing in more properties. Maybe you could even do both.

On the other hand, if you were greeted with hundreds of properties on the first report, then you would look to tighten up these parameters delivering less results. What you ideally want to end up with is around twenty to thirty results coming back that you can then pick from. Finetune your radius and dates until you have around this number of results as this will give you enough properties to pick from to make your report as accurate as possible.

You might at this stage be thinking, 'Why do I need more expensive property comparables and a few properties that are cheaper than the property I am going to value, surely I should just take similar properties?' Good question, and the reason you will want to take these with you is because it somewhat boxes in the homeowner when it comes to the pricing of their property.

Let's take the more expensive comparables you have taken with you, for example. We all know that sellers usually want to get as much money for their property as they can, so if they get a chance to push the price higher, they usually try and take it. Well, if you have comparable properties in your report which show that for the same amount of money that they would like to achieve for their home, you could actually buy a better property, then this should make them see sense and realise that no one is going to buy a three-bedroom property for the price of a four-bedroom home in the same area. The same rule applies for the cheaper property comparables you take with you, but as you might imagine you rely on those far less and it's not often that homeowners are trying to push the price down on their own home!

Now you've got this report with the comparables on, print this off and add this to the other reports you have already.

If, during the report generating process, you see any properties which you think are really good comparables, print full details off for these, as the homeowner will want to see the full details of these homes rather than just a small photo on a report. It'll also open the door for more conversation about that property and how it compares to them if they can see the size, condition and so on for that property.

The final step in your research process is to check the online planning application portal for your local council. All councils have one of these portals and the amount of information on there is just amazing. Once you've found your way onto this portal, which you can do by simply going on to your favourite search engine and typing '*your local council* online planning portal', then once on the site, simply search for the postcode of the property you're going to value and see what results come back. What you are looking for here, is any current or past planning applications that are either to do with the property we are going to value or that might have an effect on it.

There have been many times in my career when I've impressed homeowners on a market appraisal because I brought their old building plans with me from before they extended their home, or because I knew they had a planning application rejected five years ago. Honestly, for five minutes here, you can really impress a seller. As before, print out as many plans as you think are relevant. If they have extended their home, print off the before and after floor plans so you can chat about this on the appointment itself.

As mentioned previously, lots of agents find their comparables in different ways, this is just the way I have found that works for me over the years. There is always new and exciting tech coming out in the industry which will help you do all of the above in just a few clicks of a button. But for the sake of this book, I'd rather set the bar low for resources available to you, with potential to exceed the above with tech you may or may not decide to pay for on a monthly basis.

Set yourself up for success

By this stage, we should have some big boxes ticked coming up to the appointment day. We should have a strong understanding of the person we are meeting at the property, because not only have we spoken to them on the phone, but we have also met them at the property once already. We should also have an understanding of not only where they are looking to move to and the motivation behind this, but we also should have started to help out in this process any way we can. Finally, we should have a solid knowledge base about what kind of home we are going to be looking at on the upcoming appointment and should have a good range of comparables to support the figure we feel the property will fall into.

As a side note, at this stage if you don't feel you have enough clarity on what kind of price range the property is going to fall into, take a wider range of comparables with you than we have previously spoken about. I would much rather you walked through the front door and almost discarded half of your comparables due to the size or internal condition rather than not having them with you at all to use later on if necessary. The important part to remember is that if you struggle to find comparable properties to the home with all your resources available to you, then the homeowner is certainly going to struggle to find any. This should put your mind at ease as you realise that actually you are holding a good number of the cards in this situation.

Before we are in a position to go to the market appraisal, I think it's worth looking at what exactly makes a good valuer of a property. There are certain boxes that we will want to tick to make sure we come across in the best possible light to the homeowner. Most of these are just general manners, which hopefully should come naturally, but there are others as well which we will need to put some effort into before the actual appointment itself to ensure the best possible outcome for our business.

If you struggle to think of what personal attributes could make up a brilliant valuer of property, then let's make this more entertaining and look at what would make up some terrible attributes and then try our hardest to be the complete opposite of these!

In my mind, firstly, our terrible valuer would be late to the appointment, they would be dressed in a scruffy manner, and would probably smell of cigarettes. Next, they wouldn't apologise or even recognise that they were late to the appointment (which would certainly annoy me). After this, they wouldn't remove their shoes as they tread mud through my recently cleaned home. No real introductions will have been made at all and we clarified what exactly is going to happen during the appointment that day. They also would have no idea on either the local property market, or the national property, or economics as a whole when questioned. Our terrible valuer wouldn't make any comments about my property and how I could help improve my chances of selling it. They wouldn't let me know if they had any buyers at all, and oh, when it comes to price, they just tell me a figure with zero justification or background workings. Finally, a fee is dropped on me before they clear off, never to be heard of again. Just leaving a business card with someone else's name on it. Classy.

Awesome job, right?

Let's turn that frown upside down and look at how this should have gone. Our made-up valuer should have turned up to the appointment on time, if not a minute or two early, ideally. If they were running late through no fault of their own, then a phone call should have come through explaining this as soon as it was known.

Our valuer should have been well presented on the appointment and look like they have made an effort, and obviously not smelling of anything bad – especially not smoke. Their shoes should have come off as soon as they entered the property. After this, they should have explained to the seller exactly what the plan was for the day's appointment and roughly how long it would take, so they knew what to expect.

Then throughout the appointment, they should show not only their national property market knowledge but also local market knowledge and how that might directly affect the selling of this home. They also should be making positive comments about the property as they went around the home and ideally linked those back to the earlier booking conversation, such as 'This must be your lovely new kitchen you told me about on the phone, you've done a great job with this.'

When it comes to the pricing of the property as well, they should have gone through a consultative approach with the seller where they have contributed and viewed our comparables and together, they've settled on the right price range for the property, and agreeing on what would be a best-case scenario and worst-case scenario price. They should have also clearly explained the fee and exactly what they are going to do to try and sell the property to the best of their ability. Finally, they should be closing for the business, if this doesn't work at the time, then they should agree the next communication date with the homeowner.

These are a bit different right? I know I'd certainly rather be seen by the second valuer, at very least my carpet will thank me!

As you can see from the slightly tongue-in-cheek example, a lot of what we have covered is basic common sense. Be on time, be polite, be well presented and overall be interested in the property and its owner's future plans. This will give us a solid foundation to work from moving forward.

One of the pieces you need to prepare in advance before this meeting or any other meeting is the local and national housing market and any big issues which could affect the selling of the property. This is going to range from knowing huge national news such as Bank of England base rate changes and national housing market figures right down to there not currently being enough bungalows for sale in the area, resulting in them selling really quickly.

The latter of these pieces of information you will be able to see from your research in the local area before the appointment. If every property you look at is under offer or sold, this bodes well for the property you are about to go and see. If on the other hand, nothing is sold and everyone is sitting around, hoping to sell, this is a different story to talk to the homeowner about.

When it comes to national and economic news, you don't have to start reading the financial times every Sunday, you'll be pleased to know. But you do need to have a basic understanding of what is going on with the economy and any elements coming up that might shake that up a bit. Think Brexit, general elections, high inflation, all that good stuff. You need to stay on top of this. If you just watch the news in your lunch break every day or listen to a podcast covering these topics once a week, you'll have a good understanding of what's going on.

What we don't want is for someone to ask you about how the upcoming general election might affect the selling of their home and for you to reply with 'what election?'

Next up, we are going to look at what you will want to take with you on your market appraisal. There is one key rule for this, and that is to prepare to win the business. What we don't want is a homeowner turning around to you at the end of the appointment and agreeing to go on the market as soon as possible, only you haven't brought the camera, measure or even your terms and conditions with you. This would be a frustrating and annoying result, falling at the last hurdle when you were doing so well up to this point. Instead, let's plan for the best. We will want to have near to hand everything you need to get the property onto the market should the opportunity present itself. I'm not for a second saying you need to carry all this stuff with you on the appointment like some sort of estate agency camel, but it should be at very least in your car parked outside should you need to use any of it.

Inside the property nearby, you should always have business cards, a laptop, something to write on and also the research you have carried out with any marketing material you feel supports you, such as recent properties you have sold, for example. One element you should have on you at all times is your mobile phone and this should be fully charged. Although your phone can be an excellent tool in a market appraisal for things like using the calculator, the torch, the compass and so on, the most important reason for having this with you is for your personal safety. After all, you're in a house with someone who is pretty much a stranger and chances are you are on your own, so it's wise to have some sort of communication method in place should you feel in any way threatened or uneasy about being in a property with someone.

Back in your car you should have everything you need to take that property onto the market, this may well include a camera, tripod, laser measure, graph paper, property information forms and your companies T&Cs if they aren't online. This puts us in a position where we are ready to go should the homeowner instruct us there and then.

The actual market appraisal

Okay so here it is, what we have been building up to the day of the market appraisal is here, exciting right?

First things first, we don't want to be late for our market appraisal, this is not a good start in any way, shape, or form. What we do want to be is on time and prepared for our meeting. What I'd suggest we do to make sure we tick the boxes off is actually arrive at the appointment about 15 minutes early, but park just around the corner or just out of sight. Certainly, don't park in the driveway and sit in your car for 15 minutes, this would be super weird. Our goal over the next 15 minutes is to learn our comparable research as much as we possibly can.

There are going to be certain parts of the conversation that we know are going to come up over the next hour or so, this means we can and should prepare for this as much as we can. If the seller we are about to meet only bought their home only last year and is looking to move already, you know this topic is going to be spoken about and probably what they paid for it, too. Learn this date and the figure they paid for the property.

If there's a house on the market next door which has been on for a while, you can be pretty sure this is going to come up in conversation, too. Again, learn the details for this property: when it came on the market, if they have dropped the price and any other information that you think might be relevant. This is going to make you look like you know your stuff far more than having to sift through a pile of papers to find the date that next door came onto the market this year. You don't need to remember these dates and figures forever, but for the next hour they should be at the front of your mind, ready to recall when the moment arises.

As we spoke about just now, we should be looking to arrive at the market appraisal a few minutes early. Sometimes turning up on time is considered late, especially in the United Kingdom.

Before we rush to the doorbell of the property though, we should stand outside of the home and just look at the outside of the property for 10-30 seconds. This serves two purposes. Number one being that you can have a brief look at the front of the property and spot any glaring structural issues. Now, I'm not expecting you to carry out a full structural inspection of the front of the property at this stage, but if the chimney looks like it's about to fall off or the roof has more tiles missing than it does actual roof, then this is a topic to talk to the owner about later on. If the buyers don't spot it, their surveyor almost certainly will. The second reason you want to take this slightly prolonged look at the front of the property is so the homeowners see you doing it. This shows you take the properties you value very seriously and look at every aspect of the property, not just the obvious bits inside that you're about to be shown.

Once this visual assessment of the outside of the property has been completed, move onto the actual appointment for valuing the property.

Firstly, knock on the front door and then take one step back. No one wants to have someone right in their face as soon as they open the door. If you have done your valuation build-up work correctly, when the homeowner answers the door, they should know and recognise you. You have met them once already when you delivered the pre-valuation letter just a few days ago, after all.

Your first goal is to build on the foundations of the relationship you started a few days ago. Expressions like 'it's good to see you again' should be your best friend right now. This will remind the homeowner that this is in fact, their second time meeting you, should they have forgotten already. Your next job is to take your shoes off, I don't care what the homeowner says. They will say 'I always keep mine on', or 'Don't worry about those' as they point at your feet. This is a very small test, I promise you. Just take your shoes off and say that you always like to do it as it shows respect to others when you're in their home.

Our next job is to do something called signposting with the homeowner. This is a process where you explain to someone exactly what is going to happen next, so they know what to expect in the near future. You'd also look to cover a rough idea on how long each section is going to last and almost certainly how long the entire appointment is going to last. There is a good way to do this and a great way to do this.

The good way is to talk through your plan for the next hour with the owner. This could sound something like this 'Okay Mrs Jones, if it's okay with you we'll have a look around your property first of all, once we've done that, we'll have a chat about the market and where your property's value might sit. I should be all finished by 3 pm. How does that sound?'

Not a bad effort, I think you'll agree. Mrs Jones now knows what the agenda is for the next hour and knows that by 3 pm she'll be free to get on with the rest of her life.

Now let's look at the better version of this. It's going to be made better because we are going to mention earlier details that Mrs Jones will have told us when we first booked in the market appraisal. Not only showing that we know our stuff, but also that we care enough about her to remember the conversation even though it may have been a week ago. 'Okay Mrs Jones, if it's okay with you we'll have a look around the inside of your property first of all, I'm really looking forward to seeing the new kitchen you spoke about on the phone, then if we could have a look at your large back garden we were talking about. Once I've seen all of that, we'll sit down to talk about the pricing of your home and how we can help make your move to Devon as smooth as possible. How does that sound?' I feel like at this point Mrs Jones can't say no to that for a second.

Spoiler alert, I'm not actually expecting you to remember the phone call you had with Mrs Jones a week ago. In estate agency you speak to lots of people on a daily basis and honestly, it's almost impossible to remember everyone and every conversation once you get busy enough.

What I do want you to become very good at is making notes on your CRM system. This will be your golden ticket to remembering everyone and everything you speak about. If a homeowner mentions their dog's name, add it to the CRM as a note. If they mention they're off to Greece on holiday, add it to the CRM as a note. You'll come across as far more attentive and caring than if you start the conversation with 'What's your dog's name again?'

This means with the mention of the kitchen, garden, and moving to Devon, we just made good quality notes when booking in the appointment which we simply read back in the car before the appointment so it's front of mind for our market appraisal.

Next, the homeowner is going to give you a tour of their home. You need to understand that selling their three-bedroom semi-detached home is a very big deal to the owner. Chances are they have never sold a property before this, either. You, on the other hand, may have been to value five other three-bedroom semi-detached properties that week, so for it feels a bit like Groundhog Day. You cannot come across this way. This is more than likely the homeowner's biggest possession and they're more than likely very proud of it. What this all means is that if you treat it like just another product to sell, you're not going to come across in a very good light. My advice for this and for everything you do with people and property, is just be interested.

Ask questions about the property as if you were looking to buy it yourself, as these are the questions potential buyers are going to ask you when you are showing them around the property, after all. Also, you should take an interest in the owners of the property. Where did they live before they bought this property? What first attracted them to buy this home? After all, they bought the property once before so this might point in the direction of the next buyer's point of view. If you just focus on the property I assure you, you are going to miss out on the main part of this puzzle and that is the owners and making their future plans a reality.

We spoke earlier in this book about what a homeowner's ultimate goal was when it came to moving house. It wasn't necessarily just to sell their property for the best possible price, it was to get into their next property and to make this move happen. Selling their home was just a task they had to complete to make the whole thing happen. Keep this in mind when speaking to the owner on the market appraisal and don't be shy to talk about where they are moving to, why they are moving and any timescales they have set in place for this. Be aware though all of this should have been discussed when you booked the market appraisal in the first place so making the homeowner repeat themselves is not a good look. Instead prove to the owners that you were listening intently when they first booked the market appraisal and start these conversations where you left off rather than repeating what has already been covered on an earlier call.

At this stage we should have now had a tour of the property by the owner, we should have picked up the conversation where we left off on the phone and found out more about not only the property, but also the goal of the homeowner and how they want their move to progress from here. Now it's time to sit down and have a conversation with the homeowner about how you are the perfect fit to help them move home to their next property.

First things first, a bit of a golden rule to start off with here. You are not preaching to the homeowner about how great you are and how you are the best estate agent in the world. The valuation should be carried out in a consultative approach, this means that effectively you work with the homeowner to make a structure for selling their property that is going to best fit their needs. This not only goes into the way you are going to advertise the property such as price, open days and so on, but it also goes down to timescales to go onto the market and even which days would work best for viewings to make their life as convenient as possible.

As a modern estate agent, you have a whole range of options at your fingertips for selling a property. You need to find out which of these methods and techniques are going to work best for the person sitting opposite you. If a seller told me they weren't in a hurry to sell, I wouldn't be pushing them towards putting their property up for auction, for example. It's a method that has been shown to sell properties quicker than the conventional way, but generally achieves a lower agreed price overall. This would be like trying to force a round peg into a square hole. It just wouldn't fit.

A far better way of doing this is not only listening to what the seller wants to achieve, but *understanding* what they want to achieve. Once you understand this information, you are then able to make a bespoke plan on how you can turn this into a reality. Not only this but by listening to what the homeowner wants to accomplish, you can pull on certain USPs in your business which are going to make you the perfect fit for them. Now this doesn't mean tell them everything you offer to hedge your bets, instead pick on the most relevant parts of your business that will make you the ideal choice.

Once you have had the tour of the property with the owner, the conversation you have with them should have a structure to ensure you have the best possible result. I know lots of estate agents who will simply wing a valuation. Sometimes it pays off and sometimes it doesn't. If we have a structure and a process in place for this part of the meeting, then we ensure that it works a lot more times than it doesn't, and if it doesn't work, we can easily adjust and improve our processes ready for the next market appraisal.

The order of presenting at this stage should be discussing where you both feel the price for the property sits currently, then showing the owner how you are going to achieve that price and be the obvious agent of choice for them. Finally, we will put forward our fee, where we will then close for the business before the end of the appointment. Let's go through these step-by-step to ensure we have each one of these sections nailed down.

First, let's start with the pricing of the property. Remember you don't know what the property is going to sell for at this point and the homeowner certainly doesn't, this will only become apparent once you put the property onto the market and the offers start or don't start coming in. The owner almost certainly will have an idea about what they would like or even love to achieve for their home, but this may match up with what the market thinks it is worth and ultimately that is the true value of the property. What we want to do is put a price tag on the property that we feel is going to generate interest and viewings. Because as you might imagine, if you don't have any interest in the property, and you don't have any viewing on the home, then what chance have you got of realistically selling it? Very little, that's how much.

To find out what a property should be valued and put onto the market for, we are going to need to rely on the comparables we generated and printed before the appointment.

Using these, have an open conversation with the owner showing properties that you feel are similar to their home and ask them, 'How do you feel this property compares to your own?' We're trying to get to the fair marketing price for this property by working with the owner, not preaching to them. Once you've had this conversation a few times, you'll have a pretty solid idea of where they are hoping or expecting the price to be for their property by noticing how they speak and talk about the other properties we show them. From this point we can then have a conversation with the owner about where we feel the price sits for the property in the current market, what we would put it on the market for and what we would look to achieve from this asking price.

A huge piece of advice here, when delivering the price, pick a price range or bracket for the property to fall into rather than just picking one price. This is going to help you out in three ways. Firstly, imagine you were a few thousand pounds off where the owner thought the price should be for their home, not that big a deal you may be thinking? That's probably only a percent or two of the value of the property, not a bad effort. And you'd potentially be right, but remember that for the seller, that could pay for your services entirely or for an extra holiday.

By hedging our bets here over a range, we are more likely to envelop the price the owner wants. Think about it as playing roulette and covering half the board rather than just one number. You're statistically more likely to be right, the more chips you put down. The second advantage of giving a price range is you can tailor this to your homeowner's situation, showing you have listened to them. For example, you could say 'I feel the property is worth between £240,000 and £250,000, but because you've told me you're not in a hurry, let's try the £250,000 to start with.' The final advantage of doing it this way is that this is going to help you down the line if you are talking to the owner about potentially changing the price should the property not sell as in the example above. We've already said that it could be worth £240,000, we're just trying £250,000 to start off with. This makes a price change conversation a lot easier, something we'll go into a lot more detail on later in this book.

Speaking of later in this book, I'm going to bring one point forward slightly for this section. In later chapters we'll talk about how to perfectly present the properties you are selling. As you might imagine, price has a huge factor in that, because you can be the best agent in the world but if your listing is 30% overpriced then no one is coming to view it, I assure you.

When uploading a property onto one of the property portals, it is important, where possible, to ensure a listings price comes under a price point. Your first question is probably, what on earth is a price point? Well, these are the drop-down menu prices that the major portals offer you to refine your property search down by when you are looking to buy a home. Imagine you are looking to buy a property yourself at £250,000 in your town. I very much doubt you will set your price range from zero through to £250,000, wading through all the cheaper properties that don't suit you before you finally get the ones that do. Instead, you'll more than likely put a search range such as £200,000 to £250,000, showing properties that are in the right sort of ballpark for your search. Now imagine I had the perfect property for you, but I had put it onto the market at £251,000. You simply wouldn't see this home in your search results due to the extra £1,000, taking it above the £250,000 search range.

It's for exactly this reason that where possible, we should put properties onto the price points. To find these out, go to your favourite property portal and search for a property to buy, you'll see a drop-down menu that allows you to pick the price range you are looking for. These are the price points. Studies show that by hitting one of these, you can increase the views on a listing by 40%. Well worth having, you might imagine. Gone are the days where a price needed to end in 995 to seem cheap. Hitting a price point will do more for your marketing than any gimmicky price will.

Keep this information in mind when speaking to the homeowner about the pricing of their property, as by explaining the importance of this point to the seller you will show your marketing knowledge. This will work toward the best result for them in their sale because more interest in their property will equal more viewings and offers down the line. It isn't completely essential to hit one of these price points, but not coming under one that is near the price of the property is a terrible idea.

We should now be at the stage of the conversation with the owner whereby we have agreed where the price range of the property falls into. Great, this is a good box to tick. The next step from here is showing the owner how you are the perfect agent to make their properties move come true. What we are going to look at is your business' unique selling points and how they can ultimately help your seller achieve their goals. As we covered earlier, your USPs will generally fall into three categories: price, timescale, and customer satisfaction. Based on the conversation you had with the homeowner, pick ones that you think will make a difference to them. Let's pick an example to show this in action. Imagine you have just been shown around a property by the owner and during this tour, you have explored, in further detail, what their goals are for the future. They spoke about their move down to Devon where properties are more expensive than their current area, and they also want to be there in time to get into the school they would ideally like their children to attend.

Okay, so we've got two key drivers flashing at us here. One being the price aspect, as they'll want to get as much money as possible to afford to get the property they want. Also, we've got the timescale aspect for the children's school. Great, let's tick these off in the seller's mind.

We may choose to emphasise that because we have professional photography on all the properties we bring onto the market, we achieve a higher selling price than we would do without it, meaning more money in the homeowner's pocket which will help with their onward purchase. Also, due to our strict sale progression process, we're the quickest at getting our properties from on the market through to completion, meaning a better chance of getting down to Devon in time – both of which will help the homeowner ultimately achieve their goal of moving out of the area. Align your conversation and selling points with the owner's goal. Remember that we need to pass the 'So what?' test here. You have professional photography on all your instructions, why as a seller should I care? You've got super sales progression structures, why should I care about this? Make each of these conversation points and USPs so important for the seller to have in their chosen estate agent that they'll feel like they are going to make their own move tougher than it needs to be by picking an agent without these attributes. This will make you the obvious choice for instruction.

So how much do you charge?

Finally, we are going to talk to the homeowner about our fee for selling the property. Spoiler alert, in my experience, the fee you charge the homeowner for selling their property is a far bigger deal in your mind than it is in the seller's. This means that estate agents throughout the country could charge far more for selling a property if only they asked for a higher fee to start off with.

Just to put the boot in slightly more to this equation, UK estate agents charge one of the lowest percentages in the entire world. The good news is though, that (very) slowly, estate agency fees throughout the United Kingdom are heading in the right direction and are generally rising overall, which is a great thing to see. The average fee in the United Kingdom right now is still sitting around 1.2% + VAT of the selling price, though. Not exactly setting the world ablaze, I think you'll agree.

Just to compound this point, the fee charged for an estate agent to sell a property usually comes from the value of the home. This means that for almost every home you go out and value, your fee is going to come from equity that the sellers have gained just from the market going up around them, not from any particular hard work on their part.

'You can always negotiate your fee down, but you can seldom negotiate it up.'

This is a well-known expression, not only in the estate agency world, but in the sales world as a whole. It's as true today as it ever has been. Imagine you walk through the front door of a property, the appointment goes well and when it comes to talking about your fee, you confidently tell the homeowner that you charge 1% + VAT of the agreed sale price.

Do you think at any point, no matter how well the market appraisal has gone, that the owner is going to say, 'Actually you've done such a good job today that I think you've earned 1.5% +VAT instead.'? It simply isn't going to happen, I'm afraid to say.

The 1% +VAT fee is going to be the most you are going to walk out of the door with that day, so wouldn't it make sense to set your stall out higher than this? Then if the owner is looking to haggle this down, you have some flexibility to move should you even want to, but also if they don't haggle the fee down at all because you've done such a great job then you've got more than you ever thought you could get.

There are three things in life that everyone believes they can try and haggle over. They are purchasing a car, buying souvenirs on holiday and estate agency fees. What if you were looking to buy a new car and the car salesman said to you, 'There's zero flexibility on the price, it's £20,000, take it or leave it.'? What are you going to do, walk everywhere? Get the bus forever more? Sure, you've got other options and a car available to you, but if the salesman has the one you want in the colour you want, what are you going to do? Clearly, you'd just buy the car.

It's exactly the same with estate agent's fees, if you think you're worth it and you deserve the amount you charge, then the public will simply agree and go along with it. Because if you're the most expensive estate agent they have seen that day, then you must be doing something right to charge that fee in the first place.

Sometimes though, no matter how much you think you're worth your fee, people will try and get you to lower it. The main word here being 'try'. There are two aspects to think about here. Back in the diary structure section we mentioned that appointments in your diary give you power, well if you don't think the fee you are getting is going to make this worth your while and you have enough business coming in, then you can simply walk away from it. This is a good place for your estate agency to be overall and you generally find that people want what they can't have. So, if you demonstrate that you are so confident and not desperate for business in any way that you can simply walk away from it, this will make people even more motivated to work with you – which is weird, I know.

The other route to consider if a homeowner is trying to negotiate your fee down is simply to state that you will include aspects of your selling package (that you were going to originally include anyway), if they instruct to sell the home. You might look to include a video on your social media, or a premium listing on your property portal of choice, which you were going to do all along. Only now you are making it sound like you're doing the seller a favour by throwing it into the deal when really it was all going to be included from the start.

There are a couple of aspects around pricing and fee that I would suggest you have in your estate agency business from day one no matter what size of property you are going out to value. Number one is to have an idea about how much selling a property is actually going to cost you each time you do it. For every business I have ever worked with, when we have gone through this exercise, the figure is always higher than the business owner initially thought. This means that in some cases they were actually making a loss when selling a property, which is as crazy as it sounds.

To do this, take the average home value in your area and work out the average fee you will receive for it. Now, minus all the costs involved in not only gaining that instruction from local advertising and lead generation, but then also minus all costs to do with selling that home. I'm talking portal costs, listing fees, completion fees, board costs, even the amount of fuel and time you spend carrying out viewings, and don't forget your personal hourly rate. This will give you a figure that is a rough idea on how much it costs you to sell a home. Imagine this figure being £2,000 and your average fee is £2,500? You're effectively charging £500 to sell a house, which might take six months to go through, this simply isn't sustainable.

Now we have this figure, or at least a good idea of it, we can move on to step two which is putting a minimum fee in place. This will act as a hard floor for your business which you never go below. This should be a cash figure, not a percentage as 1% of £1,000,000 is far more than 1% of £60,000. Instead, you might say your minimum fee is £4,000 for example. Any properties where your percentage fee works out lower than that simply become £4,000 no matter how much you are selling the property for. Otherwise, it won't be worth your while taking that property onto the market, as you're better off spending your time focusing on clients who will pay the amount you feel you are worth.

We're now in a position where we know what it costs us to sell a property and we know the line in the sand that we will never go below. What we want to do next is work out what the seller is going to walk away with financially rather than just focusing on our fee alone. For example, let's say you achieve closer to the asking price than any other estate agent in your town. You are achieving 99% of the property's asking price when you agree a sale, whilst others are achieving a mere 97% of the asked price of a property.

In this example, you have 2% worth of value built into the seller instructing you to sell their property straight away over the other estate agent. What you'd also look to do is emphasise even further as you really want to make this as obvious as you possibly can with the homeowners. So, convert this from a percentage into a pounds and pence amount. This works in two ways: one, people generally aren't very good with percentages, especially on the spot, so you'll need to convert this to a cash amount, so they actually understand. Two, what sounds more impressive, 'I'll get you 2% more' or 'I'll get you £10,000 more'? I'd be more impressed by the money every day of the week, most homeowners will as well. So, convert this percentage into real potential money they could be gaining or missing out on. Knowing figures like this isn't exclusive to how much someone achieves for their property. Sure, most people want to get as much as possible, but for lots of the world, speed and timescale is just as important. Let's say you're the fastest selling agent in your town by four weeks, and the seller whose market appraisal you're on has been saying they want and need to move as soon as possible. Who do you think they are going to want to use? Sure, you're not going to be the cheapest, but if they want to move quickly then the figures speak for themselves – you're the obvious choice.

For most estate agents in the United Kingdom, their fees are only payable on completion. This means that the fee is only payable on the result of you selling the property for an acceptable price. If it falls through for any reason or the owner decides to take it off the market, then usually agents don't get paid. This is a rough deal for agents, so ensure that when you do get paid, it makes the ones that fell by the wayside all worthwhile.

Also, don't feel that the only fee structure you can do as well is a single percentage fee. I work with agents up and down the country that have had huge successes with various fee models and structures they have agreed with homeowners. One of the most popular is a scaled fee structure. This means that for up to a certain figure being agreed, the fee will be one figure and for anything above, the fee will increase. This can also be done over multiple steps to really incentivise an agent to get every penny for a client. Meaning that as the property sells for more, which is a good result for the homeowner, so does your fee, which is also a good result for you. Win-win all round. An example of this might be saying that if you sell a property for up to £250,000, your fee would be 1.5% + VAT. But if it sells for above £250,001 then your fee would be 2% + VAT. Therefore, you win when the client wins. I even have clients who agree that for any amount above £250,000, they get 50% of that extra, which can add up very quickly if a few people start bidding the price up. Play around and have fun with this. One golden rule of this which you may have spotted in my example, make sure there are no price overlaps. What I mean by this is our new higher fee started at £250,001 rather than £250,000 because if it were to sell for £250,000, which fee would be due? Ensue confusion from everyone.

By the end of this section of the conversation with the homeowner we should have worked out exactly what the seller is going to walk away with once they sell their property. You'd take what you expect the property to achieve when it comes onto the market and take away your fee and any other fees due. If the seller doesn't know how much they need to put aside for solicitors for example, this is an open goal for you to quote for this and potentially get paid for it further down the line. This method makes it crystal clear how you are adding value to the sale. Sure, you're charging a premium fee, but do they want the extra money you are going to get them and a quicker and smoother sale as a result? I'm sure the answer is yes, making you the easy choice to move forward with.

Closing for the business

When it comes to the estate agency world, there is one job in my experience that most estate agents are absolutely terrible at and it's a job that should come so naturally to them given what they do for a career.

Imagine the scene, you've been out leaflet-dropping in the rain for the last few days, when finally, your phone pings. You've had a lead through from one of your leaflets, yes! This is good news, you think. On getting back home, you look online at the address and see it's a good property that you think you can sell quickly and is in the right sort of area for you. You then call up the homeowner, have a great conversation with them, and book a market appraisal on their property for the upcoming weekend. After this conversation, you hand-deliver a pre-market appraisal letter when, again, you have a chat with the owner on the driveway and confirm your upcoming appointment once more. You then spend an hour carrying out research on that property, printing and preparing it all, ready for the meeting.

Finally, it's the day of the appointment, you park up outside the home and memorise as much of the property comparables as you can before you go and knock on the front door. Over the next hour, you blow the homeowner's socks off with your presentation and talk about how you are the perfect person and business to sell their most prized possession. The owner nods along and seems to agree with everything you say throughout the appointment. Then you say 'Anyway, thank you for having me out to see your property today, you've got my number so when you want to sell your home just give me a call and I'll come and see you and take it onto the market'. Excuse me! What on earth just happened? Talk about snatching defeat from the jaws of victory!

You might look at this story and think 'that surely doesn't happen?' I assure you, this happens throughout estate agency offices all over the country and even the world daily. Estate agents do 99% of all the hard work, then pack up their bags and go back to the office just when they could have really easily just nudged home to victory with that extra 1% of hard work, or even less. I suppose the big question here is, why? Why, in this example, did our salesperson do all the upfront hard work but simply not close for the business? Now, this isn't a psychology book, and I'm in no way a psychologist, but I know enough about people and myself to understand that no one likes to be rejected or have people say no to them. Which is why many estate agents don't allow themselves to be in a position where someone can actually do this to them and make them feel this way. And honestly, I get it. No one likes to feel they have been refused or closed down, be it professionally or personally.

I can't be clear enough on this. It is important for your business to get to the levels you want it to be at, that you close for the business. We're going to run through some various options shortly, but what you'll discover is that really it doesn't have to be a super complicated sales close from a fancy sales book. Simply just asking someone, 'shall we get you on the market then?' will get a better result than saying nothing at all, walking away from the customer and not asking for the future business.

Here's a little trick I use personally to push myself to ask for the business whenever I possibly can. And actually, I use it for most aspects of my business, whether that's speaking in front of a crowd, recording a video to put online, asking for the business or basically anything that pushes me a little bit out of my comfort zone. Imagine a future where your business isn't doing well. In fact, it's doing so badly that it's time to close the doors for the last time and it's now time to inform your loved ones that it hasn't worked out for you and you have to close your business down. Just imagine how tough that conversation would be to have with your friends and family. Pretty tough, right? Now you've got two options ahead of you. Either you ask for this business on this appointment, or it's the conversation with your family about shutting your estate agency down. Which one are you going to choose? Which one is the easier option?

Well, I very much hope that you felt that asking a stranger – who has been telling you for the last hour or two how they want to sell their home – if they would actually like to sell their home with you, is a far, far easier conversation than telling your loved ones that you are closing your business down because it didn't work out.

This is how seriously you should look at closing for the business on market appraisals. I assure you that you don't need to be the most amazing valuer of properties or even have that much of an impressive bedside manner with homeowners. If you ask for the business, you will get it over someone that is a great estate agent but doesn't ask for the business. Just ask the right questions at the right time and it will overcome many shortcomings elsewhere. This doesn't mean we don't have to become all round great estate agents with amazing offerings and pitch, it just simply means that if you don't ask, you probably won't get. Trust me, with all these sorts of things, it's a bigger deal in your head than it is for the person you're asking.

Sometimes with sellers, they want to instruct the estate agent sitting opposite them but simply don't know what happens next in the process, they don't want to look stupid and say the wrong thing. After all, chances are this is the first home they have ever sold. You've probably sold multiple properties this month and this valuation is one of many. So, who do you think has a better idea of the next stages from here? Take their hand and guide them through what happens next. But don't literally take their hand, that will come across as very weird and inappropriate.

Now we have a solid understanding of how important closing is in your business, we're going to have a look at a few examples of various ways we can close for the business and effectively ask the homeowner if they would like to sell their home with us. Some of the below examples you may feel would work for you whilst others, you might find, don't suit your personal conversation style. That is absolutely fine. As we spoke about previously, the important part is that you ask for the business in some way as some way is better than in no way.

Let's start with the most basic way of closing for the business, and this is simply by asking a question which has two answers – yes or no. This is officially known as a 'direct close' as it leaves very little space for alternative answers outside of this. Although it's called a direct close, we can soften this up when speaking to people and I recommend you do. In an ideal situation, we should be closing for the business without the owner even noticing we are. It's just an organic flow of conversation that ends up with us taking the property onto the market or at least putting the next stages of this into action.

A very crude version of this direct close might be something like 'Do you want to instruct me to sell your home?' As you might sense from this, it's very to the point and could easily be said by some kind of estate agency robot in 50 years' time when AI finally takes all our jobs. The answer to this question is either going to be 'yes, I'd like to instruct you' or 'no, I don't think I will, thank you'. Okay, so let's try and soften this up a bit and add some personality to it, after all, we aren't all robots quite yet. You could instead try saying something like, 'Shall we move ahead and book a day for our photos to be taken of your home?' or 'Right then, shall we get your property onto the market ready for the weekend?' As you can see, these are far softer versions of the earlier question, but the results are the same.

In a perfect world, you should try and link any close back to the conversation you have already had in the meeting. You might have mentioned that you get most of your viewing requests come through on a Monday so you could include this, or that your photographer is really busy at the moment so it's important to get that booked in soon. Either way, we have linked back to previous conversations to help push the conversation in the direction we want it to go in.

So now we've looked at a very direct way of closing for the business. Let's look at another route we could take the conversation. This next option is called an assumptive close. Slight warning on this one, it takes either more confidence than the direct close, or if you don't have the confidence currently, a little bit of poker face will help you achieve this one. This close relies mostly on that confidence or at least the feeling of belief in yourself and the next steps at the end of a market appraisal.

To action this close, you just have to assume that the person sitting opposite you wants to sell their property with you, because why wouldn't they? Everyone else does. With this in mind, just explain to the homeowners what the next stages are and what we need to do to get their property onto the market. As you can tell, there aren't really any questions being asked here, more statements made about what you are going to do next to get them onto the market. As you can see, this is where confidence is going to need to be in place and you'll have to have faith in yourself to push forward with the next stage of the instruction. An example of this might be saying something like, 'Okay, sounds like we're on the same page with regard to selling your property, I'm going to pop to my car now, get my camera and we'll get things underway and listed for you by tomorrow.' As you can see, no question has been asked of the homeowner, you've just got on with it! You almost need this mindset of, 'everyone instructs me, why would you be any different?'

Okay, so you might be thinking that an assumptive close sounds a little bit like diving into the deep end of closing, and for some it might be. So, let's look at an option which requires less confidence and, from personal experience, works really well. I use this one all the time in my day-to-day. It's called an alternative close and it relies on us asking a question with two or more possible answers, but no matter which answer is given, it's good news for us. Sounds complicated but I assure you it really isn't.

A good example of this might be 'Okay the next step is for us to book the photographer in to take photographs of your home, which day would be better for you next week? Tuesday or Thursday?' As you can see from this example, neither option here is 'no, I don't want to book the photographer yet, thank you.' We really don't mind whether the photos are taken on a Tuesday or a Thursday as long as this property comes onto the market with ourselves, that's the important bit. Another example could be 'Would you like to come onto the market for offers in excess of £240,000 or an asking price of £250,000?' Again, neither option is a bad result for us, we succeed with this question no matter which of the two options they pick from this example.

Next up, we are going to look at a method called the carrot and the stick close. This is a process where we would demonstrate either the positives of doing what we would like them to do or, highlight the negatives if they don't act in alignment with this. Think about it almost like a good news/bad news close. An example of using the 'carrot' approach might be, 'if you sign up with me today, we have a promotion on where we'll throw in a premium listing on your portal listing.' As you can see, the carrot here is the included premium listing which we are using to sweeten the deal. On the other side of the coin, we have the stick approach, an example of this could be 'I know you mentioned you wanted to go onto the market in February, well most of the bungalows come onto the market in January, so you'll miss out if you're not sold before then.' The stick in this equation is our homeowner missing out on those bungalows coming onto the market in January by waiting another month before listing. Ideally the perfect use of the carrot and stick method should include a combination of both aspects of this question. Not only rewarding the seller for acting in line with what you want to achieve, but also knowing and understanding that if they don't follow this process, there's some sort of stick waiting for them just around the corner.

Finally let's look at the cautionary tale close. This closing method you probably won't be able to use from day one of your estate agency launching but very quickly, as you deal with more and more of the general public, you'll have lots of material to help you effectively deploy this. The reason being, this close relies upon you having had other clients who were in the same position that your current client is right now. It looks at what they did and how it worked out for them.

Let's look at an example for this one. 'Mr Jones, I understand what you're saying about waiting to find a property before you sell your own home, but I had a client just two weeks ago who felt the same way and did exactly the same thing, and since then they have missed out on three different properties that would have been perfect for them, because they weren't on the market.'

As you can see from this example, we have understood what the homeowner is looking to do, and we've given an example of someone else who was in the same situation they were in only a few weeks ago, and how it ended them. I've gone glass-half-empty in this example, but you could quite as easily say something with a positive result as well. I find from experience, though, people are more worried about a negative outcome than they are excited about a positive one. So, if in doubt, choose a negative ending to the story as it's more likely to resonate with the other person.

When it comes to closing for the business, there are thousands upon thousands of sales books written on this subject alone. The number of ways to ask for the business goes into probably millions of different methods and formats. Though no matter which style of closing you feel fits your personal preference, the important thing is that you do ask for the business and close for it. If you don't, you are leaving so much on the table to chance. After all, the reason you have been invited out to the property is because the homeowner more than likely wants to sell the home so what have you got to lose by asking if they would like to proceed with you? I assure you the upside is far bigger and better than the downside.

After the market appraisal

Okay, so we are now at the stage where we have completed the market appraisal and we have demonstrated to the owner why we're the perfect choice of estate agent to sell their property. We have most definitely tried to close for the business as we are keen to get this property onto the market sooner rather than later. If there is any reason why the property doesn't come onto the market straight away, have a think about what you could change next time in your process so that for the next market appraisal, you can go straight to signing on the dotted line.

For example, if at the end of the market appraisal, the owner says, 'Thank you for coming out today, I'll speak to my wife and come back to you after the weekend.', where do you think you went wrong? That's right, at the booking stage. You should have booked the appointment at a time where both owners of the property could have been in so you would have stood a better chance of being instructed there and then. Review your processes constantly, and what you'll end up with is a system that works more often than it fails. Sure, you can't make everyone happy all the time, but for most people your process should be as bulletproof as it possibly can be.

I'm going to be glass-half-empty here and go in the direction of the worst-case scenario, that being that the owner from the market appraisal didn't agree to come onto the market with you there and then. I'm sure that during your presentation to the owner, you spoke about the excellent personal service they would receive when interacting with your estate agency business. Well, we have another opportunity coming up to not only show that off but also to close for the business all over again.

Statistically, when selling their home, most people in the United Kingdom book three estate agents to value their home to get a good cross section on not only the value of their property but also which agent will align best with them personally. Already if you're following the processes in this book, you should be the first agent they see back when we hand-delivered the pre-market appraisal letter to them before the valuation of the property took place. But we also want to be the last agent that they see, as well. This is where the next stage comes in.

After we have carried out the market appraisal and agreed a future time and date to speak to the homeowner, we should be hand delivering a post-market appraisal letter to the property that summarises not only what we have spoken about that day, but also includes any details that may help the homeowner off the back of our conversation with them. Again, this is a good chance for us to go above and beyond what other agents are doing in our town.

As a worst-case scenario, this hand-delivered letter will demonstrate our personal service to the seller once more and will give us another chance to close for the business. Most sellers have all the market appraisals on their property on the same day, so chances are that by the time you have gone back to your office, sorted out this letter and returned to the property, one or maybe two of the other market appraisals will have been carried out by the other agents. During the market appraisal, you could also ask what time and what other agents they have coming out to value their property, which would make far less guesswork involved with this part of the process for you. What we can do to bolster this section even further is include other property information in this pack that will potentially help the homeowner and their onward move.

Let's say for example, during the market appraisal, the owner mentioned how they would love a bungalow in a certain area of your town but simply couldn't find one. What we should be doing here is helping the owner in this part of the process if we haven't already done so earlier on. For this example, you could look on Rightmove Plus after the appointment, in the same way we spoke about in earlier chapters and look for suitable bungalows that have been taken off the market over the last few years. Print these withdrawn bungalow details off and include them in your marketing pack you're delivering to the owner. Then, when the owner answers the door to you, you can then explain that not only have you included the post-market appraisal letter summarising everything discussed on the appointment, but you have been back to the office and highlighted some potential properties. And that if they like the look of them, you'll contact the owner to see if they would be open to a one-off viewing on their property. If you didn't look good in the owner's eyes beforehand, you do now. This sort of proactivity is going to set you apart from the rest and all it took was a few extra minutes and some thinking outside the box. Always look to go above and beyond at this stage, as it'll make a big difference.

To be crystal clear, right now you should be looking to make conversation with the owner once more when delivering this letter and look to close for the business all over again. After all, they may have wanted to hear from the other agents before they decided. Well, that has now happened, so let's decide, shall we?

If you aren't in a position to sign up the business again at this point, then reconfirm your next catch-up phone call with the owner. This might be as simple as 'speak to you on Monday!'

If you'd like a copy of an example post market appraisal letter that you could use for this. Simply scan the QR code and you'll be taken through to a template you can use for exactly this task

The chase has begun

'The definition of customer service is phoning them before they phone you.'

I love this expression. I use it all the time in my day-to-day workings because it is so true. Never in your business should you leave the ball in the court of the homeowner or applicant for that matter, with them calling you, seriously, never. I don't care whether they are off to the Caribbean for two weeks and they'll 'give you a call when they're back', or they say they'll 'call you once they have 'found a property to buy.' It's your job to be proactive and be on the front foot with communications. This means you are always calling them, they are never calling you.

Call me when you're back from the Caribbean? What date are you back? Insert note in diary or CRM system to call Mrs Jones upon their return, asking how their holiday was, and if they have decided to go onto the market. This in no way means you should be pestering people, but you should always be trying to speak to them rather than sitting back and waiting for the phone to ring. After all, you're keen to sell their property, aren't you?

When dealing with members of the public, you'll find that some people are fantastic at coming back to you whilst others leave a lot to be desired. This is a polite way of me saying, dealing with the general public can sometimes feel like herding cats, and getting them to return your calls is no different to this. Putting this to one side though, we need to make sure that we make the process of staying in contact with us as easy as we possibly can and keep ensuring the owners not only know that we are keen to sell their property, but also make the process of touching base with us as frictionless as possible.

For this reason, if we are not successful in getting a market appraisal converted into an instruction, we should then ensure we have a robust follow-up process in place to make sure that this potential instruction does fall 'off of our desk' never to be seen or spoken to again. For some sellers this could involve a call every couple of days, whilst others you might feel a call every six months might be more appropriate. The important thing is that the contact never just stops and dries up one day. Basic use of your CRM system makes this job really easy to enforce on a regular basis. My golden rule on this is, if you are ever in doubt about how soon you should contact a homeowner, always go for the nearest option. It's better to be early to a party then turn up three days later, when everyone else has gone home.

A good exercise when tracking potential instructions that may come onto the market with you in the future is to keep a list of these potential instructions. This could be a list within your CRM system, it could be a spreadsheet, or even my personal favourite, the white board. I'll use the latter as my example as this is the most basic and universal method out of the options above. On one side of your whiteboard, write a list of all the potential homes that you may get onto the market in the future. These could be properties you think are coming on next week, whilst others might be a few months or even years. In the middle of the board next to the properties, write down what is stopping that property from coming into the market today. Then finally, next to this column, produce another one with the jobs you can do to assist that property to come onto the market sooner rather than later.

For example, you might have 123 New Road which you went to see last week. The factor holding them back from coming onto the market – which would go in the next column – might be that they want to find a home locally to move into before they go onto the market. In the final column, you would list all the jobs you can do to help them find a home. This could include leaflet drops, social media posts, VIP letters, withdrawn letters and so on.

Another example might be 456 Old Road which you went to yesterday. One of the factors that you might highlight as a potential blocker to them coming onto the market could be that just one owner attended the appointment instead of the two that you expected. The solution to this could be a screen recording video to send to the other homeowner who couldn't attend, running through what you spoke to their partner about. This could highlight which comparables you looked at, how you are going to market the property and how you arrived at the price you did for the home.

The very obvious next step is to put into action what you have written down in the final column of this exercise. By doing this you are not only improving the chance of this seller coming to the market at all, but also pushing yourself firmly into pole position to be the agent of choice for them to pick to work with. When you are doing these tasks, let the homeowner know. Gone leaflet dropping in the rain to find them a house? Send them a video making them aware of this. Always make sure you are your own biggest cheerleader, if you've done a good job for someone, let them know!

One-off viewings

Just because a homeowner doesn't want to instruct you to get their property onto the market as soon as you possibly can, doesn't mean that they wouldn't be open to exploring this option sooner than they expect should a potential buyer fall into their lap.

A process that I have implemented and sold copious amounts of properties from in the past is one-off viewings on properties that aren't currently on the market. It's relatively simple to set up, as I'll explain. Whilst in the closing stages of a market appraisal and you understand that the property isn't going to be immediately going onto the market in the short term, just mention to the owner 'On the off chance I speak to a buyer who is specifically looking for a home just like yours, are you happy for me to run a potential one-off viewing past you?'. Newsflash, everyone says yes to this, because what have they got to lose?

Imagine their surprise when you give them a call in the coming weeks to pick up this conversation. 'Remember as I was leaving, Mr Jones, you mentioned you'd be open to a one-off viewing on your home should I find the perfect buyer? Well, great news! I've found the ideal person for your home. When would be good for them to come around to take a look?' Also, if you're super smart about this you can get someone around to view this property who also has a property you can sell if they find their dream home. You're literally making two potential sales out of nothing here.

Let's play out the options here. The best-case scenario is the buyer comes around, loves the house, lists their own with you to sell and away we go. The other option is the buyer who comes around, doesn't like the property for some reason and doesn't want to go ahead with it.

In this situation, the person who viewed the home thinks you're great because you're going above and beyond to try and find them a home, and this is only going to push you closer to being their agent of choice. On the original property, if they are open to a one-off viewing on their home then they are clearly ready to sell, so let's have a conversation about getting onto the market sooner rather than later.

A couple of key points to cover here before we head away from this topic. You would always want to get your terms and conditions signed by the seller of the property. You can clearly state in the T&Cs that they're only applicable for this one-off viewing with the Smith family. If you don't, you're going to potentially have an uphill struggle should the owner decide to go behind your back with their newfound buyer. Not great business.

The second key point is that if this one-off viewing deal did come together, we would not only make full property particulars for the home we have just sold but we would also mark it up for sale, if only for a few hours before marking it as under offer online. You might be thinking, 'What's the point? It's sold already.' Well, I'll tell you. We need full details for surveyors and solicitors for one. Second of all, and most importantly, think of all that positive publicity you are going to miss out on should you not tell the world about this brilliant job you've done. The reason we will mark the property for sale for a few hours, then mark it as under offer, is for the benefit of your average selling time. I don't care which estate agency you run in the world, let alone the UK. Add a new property selling time of two hours into the mix, it is going to boost your average selling time by some margin. A nice little bonus.

Listing a property onto the market

We have now arrived at a really exciting stage in your estate agency journey – taking a property onto the market. Listing someone's home, especially for the first time, is a key part of an estate agent's journey. Mainly because let's be frank, if you haven't got any properties to sell then you are going to be in trouble very quickly.

As we know, when it comes to selling homes, we can never guarantee that a property is going to sell, and as we spoke about earlier, we can never know exactly what price a home is going to sell for either. But what we can do is put all the marketing TNT we possibly can behind the property so that when it does come onto the market, we are giving it the best possible opportunity of not only selling, but also going for a great price as well.

In this section we are going to look at how to take a property onto the market so that it will be punching well above its weight. We'll look at not only the processes in the property that will make it a success, but also, we'll look at how you can leverage this property to get even more properties onto the market, which is going to be great for your business. After all, what's better than having one house for sale? That's right, two.

First of all, though, let's look at the number one job of your listing. Once we establish this, we can then work backwards from there. So, what do you think this might be? To sell the property? To show off your estate agency and what a great job you do? Well, these are both really good answers, but I would always see the number one job of a for sale listing to be to generate as much interest in the property as possible, and to get your office phone ringing as much as we possibly can. More phone calls not only equal more potential buyers, but also equal more opportunities for you to convert these phone calls into market appraisals, third-party income, future clients and so on. All of which will be good for you.

The way I have always thought about property adverts is comparing them to an online dating profile for the property world. First of all, we don't want to give away everything. We want people to be keen to investigate the property further.

Just imagine setting up an online dating profile for yourself with 50 photos, a bible-length description stating everything about you: what you do on Monday night, where you favourite holiday was, where you're from and what your favourite meal is. Everyone would think you're an absolute psychopath and would rightly swipe left. What would be a far better route to go down? Perhaps picking a few photos where you look your best, a short description that lists a couple of interesting facts about you, then sitting back and waiting for the matches to come in. More isn't necessarily better. This is the same mindset you should have when marketing your property. We don't need to see what colour the downstairs toilet's carpet is, we just need to know it has one.

Thinking back to your personal dating profile, do you think it would be better to put some average photos up first, and wait to see how these get on before dropping some of your grade-A content on the dating site? I'm hoping you were shaking your head on that last one. I'm thinking you would say that from day one, you would be dropping your top-quality content on the site to give yourself the best chance of making the biggest splash possible with whoever you are looking for rather than sandbagging your better stuff as some kind of Plan B.

This happens with property listings every single day. Agents up and down the country give away too many details that just aren't important on their listings and if anything, push people away from being interested in the property. Then to make things worse, when they're a couple of weeks down the line and aren't getting traction at all is when they'll look at what they can add to the listing to hopefully drag it out of the proverbial gutter and onto the straight and narrow.

To be crystal clear, when they launch, your listings should not only look their absolute best, but should have every piece of supporting marketing engaged from day one. There are two very good reasons why this is the right route to go down. First of all, like most things in this world, your listing is going to have a honeymoon period. This is the first three weeks when a property comes onto the market. It's new, it's fresh, buyers haven't seen it yet. This is the part of the selling process and marketing journey where the property will more than likely be getting the most interest it is ever going to get, as very soon it'll be old news and there'll be new properties on the block. The second reason, which aligns with the first reason, is that when a property comes onto the property portals as new instructions, the portals will send this out to anyone who has registered on their site and saved this search when looking to buy. This means that if you have a three-bedroom semi-detached home in a certain village or town coming on the market, anyone that has been on that portal and highlighted that type of property in that village or town as a potential purchase will receive a marketing email from the portal informing them that a property matching their criteria has come on the market.

So how many people do you think get these emails? A couple of hundred? A couple of thousand? Well, it varies from place to place throughout the UK, but in my experience most areas have tens of thousands, whilst some more built-up areas go into the hundreds of thousands. That's one big mailing list your property is going out to and I'm willing to bet it's a fair amount bigger than your mailing list of potential buyers.

If you wanted a third reason to make sure your property is looking 10 out of 10 when you launch it, just think of that email going out to tens of thousands of buyers and potential sellers in and around your local area, but you've done a terrible job of presenting the home. This isn't exactly the best advert for your estate agency business, I think you'll agree. On the other hand, if you do have your new listing looking absolutely spectacular, this can be a massive opportunity for you to show the locals in your area exactly what you can do, showcasing you as an agent who does a brilliant job presenting their homes.

Hopefully you know now that when you put your properties up for sale, they should be as good as you can possibly get them, and you should be throwing everything at it from day one. No warning shots, just drop your marketing nuclear bomb straight away.

The take-on

When taking a property onto the market, most agents book in a separate appointment to return to the property and start the ball rolling on the marketing. It could be the next day or it could be a few weeks' time once a couple of pieces of work have been carried out in the property. What I would recommend is always try and get as much as you possibly can, while you can. Imagine you're back on the market appraisal and the homeowner you've met today has agreed to come on the market with you to sell their home. Would you just walk out the door and see them in a few days' time? You could do, but you're running the risk of potentially losing this business, as another agent could swoop in and sign them up right under your nose. Just imagine how annoying that would be. Instead, you should get as much done on this first appointment as you can. This could include getting your terms and conditions signed and could even include drawing a floor plan, for example. You can then get the rest of the details done later. The more you can do at this initial stage, the less chance you have of losing the business. Even if you hypothetically ignored the contractual part of proceeding and just focused on getting photos, floorplans, and description taken care of on the appointment, do you really think the homeowner is going to want another estate agent doing all that all over again so they have to tidy up for a second time? I very much doubt it.

We can take this even further. Imagine you've got a property whose owners have said they want to come onto the market with you, but they need to finish some decorating over the coming week, first. Option one could be calling them every week or so to see how they're getting on. This is fine, at least you're staying in regular contact with them. What would be better though, is letting the homeowner know you'll come around as soon as possible and do everything you can that won't be affected by the decorating. This could include having all compliance paperwork signed, floorplans produced, and the description all done. This not only means that when the property has been decorated, all you have to do is take photos and you're good to go. But also, by doing the work beforehand, it ties the owner to selling with you. Because will they now want any more estate agents coming round their home and measuring up? Not if they can avoid it. The instruction is as good as ours.

For the sake of ease, in this next section, we are going to book a time a couple of days after our market appraisal to meet the homeowner again and take the property onto the market. In this appointment, we are going to complete all of the tasks to ensure we get this done. Hopefully, you'll have a few ticked off already.

Okay, let's get the elephant out of the room on this bit, as we're going to have to talk about compliance. Something that in no way interests me any more than it interests you, but as estate agents in the UK, the government sees you as the first line of defence against certain financial crimes such as money laundering. Which does make an awesome-sounding business card title. Also on this subject, as a brilliant get out of jail card for me, this is only meant as a guide to the compliance rules for getting a property onto the market, as the rules and regulations can change on a regular basis and I'd hate for someone to get into trouble over a new rule I simply hadn't predicted in this book. My advice would be, if in any doubt about how to compliantly take a property onto the market for sales, consult with a compliance company who specialise in this sector. Trust me, there are plenty to choose from.

When taking a property onto the market and dealing with the homeowner, there are two questions you need to answer. They are, firstly, can I prove the person in front of me is the person they say they are? And secondly, do they even have the right to sell this property? If you can't prove either of these, it's going to be a bit of a nonstarter for you straight away.

Starting with the first problem we are going to have to face, is this person who they say they are? As you might imagine, this is photographic ID time for all legal owners of the property. Think passports, driving licence and so on. To answer your next question, bus passes don't count. You can find a list of what you can accept for this on the government website if you are ever in doubt at any stage of the process. Sometimes you may be faced with certain clients who may not have a driving licence or a passport, but you can make up for this shortcoming with a selection of other documents which will tick the boxes for this section instead.

Next up, let's look at how we can prove that the person looking to sell the property we're standing in actually owns it, and isn't a tenant who is super keen on selling this rental home they've found themselves in. This is going to include paperwork such as land registry documents, mortgage statements, property deeds and so on. This isn't to be confused with someone proving their 'proof of address' which can be done with something like a utility bill. As you'll know, just because someone lives in a home and pays the gas bill, doesn't necessarily mean they have the right to sell it!

Once you have copies or photographs of these documents, upload them to your CRM system. This is one of its core jobs: a safe place to store customer information. We've all heard those stories of people who leave plans for nuclear submarines in a pub toilet. Well, don't be one of those people. Snap it, upload it and delete from your phone, leaving it safely held on your password protected computer system to be called on if you need it in the future. After all, if you ever had an audit in future, lines like 'I lost that document' or 'that's on my old phone' are not going to make you pass with colours.

Now let's move onto getting your terms and conditions signed by the homeowner. As you might imagine this is a key part of the process for you because it will not only outline what is expected from you as an agent selling the property but will also spell out exactly how much you are going to get paid at the end of the transaction. And how long this homeowner is tied to you as their selling agent of choice. A couple of golden rules here: firstly, try and get this signed as soon as possible. This document commits the owner to selling their property with you, which is a good start but also shows that you are both on the same page moving forward. After all, I'm not sure many people just sign anything that is put in front of them without giving it some kind of thought on how it might affect them. The second golden rule is to make sure this document is signed by all legal owners of the property. I have heard stories in the past where estate agents have had calls from husbands and wives who have had no idea their partner is putting their property up for sale without their consent. As you might imagine, not only is this a very embarrassing situation for all involved but also a non-compliant situation for the agent, too. They should have known better, really.

These days, most agents have their agency agreements uploaded into some form of online signing platform so that they can quickly and easily send their agreement over to the sellers as soon as they're given the green light. Also, this allows you to add all owners of the property onto this signing route ensuring that everyone signs exactly the same agreement no matter where they are in the world. This will hopefully prevent any potential misunderstandings. If you're slightly more old-school than this and are still using a paper and pen, this is absolutely fine, but I would still, as soon as you have the agreement signed, file it away and upload a photo or scan of the agreement onto your CRM system again, just in case you lose the original. Which happens more than you might think.

Finally, we are going to look at property information forms, also known as PIFs, and why these are so very important for your business. This is a form that will be completed by the homeowner before the property goes onto the market. It will ask them lots of questions about their home and will highlight key facts which will be important for anyone that might be looking to purchase the home.

The first reason why this is important to have is because you always want to appear knowledgeable about the property you're selling. Answering every question with 'I don't know' isn't going to fill anyone with a huge amount of confidence that you're the sharp estate agent that you want to be seen as. Sure, we can't prepare for every question that someone asks us when they look around a property to buy, but most people buying properties are highly predictable in what they want to know. I've never known whether this is because most people are very similar to one another, or whether there is a genuine lack of knowledge of what questions to ask when looking to buy a home. Whichever it is, the questions you are going to be asked on a viewing will be very consistent from one appointment to the next, so you should know with some certainty what people are going to ask you before you even start the first viewing.

The property information form allows you to gather all this information beforehand, so if anyone asks you how old the boiler is, for example, you'll know the answer. Or if they ask you if the loft is boarded, then again, we have the answer all lined up and ready to go. Not only does this give the buyer a better viewing experience when looking to purchase a home, but it also paints a far better picture of you as an estate agent and an estate agency business.

The second reason why this form is crucial to you is because it becomes your get out of jail free card for the property. I should point out that I don't mean this literally, but having it filled out right at the start can help you with a potential problem down the line. Imagine you have just agreed to a sale on a great property, the buyers are over the moon and the seller is hugely impressed with what a great job you have done. The survey on the property is booked quickly, which is always a good sign. However, once the survey has been carried out, you hear from the buyer that they have found Japanese knotweed next to the home. This could be a disaster for the sale. The buyer relays this information to you and asks you to speak to the homeowner about this issue and how this might be resolved. Now imagine, in that conversation with the homeowner, they say 'You knew about the knotweed all along, I told you about it when you first put the property onto the market!' How would you prove that, actually, you had no idea about the knotweed and this conversation never took place? You couldn't. It would be your word against the homeowner's, and I'd imagine the buyer wouldn't take much convincing to believe that you had known all along but kept quiet so you could get the property sold and your commission paid. This is not a good situation. We're in between a rock and a hard place. I'm sure the buyers would be very annoyed if they thought you knew about this issue all along and they would be well within their rights to try and recoup some of the costs of their attempted purchase from you.

The property information form may well come to your rescue in this situation, as it's a document where the homeowner needs to also disclose any reason, obvious or not, that they know of that might affect the property sale. This doesn't necessarily mean issues with just the property as well. This could also include a next-door neighbour who is verging on psychopathic that the owner has called the police about on several occasions. Once they have filled in the form with all of the information about the property that they know, they then sign the document to confirm that it is correct to the best of their knowledge. Sure, they aren't expected to know everything about the property, but if they had subsidence, or the neighbour is taking the fence down with a chainsaw at three in the morning, I'm sure these are subjects that would spring to mind when completing this.

As you can see from the two massive reasons given, it is paramount that you complete a property information form when you take a property onto the market. Not having this in place can leave you exposed not only to looking like you don't know what you're talking about inside a property you are looking to sell, but even worse, can also can leave you exposed as a business as a whole, to a client who sees you as an easy scapegoat in the equation.

Next up, we are going to look at how to present your properties online so that they generate as much interest as possible. Notice I've not said to sell the properties as quickly as possible. As we spoke about earlier, the job of your listing isn't to sell the home, that's the job of the viewing. The job of your property listing is to get your phone ringing with opportunities for you to grasp with both hands and get as much as you can from them. That means that we only want to highlight the best bits of the property we are selling, to entice people to enquire about it. More enquiries equal more opportunities for you to benefit from. It's as simple as that.

To set ourselves up for success here, we need to look at the data on what makes the ideal property listing. Luckily, property portals actively encourage agents to produce their listings in a certain way so that they perform better on their sites. It's good for them, and it's good for you. But in spite of this, many agents up and down the country chose to ignore this advice and instead of looking at millions of data points which all say you should do X on your instructions, they go for old reliable Y which they have done for the last 20 years as 'it's done okay so far.'

We are going to follow the more scientific route here and work through what actually works when listing a property rather than just focusing on old wives' tales about what once sold a property in a week back in 1986.

How do I look?

Firstly, let's look at preparing the property for marketing. In my experience, most of the public generally fall into two camps in this, either: you can eat the dinner off the floor because the house is so tidy or the dinner from last night is still on the floor because it is so untidy. There is usually very little between the two.

It's your job as an agent to advise the homeowner of any changes they can make that will increase the chances of them selling their home. Also, this will make your job a lot easier because not only will it make the property present better for your property details, but it will also help when you show potential buyers around the home.

I'm not for a second saying that you should be telling homeowners to spend vast amounts of money on renovating their property, but what you should be doing is actively giving them advice on small tasks that will have a big impact on the selling process. This could be hiding more boxes in the garage, tidying up, or putting in a couple of air fresheners to cover the smell of the dog. Though as you might imagine, it's important to try and be tactful with these conversations. No one wants to hear that their home smells, instead, just talk about it being a better buyer experience if there are some air fresheners in the property.

The camera never lies

As you may expect, photographs are a key part of any property listing. They say a photo can say a thousand words, and they are absolutely right. Imagine a photograph of a dark dingy room, curtains drawn and food bowls all over the floor. Straight away, you assume the house is going to be a mess throughout and this one won't be the one for you, stopping you from visiting the property and discovering it is in fact, the ideal home for you and your family. The 'thousand words' for this property photo though would start with 'dark' and end with 'messy' with little improvement between the two.

The photos you take of your listings will also act as a digital shop window for your estate agency business. Imagine a company with poor photography on the properties they're selling, straight away, not only would you assume this isn't the property for you, but also that this is not the estate agency you want to use to sell your own property. If they can't even take good photos of a home, what's everything that I can't see going to be like? This is why it's always important that your photographs are absolutely 10 out of 10. Lots of my clients outsource their photography to a local professional photographer for exactly this reason. It makes their properties look better and makes their estate agency business look the best it possibly can online. Sure, they might end up paying for these photographs in the short-term, but I would say this is a worthy investment in the long run.

The statistics even back this up, as studies have shown that properties that have professional photography on them actually sell for closer to the asking price than homes that don't. How much closer, you might be thinking? Well, around 2%. That means that for the average home in the UK, having professional photography as one of your USPs could potentially increase the amount your seller ends up with by around £5,000, which for most agents will pay for themselves and more.

Remember that the next time your potential seller is trying to haggle you down by 0.25%!

With our photographs of the property, we should be looking to highlight the best possible aspects of the home and make everything look its absolute best. The portals recommend that for the average home, which around 90% of all listings will fall into, we should have between 9 and 12 photos displayed online. As an absolute worst-case scenario, if we're taking on the world's smallest studio flat, we should have a minimum of five photos in place. But it's important that where you can, you get up to at least the nine photos. For most homes though, your biggest issue is going to be trimming the fat from your photographs and actually getting down to the ceiling limit of 12 photos, especially if you have an overly keen seller who wants you to upload every inch of their property. If you find yourself in this situation, you need to reassure the seller that you're using the facts to sell their home, rather than just the aspects they would like you to use.

To be 100% clear, just pick the 9-12 photos that show off the best of the property. This is a dating ad for the house you're putting onto the market. We don't need to see everything at this stage.

The order in which you put your photographs online is also important, as we want to start with our best foot forward. In the same way that you'll never get seen if you are on page nine of Google, the first few photographs we put online are going to be viewed more than the rest. So, it stands to reason that we put some of our best photos first. Typically, the order of your photographs should be a front shot of the property, then the living accommodation, followed by the bedroom accommodation and last of all, the garden photos. But since the pandemic, more and more people are looking for a property with some kind of outside space. This means that one of our garden photos – and I'd suggest the best one you have here – is going to be promoted into the first four photographs on your listing. This can include any outside space with the property, so if you're selling an apartment with a balcony, this balcony photo would need to appear within the first four photos of your instruction.

If you're working alongside a professional photographer, they will have a good idea about what will look good for property photographs and what won't. If you're thinking of taking the photographs yourself, I would suggest you look into a photography training course, as taking great photos isn't as easy as simply pressing the shutter button, as you'll soon find out.

When taking great photographs, a lot of producing the best images comes down to the prep work involved beforehand. As we covered earlier, by now you should have advised the owner to have a nice clean home and to have the property as photo ready as it can be. But there are still lots of small mistakes that I see agents make time and time again when they take property photos and I bet if you go onto your favourite property portal, you'll spot some of these within minutes, if not seconds of your search results coming in. They include such aspects as: cars on driveways, clothes in the washing machine, the TV on, washing up liquid and bowls on the kitchen side, tea towels and oven gloves in the kitchen, bins in photos, bath towels in the bathroom and finally my personal pet hate, the toilet seat being left up… Ladies, I'm with you on this one 100%.

As you see, none of these things require massive fixes or will take much time to sort out, but you need to have a keen eye for what is going to stand out in your photos for the wrong reasons, otherwise, whilst reviewing your photos later on you'll wish you made some small changes before you started snapping away.

Where's the floorplan?

Next up, let's look at floorplans. I read an interesting statistic some years ago that said that 50% of all homeowners wouldn't instruct an estate agent who doesn't produce a floorplan for a home they are selling. So, with this in mind, not only are you producing a floorplan to help show off the layout of the home you're about to sell, but also, you're producing it to impress any future sellers who may want to use you to market their home in future.

Floorplans act as a helpful guide to the property layout and should therefore, be on every single property you bring to the market, no matter how small or big the home is. But we can do better than a boring old two-dimensional floor plan like most agents. For little or no extra work we can not only have a 3D floor plan, but also a plot plan for the entire home, showing exactly where the property sits on the site itself. This will show not only how big the gardens are but also the layout of the outside of the property, which will give buyers a good idea of what they are going to view before they even park up outside.

I will, at this stage, add a caveat to adding a plot plan onto a listing and that revolves around the size of the garden on the home. If you have a fairly small or normal size garden compared to the size of the home, then the plot plan attached to the floorplan for the property will work perfectly fine. The times where it doesn't work very well is when you have a large amount of land with the property and a fairly modest-sized home. Imagine a small bungalow sitting on 10 acres of land. The plot plan would be a huge expanse of green outside space and after you zoom in a few times, you'll eventually realise that there is a bungalow in the middle of the plan, with a layout sketched out. In this sort of situation, you'd be far better off attaching a separate image or plan highlighting the outline of the land around the property and this image won't be directly attached or affect your floor plan.

Lots of professional photography companies include a floor plan as part of their package when they produce professional photographs of the property, or you can simply produce these yourself. With a bit of practice, you can produce an accurate plan of most homes in 30 minutes or less. No matter who produces the plan, it's important that you review it once you have completed it. I'd make sure that all rooms have doors, windows and that any other large aspects are covered in the plan.

Talk to me

Property descriptions are a key aspect of any listing. Get them right, and you'll boost intrigue and excitement about the property you're bringing onto the market. Get them wrong, and the only thing you'll see is tumbleweed rolling past your new instruction.

Your description will fall into two camps, one is the initial description which sits next to the listing on the search pages of the portals and is capped at a relatively small number of characters. The other part is the full description which, as the name gives away, is where we can describe the rest of the property. The expression goes that once you have written the headline for a published piece, you have spent 80% of your marketing money. The following 20% is in the main text of the article. This shows the value of having your initial description of the property pop as much as you can, otherwise no one is going to look at your full description and you might as well have just saved your time and effort.

To start off with, let's take a look at some information that portals will automatically upload for us when we put a property live on their websites. This information will include the road, the area, the price, how many bedrooms, how many bathrooms, the style of property and your estate agency details.

With all this in mind, you might imagine you're wasting your time writing an initial sentence like:

Chris Webb Estate Agents are proud to bring to the market this three-bedroom, two-bathroom detached home in the popular area of New Village.

Even if we uploaded the property online with no text at all (which I don't recommend, by the way) we would have known all that information already from the information the portals automatically pull through. This is just a huge missed opportunity for you and your business to get across how great the property is you are looking to sell. In these sorts of situations, we need to make the property stand out in a crowded marketplace. I would recommend either telling the potential buyers something they don't know about the property that will attract them in, telling them who this property would be absolutely perfect for, or both, if you can.

An example of this would be:

Have a look at these amazing views over the New Valley! If you're a growing family looking for your forever home, look no further!

Or

Wow! This is the perfect home for a first-time buyer, just a short distance from the town centre!

In the above examples, not only have we told the potential viewers something they may not already know, that being that the property comes with amazing views of a nearby valley or is close to the town centre. We have also highlighted that it would be perfect for a family looking for their forever home or a first-time buyer. Both boxes ticked and we have made a splash for our property listing in the first couple of lines alone.

Only if we have made a good impression to someone viewing the initial part of our listing on the search page will they then click through to look at the full details. This is where it will lay out the full description of the property for them to read. This conversion from search result page through to clicking into the advert for more details is tracked by the large portals and is something we'll go through later in the book, called the click-through rate or CTR for short. As might imagine, the golden rule here is the higher this conversion rate the better, as more people are interested in clicking on your listing for further details.

Now we've got potential buyer's attention with your catchy introduction to the property, and they're reading our full description. We need to look at the same rules that we have applied throughout this listing process. That is the understanding that the text we enter here should be focused on getting your phone ringing. The full description is not an autobiography of the property or some structural survey for the home. Instead, it should highlight the best parts of the property and push people to make contact with your business.

Personally, I would always divide this into two halves. One is going to talk about the property itself, well, the best bits of it at least, and the other is going to talk about the area the property sits in.

With the first section, we should be looking at getting across the best aspects of the property as soon as we can. Lots of agents make the mistake of going for almost a guided written tour of the home starting at the front door and going straight into the downstairs WC, then onto the rest of the property. Best foot forward doesn't mean talking about the toilet in the first two lines, I assure you. Instead, what we should be looking to build on is our initial headline. You've mentioned this would make a brilliant family home. Okay, so what's important to families? Kitchens, living rooms and gardens. So, let's start with these shall we?

You don't need to go into every detail about every room either, just highlight the main points that will be of interest to people viewing the property. Had a fancy kitchen installed? Name the company who installed it. Got built-in appliances in the home? Say so. The property has an amazing wood burner? Great, tell me about it. What we don't want to know about, though, is how many plug sockets there are or how the current carpet was lovingly installed 15 years ago. Finally, we should include details of the less exciting rooms of the house, but these should all come towards the end of the full description of the property.

Next, we should have a paragraph all to do with the local area that property sits in. This could include if it is close to the town centre, bus stops, mainline railways, schools and so on. Think about this section as a bit of an overview of what makes this the perfect area to live in for the people we have highlighted so far. If you suspect the buyer of this property is going to be a young family, highlight local primary schools, secondary schools, community centres and parks. Effectively paint a picture of the local area, the amenities it offers and state why this makes the property perfect for them.

Now we have the initial text and our main body of text completed for our listing, the next area we want to focus on is the bullet. These are short snappy points about the property which people can quickly look at and assess if they want to read more about the home. For most portals, we can have up to 10 bullet points. I would suggest you use all of them. As before, let's try and not repeat information that the buyer already knows from the portal such as number of bedrooms, bathrooms and so on. Instead, include information that they won't know such as 'large double garage' or 'over one acre of gardens.'

The importance of keywords

There is a very good reason why we want to use all 10 available bullet points and that comes back to something called keyword search. Imagine you are looking to buy a property yourself, you go onto your favourite portal and type in the type of property you'd like to buy along with your preferred price range. After this stage though, most portals allow the user to refine their search down even further by adding keywords into their search for anything specific they're after. These are all the aspects of a property that you would expect people to be searching for: garage, garden, parking, annexe, land, and so on. These keywords will narrow down the search even further, highlighting properties with the features that we have typed in.

For this reason, it's really important that if you have any aspects of your property that align with someone's keyword search, that you include this in one of four places on your listing. Those four places are, in the initial text on the search page, in the main description, in the bullet points and in the premium listing label, something that we'll come on to very shortly. Therefore, if we have a property which is currently divided up into an annexe, for example, it's important that we make sure the word 'annexe' is included somewhere in those four places. If you don't have these keywords somewhere in those four places, you'll find your property will fall down the pecking order on the portals, making it far less likely to be viewed.

If a potential property buyer carries out a search for a property to purchase in a certain area, most portals will bring back the results in order of asking price, starting with the highest and working backwards down to the lowest. If the searcher has included one keyword in their search, such as 'garage', the portal will list all the properties that have that keyword, in price order first, but will then also list starting with the most expensive property and working through to the cheapest properties that don't have that word. The same rules apply if someone is searching for properties with two keywords in them, such as 'garage' and 'parking'. First in the list would be properties with both keywords, in price order. Then a list of all the properties with just one again, in price order. And finally, the properties with no matching keywords, again in price order. Effectively, by missing out one or multiple keywords that someone is looking for, we have demoted ourselves down potentially pages and pages of portal listings which are simply going to be seen by less people than if we were to appear at the start of the search results. For this reason, it is important that you list as many keywords as possible in your listings that are relevant to the property.

Have you got a premium listing?

As mentioned in the previous section, the final place that online portals search for keywords is the premium listing label attached to the property listing. Premium listings are an additional feature sold by the portals to estate agents and they are designed to help your listings stand out from the crowd. They do this by not only showing more photos on the search results page but also adding labels to the listing that highlight a key factor about the property.

There are hundreds of options for these premium listing label options. Everything from 'star buy' through to 'generous garden'. By default, this label will just state 'premium listing' which I assure you no one is looking for in their normal search criteria. Instead, we should change this label to match up with one of the keywords that align with the property we are selling. For example, 'star buy' as mentioned earlier, I can't imagine many people searching for those keywords. Whereas 'generous garden' includes one of the top-ranking keywords people search for, garden. This should be the approach we take when choosing a premium listing label to go with our property. Find the highest-ranking keyword that fits the property and use this as the premium listing label.

Premium listings vary in success, but the statistic I have heard historically is that they increase the number of views on a property by 65%. Which in my mind, is well worth having. Not only because it makes the property stand out, but because it makes you stand out as an agent in a busy marketplace.

We spoke in the fees section earlier about aspects of our marketing we can potentially include to sweeten any deal conversation we have with a homeowner who is currently on the fence about our commission. These are aspects of our marketing that we were potentially planning to include anyway but have thrown them into the mix to make it sounds like we are throwing in a bonus. Premium listings can be a great add-on for this sort of conversation or sticking point over your fee percentage.

Video tours

In this next section, we are going to look at video tours on our properties. Video tours became hugely popular during the pandemic, which shouldn't have really been much of a surprise when most people couldn't leave their homes and videos on the internet were about as close as you could get to the outside world. Even though those days are fortunately behind us, video tours still live on and are thriving in the post-pandemic world.

Recent figures show that by having a video tour attached to your online property listing, you increase the number of views on that listing by 8% and increase the number of leads by 6%. Which, for the sake of recording a video, is a strong jump up in views and leads that we want for our property.

To start this section off, I'd like to slightly reprogramme your thoughts on what a video tour is. If you close your eyes now and imagine a video tour, you might be thinking of a video which starts at the front of the property, meanders from room to room, finally finishing in the rear garden of the property.

To be clear, this is in no way what I would like you to produce. Just like how we don't want to give away all full details of the property we're selling by uploading a huge number of photographs, the same rules apply for video tours. If we have a video uploaded online that gives away 100% of the property, where is the motivation for a potential buyer to pick up the phone and talk to us? Similar to the photos, we want to not only show off the best of the property, but also show that we have a brilliant opportunity to introduce you and your agency alongside the listing.

Firstly, a video tour of a property should be presenter-led, meaning that you have an initial introduction about who you are followed by an introduction to the property you're at today. All we want to do for the core part of the video is to show off one or two parts of the property we think will get the phone ringing. This might be the recently installed kitchen for example, or the extra-large garden. Effectively, you want to show off the best feature of the property and highlight it in your video. Once you have done this, you should have some sort of call to action at the end of the video which tells the viewers what to do next. This lets people know what the next steps for seeing more of the property are.

As an example of this, you could say something like the following:

Intro: Hello, It's Chris from Chris Webb estates, you join me today inside number 123 New Road which we have just put on the market in the super village location of Old Village.

Core: As you can see, the property has recently benefited from a brand-new kitchen which the owners have had recently installed. This is complete with built-in appliances as well! I don't expect this one to hang around in such a popular location.

Call to action: If you would like to have a look around this stunning property and look at this glorious kitchen, give me a call on 123456789 to book your slot.

As you can see from the above example, it's short, sweet, and just shows off the best bits of the property, leaving the viewer wanting more. We've also introduced ourselves, as well, so when they do book a viewing or a valuation, they know who we are which is a bonus. The best thing about this layout is that you can swap in and out sections of the above, too.

If you struggle to think about what to say from one video tour to the next, simply keep the intro and the outro the same, but change the address, obviously. Then, just add a new core message in the middle of the video for the new property you're recording that day.

Once we have our video tour recorded, you will want to add this to your listing which you can do via most CRM systems. The way that most portals work is they prefer if this video is uploaded onto a YouTube or Vimeo channel. Out of the two, I'd suggest because as we covered in earlier chapters, this is going to help you with your Google ranking as an added benefit. Also, by going down this route, the video platform is better integrated with the portal, meaning a better customer experience which effectively means they stay on the same browser page rather than being directed onto another website and the back-and-forth that comes with it.

Online viewing stickers

Finally, let's look at a really easy way of getting a little bit more traction on your instructions with just a few clicks of your mouse. The online viewing sticker, similar to the world of video tours, is still a leftover from the pandemic which has stuck with us long after it has finished. Effectively, this sticker was used to highlight properties where you were able to do an online viewing. So, if you couldn't leave the house for example, the estate agent would either send you a prerecorded video tour of the property, or they would go to the home, facetime you and show you around this way.

As you might imagine, when anyone is looking to buy the biggest financial commitment in their lifetime, they are keen, where possible, to go and view homes first-hand rather than watching online. But, by having the online viewing sticker attached to our property listing, it simply means that if anyone wants an online viewing, they can hypothetically have one. This will by default, increase the amount of traction and views our listing will get online.

I advise all my clients to turn this sticker on. It takes a few clicks of the mouse, and you will get extra views on your listing and generally won't have to do any online viewings at all. In fact, of all my clients in the UK, I don't think a single one has carried out a virtual viewing yet, they've just benefited from the increased traction on their stock from doing this. It's a real easy win for you and your listing.

If you follow all of the advice from the last couple of sections, not only will you have a great-looking property released onto the local market, but also you'll be able to take full advantage of all the tools at your disposal to not only promote that property as well as you possibly can, but also promote your business as a whole to entice new clients towards your estate agency.

If you'd like a guide showing you how to get the most out of your listings when you come to the market, you can find one here by scanning the below QR code.

You can also find the current top 20 portal keywords at the time of writing this book by scanning the QR code below:

Once you have completed and put together your draft property details for the home you are about to sell, it is crucial that you get the sellers of the property to sign off on the details you have produced, to ensure they are 100% happy with what you have created. This is important for two reasons. Firstly, the owner may not be happy with certain aspects of the listing you're about to put online. This might include certain photographs or even personal effects shown in the images you're putting online, that you simply wouldn't have known about.

The second reason is to make sure the owners have approved all the aspects of the property you have mentioned in your description. This could include topics such as built-in appliances or the property having a certain number of parking spaces, for example. Similar to the property information form, this forms a bit of insurance for you that the owners have approved and agreed with everything you have said. Therefore, there should be no issues or confusion when potential buyers come to view the home. I'd suggest you get this approval in writing in some form, because if the owner just verbally agrees to the details being correct, this can be very hard to prove down the line.

Leveraging what you've got

In the next section, we're going to look at how to correctly leverage a property that we put onto the market. Remember, the number one job of an estate agent at any one time is to get properties on the market, so that's exactly what we are going to focus on in this next section. We're going to zoom in on the processes and structures we can put in place to leverage our instructions and gain more properties to sell off the back of them.

To start off with, let's divide this topic into two halves. The first half is going to be looking at marketing methods we can deploy in the real world, to boost our presence in a local marketplace. In the second section, we'll look at what marketing methods we can deploy in the digital space to ensure we get the maximum bang for our buck off the back of our new listing online.

Before we get into that though, what is the perfect result in an estate agency business when listing a property? If you look at sport, 10-pin bowling for example, a score of 300 in a game is referred to as the perfect game as it's the highest score you can possibly achieve. In a round of golf, the perfect score would be 18, as it takes you one shot per hole which I'm going to go ahead and say has never been done before. So, in an estate agency, is listing a home on Monday, selling it on Tuesday and cashing the money on Wednesday a perfect result? I'd say this is a good result, but it is far from the perfect result, as by the time Thursday comes around, you're back to square one with nothing to sell all over again. No, the perfect game in an estate agency involves putting a property on the market for a set period of time, getting lots of instructions off the back of it, then selling the home as well for over the asking price. Then even once the original property goes through, we'll now have lots more homes to not only sell, but leverage all over again and the story repeats itself over and over, growing with each chapter.

It's for this reason that we should have a structure in place when it comes to when we want to start viewings on a property. Because we want to strike a balance between selling a home too quickly and getting no leads off the back of it, or taking too long to sell the home and it drags down our overall average selling time, or even worse doesn't sell at all.

I've found personally that the correct balance for this sits at around 7-10 days once a property comes onto the market, which should be pushed towards the nearest weekend with this timescale in mind. Imagine you're bringing a house onto the market on a Wednesday afternoon. Great, let's start viewing on Saturday in a week and a half. This clear space allows you time to not only generate more interest in the property which will help increase competition on the first day of viewings, but also allows you more time to generate leads into your business off the back of your property-specific marketing.

It's up to you how public you want to make this message of starting viewings, some agents will put this information all over their online advert that 'Viewings are on Saturday 1st between 1 pm - 3 pm' but personally, I wouldn't do this. It sets you up for a fall. Imagine the property doesn't sell on this date and you've got that all over your advert, it doesn't look good. Instead, I would keep this date between you, the owners, and the viewers of the property. If anyone enquires about viewing the property, simply say that's the day when the first viewings are taking place on the home.

Now we have bought ourselves around a week to 10 days to get some really solid marketing out in the local area, showcasing what a great job we're doing selling the property down the road. To start off with, let's go for an estate agency classic, that being the old reliable For Sale board. It truly is a classic for a reason and the expression 'boards breed boards' is as true today as it ever has been. These little rectangles of marketing magic simply work, so with this in mind, we should try and get one erected at every property we bring onto the market and sell.

Sometimes, though, homeowners will say that they aren't happy having a board outside their home, which I always laugh at inside because they're about to go onto one of the top 10 websites in the UK which gets millions of views a day. So, I wouldn't worry too much about Mrs Jones in number 7 knowing you're moving, the whole world can look inside your living room over the coming 24 hours.

Rightly or wrongly though, if a homeowner doesn't want to have a board, this shouldn't be the end of the conversation. Ask again in a few weeks' time. Ask when the property goes under offer if you can have a sold board, or once the property exchanges, if you can have the board up for a week before completion takes place. No matter how long you can get the board up for, I'd suggest you try. Even if it's just a week, persistence is key on this one. Don't just hear the first no and give up forever.

Now that we have hopefully placed a For Sale board up outside the property and the listing is about to go online, all the neighbours will start to find out that one property in their street is about to go up for sale. Yes, even Mrs Jones in number 7. We know this because we are going to deliver a leaflet to all properties within a radius of the property we are selling, telling them exactly that. In the property industry, these leaflets are known as 20/20s. They're called this because historically, estate agents delivered 20 to one side of the street and 20 to the other side. This tactic still remains but we need to inject some steroids into this equation to get the most out of this process. Firstly, we need to simply deliver more than 40 leaflets in total. You'll be very lucky to get any traction off the back of such a low number of marketing collateral going out. As we spoke about previously, sales and marketing is just a numbers game, the more of these we can get out the better our chance of getting a reply to one of them. For the average property you have coming onto the market, I'd suggest 250-500 of these going into the local area. For a really great property in your core patch that you would love more of, you could even do 1000+ of these.

For most homes you deliver to, in fact about 99% of all properties you deliver to, the lifespan of this leaflet is going to be about three seconds before it finds its new home in the recycling bin. It's for this reason we want to get as much information across in a short period of time as we possibly can before this glorious binning takes place. One main point that I would love to get across before our leaflet finds its new home is a good-looking picture of the front of the property we've listed which locals will look at and recognise as in their local area. Next, I would like to get across the name or logo of your agency alongside a great photo of you. It almost doesn't matter what we say on the rest of the leaflet, it could be 'for sale', 'sold', or 'to let'. The message doesn't matter for the majority of people because all they will see is a property that looks like theirs with an estate agent's details on there. Their mind will fill in the gaps between.

It's important to have some text on the leaflet of course, as the 1% of people who actually take time out of their day to read all of the marketing material will want to know what's going on with the property. With this messaging, less is more. Do not include multiple paragraphs or copious bullet points trying to cram in as much information and as many USPs as you can, you'll bore the 1% to death. Instead, just focus on a key message of 'we've brought a property onto the market near your home. If you'd like to know what yours is worth, give us a call', or words to that effect.

If you scan the QR code, not only will you be able to see some great examples of how these look, you can actually order your own directly from this page once you have uploaded all the information needed to produce them. How cool is that?

Okay, so by now even if we haven't got a For Sale board up outside the property we're bringing to the market, all the neighbouring properties around the home should know that we are selling a property within their local area. If you have managed to get a board up at the property as well, this is another touchpoint for the locals in that part of your patch.

Next, we are going to hit the phones to try and not only generate more interest in the property, but you guessed it, we're also going to use this action to try and get even more new properties into your business.

Let's start with the lowest hanging fruit in this equation. This is going to be owners of properties you've been to value before, who may want to buy the property you are about to bring onto the market. Instead of these old valuations seeing your new listing online and calling you, feeling slightly let down that you didn't call them about this potentially perfect property, don't you think it would be a better customer experience for you to pick up the phone and run it past them first of all?

This is exactly what we are going to do now. First of all, find people from previous market appraisals and have a look at what they are looking to buy. Your CRM system should be your best friend here provided you converted and added any market appraisals you have been to into applicants on your system. This means they will show as being a potential listing for your business, and also a potential buyer down the line. If any of these old market appraisals are close to matching, pick up the phone and use the following sentence, 'I'm just about to take a property onto the market and as I walked out of the front door, you jumped into my mind. I thought it would be perfect for you, so I wanted to run it past you first before I put it onto the general market.' Not only does this make the homeowner feel like a VIP as you thought of them, first. But it also means you are far more likely to be instructed to sell their property with customer service like this. Also, if they do end up wanting to buy this home, you're an absolute shoo-in.

Spoiler alert, we're going to have this conversation for every market appraisal done for people searching for something close to the property we're bringing onto the market. With this in mind, you are going to be telling a lot of people that you 'thought of them' on this one. It'll make everyone you talk to feel special and make you look like an awesome estate agent.

Notice how I've said anyone looking 'close' to the property we are selling. I don't mean geographically, though in reality, that might help as well. I'm talking about not a 100% perfect match for them but not a million miles off either. After all, with most market appraisals you've carried out, you're looking for a good reason to touch base with the owners and talk to them – and this listing could be the perfect excuse for you to do just that.

Imagine you have a three-bedroom semi-detached house coming on the market. I'd not only call everyone looking for a three-bedroom semi-detached, but I'd also call everyone looking for a three-bedroom mid-terrace and anyone looking for a three-bedroom detached. I'd also potentially talk to anyone ideally looking for a four-bedroom in the same sort of price range as well, even though I know chances are, it won't be right for them. I'd even look at talking to anyone looking for a two-bedroom home with the goal of them talking to my mortgage advisor who could give them a larger budget to look around with, making this property suddenly achievable for them.

This listing is just a good excuse to get on the phone with these people and ideally sell them the property we've just listed. But as a worst-case scenario we can have a conversation with them which will lead into talking about their own property and whether they're ready to go onto the market yet. At the very least, they'll feel like a VIP in your business because you called them first, prioritising them, and people like to feel special.

Once this job has been carried out, we are going to rinse and repeat, but with one small change. This time, we're going to call anyone who has viewed a similar property with you recently or has registered looking for a similar property, but who also has a property to sell locally. These might be viewers who currently have their property on the market with another agent, for example. They are going to come next in the pecking order because like with the people you went out to value in the past, we have an opportunity to get another property onto the market off the back of our listing. This will also make them feel important and this gives us a good opportunity to talk about their property as well. We use exactly the same message as before, 'I've got a property coming onto the market, and as soon as I stepped out the front door, I thought of you…'

Once we have had this conversation with those potential buyers and potential instructions for ourselves, we're going to move onto the next category which would be registered buyers and viewers who don't have a property to sell. This part of the exercise is purely to try and generate interest on the property we are selling. Because if we have done our job correctly here, everyone with a local property to sell that we could help with has had a call from us already.

When we put the property for sale on the property portals, we should start receiving phone calls and enquiries about the property, if we've done our job correctly so far. This is going to be a gold mine of opportunity for your business. So much so, that this book has a whole section on it later for us to work through, to ensure we get the most out of these communications, exploring how we can diversify the income into the business on the back of these conversations.

Now imagine that we have fast-forwarded a week or so from the launch of your newest listing going up for sale. Your marketing has done its job and you're lining up to have a solid turn out of viewings on the property you have listed. What are some basic factors that we want to happen on the day of the viewings? Number one is to make sure that everyone actually turns up, this would be a good start. Number two is that we want everyone going to the property to understand that it's a busy day and a popular property, so if they want to go for it, they'll have to act fast to avoid missing out on this great opportunity.

With this in mind, let's put a process in place that ensures as much as we possibly can that the above is going to happen. The day before the bulk viewings commence on the property, block out a timeslot to call everyone booked to view the property the next day. In this call we are going to talk through a few points with the viewer. Number one is:
'Just checking that you're still coming tomorrow?' because we want to make sure we're not waiting around for them to turn up if they are not going to come at all. Secondly when they confirm they're coming,
'That's great news. Just to let you know, it's a really popular property with lots of viewings on it tomorrow so if you could turn up as close as possible to your allotted time of 10.30 am as possible that would be really helpful'. You may even drop in the number of viewings if it's a big enough number, though if it's anything below seven viewings, I probably wouldn't, as it doesn't sound impressive enough. We have confirmed that the viewer will be attending the appointment, and they now know that it's a popular property and it's certainly not just them viewing. Time to crank that up a bit.
'Just to let you know the property isn't going to hang around for long with the amount of interest it has generated, I'd hate for you to miss out due

to not having something like your mortgage or solicitor in place, do you have that sorted already?'

You could even emphasise this with a real-life example of someone that didn't have their mortgage or solicitors in place and actually did miss out. 'I had a client just last week that missed out on their dream home because of this, and I don't want you to be in the same situation.'

This gives you a really good opportunity to refer to your local mortgage broker or solicitor to potentially earn some further income. Something we'll go into far more detail on in later chapters, as this is really important diversified income for your business.

As you can see, leveraging your listings to their full potential when they first come onto the market is key to helping your estate agency business flourish. It's for this exact reason I've created a leveraging guide on this subject. To access this guide, simply scan the QR code below.

Advertising online

At this stage, we should have a really good span of marketing in the local area around the property. Not only have we had the board go up outside the property but also around 500 homes around the property have had a leaflet through their front door saying we have a local home up for sale. We've also spoken to all applicable market appraisals and potential viewers with and without a home to sell.

Next up, we're going to focus on how to make a splash online as well to ensure traction for the property from this angle of marketing. To do this, we're going to produce multiple pieces of content that are not only going to showcase the property, but also give us a chance to show off our estate agency as well to gain further traction in the local area.

To start with, we are going to produce something I like to call 'the street sign teaser video'. Like all the videos we produce, this is going to be presenter-led, by you, which means, yes, you need to be in it. This video is simply you standing next to the street sign where you have a property for sale, giving people the sneak peek that you have a property coming up on that road. This video will be short and sweet, lasting less than a minute. And like the rest of our videos, will be made up of three parts: the introduction, the core message and the call to action to close things off.

The message would go something like this:

Intro: Hi! It's Chris at Chris' Estates here, as you can see, today I am out on New Road.

Core: I've got some really exciting news if you're looking for a large family home in this area, because I have one coming to the market really soon.

Call to action: If you'd like to have some more information on this property before it comes to the market, DM me on here and I'll tell you all about it.

That's it, certainly not longer than 60 seconds with a bit of a tease about what we have coming up, with a call to action for those looking for that sort of property. This video should be posted onto your social media account before the property goes live online. I'd also upload this video to your YouTube account as well, you should know why this is important already.

Now we have video one in the bag, it's time to move onto video number two, which we can actually record just a few moments after we have finished recording video number one. For this next video, it's going to be the next stage of teasing the property out into the public eye. To produce this video, we are going to be located at the best feature of the property we are about to sell, very similar to the video we recorded for our video tour of the property earlier on. This video is purely about showcasing this feature. Set your camera tripod up so it can be seen behind you and record a video that goes a little something like this:

Intro: Hi again, It's Chris at Chris' Estates here. A few days ago, I posted a short video about a property in New Road that I'm bringing onto the market for sale.

Core: Today you join me as I'm taking photos of this lovely property and I wanted to show you behind the scenes so you could take a look at this amazing kitchen the owners installed only last year. Isn't it lovely? Loads of built in appliances as well!

Call to action: If you would love to see all of this property including this wonderful kitchen, give me a call on 123456789. Don't take too long though, this one will be snapped up quickly.

Post this video on your social media accounts and YouTube a few days after your first 'the street sign teaser video' video has gone up. This could be a couple of days before launching the full listing online. As you might imagine, it's important to get both these videos posted before the full listing goes live, otherwise you're doing a sneak peek on something that everyone can already see full details for.

Now we have two videos recorded for our social media account, both completed within 10 minutes. Once you've done this a few times, you'll be able to record both in under five minutes in total.

Time to record one more video before this section is complete. Now, this video we can record or rerecord at a later date should you choose to, but I have always recorded this one in advance and then if I wanted to redo the video later down the line, I can.

This video is going to state that we have just started viewings on our new listing on New Road and it's proving hugely popular with everyone who has looked at it so far. Let me know quickly if you'd like to have a look around the home too, before it gets snapped up.

You might be thinking at this stage, wait, we haven't even put the property online yet, let alone got any viewing for it. Is this a bit presumptuous? Well, yes in a short answer, it is. But we want to be prepared and I'd rather we had this video as a backstop and recorded another one down the line, than us being too busy to post anything at all on the topic. Some of my clients will even record a video saying how they have now agreed a sale on the property at this stage, as well. Now, *that's* being prepared in advance!

We're going to roll out the same structure as before with you leading the video, which will look something like this:

Intro: Hi, Chris from Chris' Estates here, you join me again today in New Road, at the delightful family home we have for sale here.

Core: We've just started viewings on this property today and it's proving to be really popular with everyone that has looked around it so far, with some brilliant feedback and interest.

Call to action: If you'd like to have a look at this property before it gets snapped up, give me a call on 123456789 to book a time to view this wonderful home.

Again, as before, short, sweet and to the point. We should be looking to post this video on the day the viewings start on the property. As mentioned before, if you want to record a different video on the day you start viewings, that is also fine. The important thing is that it happens.

Not only is this process going to help sell the property and bolster our local standing as a great estate agent, but it's also going to give us so much content for our social media accounts. Imagine you are taking one property to the market a week. That property will have three of these videos posted about it, just on listing the home. That's 12 videos per month on your social media account, purely saying that you've brought a new house to the market. Suddenly, having a lot to talk about online doesn't seem so hard, does it?

With any of these videos I would be asking your sellers to share them on their personal social media accounts as well. Chances are that if the owners have lived in the area for some time, they will have strong local connections that will watch your video, and usually these connections comment and like in higher numbers because they know the owner of the property. We all have one usually a more mature family member who we roll our eyes at when they comment on our personal social media posts. Well effectively, we are going to take advantage of that process to give more local traction to our listing and also our business as whole.

Finally, we're going to look at sharing our listing on local community Facebook pages for the area we are selling in. Most areas, villages and developments have a Facebook group these days. A group where locals can complain about the bins not being collected on time or put a post up to see if someone has found their child's bike in their garden.

Firstly, you'll need to join these groups. If you have set up your Facebook account correctly to start with, you should have done this already, but if not, you can join them now. Once accepted in the group, you can post something along these sorts of lines.

'Hello everyone. You might have seen that I have just put a property up for sale on New Road which I expect to be really popular in such a lovely part of town. I know lots of people locally have friends and family who they have spoken to about moving closer to them into this area. With this in mind, I thought it was worth adding this onto the group here so you can tag anyone you might know that might be interested in this property. Thanks.'

This is a good move, as it connects you with other local homeowners in that area who might be interested in selling their own home down the line, but also the members in this local group are going to do the leg work for you by tagging potential buyers. Once they start commenting and tagging friends and family, firstly make sure to reply, and secondly, direct message anyone who is tagged with a full set of details and ask them if they would like to take a look around the property on the upcoming launch day. Remind them to be quick, it's going to be busy!

As you can see from the amount of information covered, when it comes to taking a property onto the market, there's a lot to remember to ensure that by the time you walk out of the front door of the property, you have every piece of marketing lined up and ready to go. For this reason, I've created a checklist for taking a property onto the market which you can find simply by scanning the following QR code.

Protecting your stock

As we touched on in earlier chapters, looking after the sellers currently on the market with you is a crucial job for any estate agency business. This is typically known as vendor care. There is no point throwing huge amounts of time, effort, and resources at trying to gain more instructions to sell if you're losing more than this from the stock you currently have up for sale. Sure, listing 10 houses in a month might sound like an amazing month, but if you have had 11 de-instruct you, is that really an amazing month? I'd say not.

In our diary management section of this book, we discussed how once a week we should have a time in our diary set aside to speak to our sellers. When you first launch your business and you only have a handful of properties up for sale, this might only take you an hour or so. But fast forward a year, you may have to put a whole afternoon aside to contact everyone selling with your agency. This in itself, is a very first-world estate agency problem to have, I think you'll agree.

As a bare minimum, if a property is receiving no interest and no viewings over any week, they should most certainly get a call from you to update them. Even if a property has received multiple viewings that week, I would still pick up the phone just to recap what's going on with their property sale. Notice how I have said call and not email, text message or voice note. Unless specified otherwise with a homeowner, I would always, always pick up the phone for your vendor care process. As we spoke about earlier in the book you can get so much more from a phone call with regard to tone of voice, if they are happy, sad, or even on the train. This simply doesn't come across in many other formats of communication. So, I would always pick up the phone unless a homeowner has specifically asked you to update them in a different way.

There are a couple of golden rules when it comes to vendor care. Number one is that as activity decreases on a property, then the amount of outgoing vendor care should increase to compensate for this. Let's look at an example to show how this works.

Imagine you have a launch day for a property booked in for the coming weekend, you have six viewings booked and everything is looking good. Would you still give the owners a call to communicate this? Absolutely. It's an easy call for you to make and should last no longer than five minutes. Now picture that you've got a home that's been on the market with you for four months, the viewings have dried up and nothing much is happening with it. So, you think 'the owner knows it's a quiet market at the moment' and you don't give them a call. This is a big mistake. You might have gotten away with not calling the owners of the first property because they know you're busy trying to sell their home. But the other one is probably reaching the end of their tether on selling and may well look to de-instruct you from selling their home. All of which could have been avoided if you just picked up the phone to them to update them on your efforts to sell their home despite the quiet market. We should be calling all our sellers no matter what is happening with the property market or their home, but the less traction their property is getting, the bigger the need for you to talk to them.

The next rule here is the core job of your vendor update. This is to communicate to the homeowner what you're doing and how hard you're working to try and sell their home. Imagine you don't speak to someone who is on the market with you for a whole month. Do you think that property's sellers think you're working so hard in the background to try and sell their home that you haven't got time to call them? Not for a second. They will think that you have forgotten all about them and have moved onto the next property, or even the golf course. This is why, when speaking to homeowners about selling their home, we need to highlight exactly what we have been doing to try and sell their property. Also, a big part of this conversation will be what has been working well so far and putting a plan in motion to keep interest in their property high.

There are other key topics that we would speak to our sellers about, one of the biggest is the online activity for the property as this can tell a story in itself. Firstly, we would look at the number of searches a property appears in over a weekly basis. This will let us know if it is the style, type, or area of property people are looking at, at the moment.

Fairly early on you'll get an idea about what good looks like for these figures as you compare them to other properties you have on the market. This is going to be made up of a selection of searches from your chosen portal and some of this search result could be from people only looking in the street we are selling on, for example. Whilst other search results we appear in could be from someone searching the whole of the UK. So, we need to keep this in mind when we are looking at the figures.

Next up, is a subject we highlighted earlier in the book and that was click through rate, or CTR for short. CTR is the percentage of people who click through from seeing the property on the search results page, through to looking at the full listing with more details. So, if our property appeared in 100 search results and five of those people clicked on our property to look at more details, we would have a CTR of 5%. This 5% figure is about average for most properties that appear online, but as you might imagine, you're not here to be average, so I would be looking to have a CTR of around 10% on all your instructions, which is possible if you're doing your job correctly and marketing the home you're trying to sell.

Another topic we should be talking to the owner about is any potential activity we have coming up on their property. This could include conversations you have had with potential buyers on the phone, details requests and so on. It's another chance for us to show how hard we've been working in the background to sell their home. We should also be looking at providing an overall viewing feedback recap to the seller. This could be fairly high-level, looking at the total number of viewings we have so far, but should also point out any themes or common feedback from the viewings we've had and offer advice moving forward. We are going to go into this in more detail in the following section where we talk about reviewing properties and getting properties that aren't getting any traction sold.

Notes from all your conversations should be added to your CRM system, because I promise you, as soon as you start doing multiple updates in a day, they will start to blur into one very quickly. So you'll need these notes to fall back on to ensure you are continuing the theme and message from the last time you caught up with the owner.

Although, as we have discussed already, the telephone is going to be our best friend when updating our sellers, it's still a good idea for most homes you are selling to set up a WhatsApp group which includes all the owners of the property. This is in no way a shortcut to not pick up the phone, instead, this should be used for low-level communications with the homeowner, such as confirming viewing times. This can be an especially powerful tool when you are having to deal with multiple parties who are trying to sell a property with you. This could include sales which involve clients in different parts of the world, probate sales where you have multiple members of a family selling a home, or even divorcing couples who don't speak directly anymore. This can be used to ensure that everyone is on the same page and in no way can anyone be out of the loop on the sale.

I assure you, although this section of the book isn't the longest, it is one of the most important parts of your businesses as a whole. Good communication is always listed as one of the top reasons to work with an estate agency. It's also one of the biggest reasons, if not the biggest reason for sellers falling out of love with their current instructed agent. Sellers that you communicate with on a regular basis will stay with you for the long run. Sellers that you do not communicate with or keep in the picture with what you are doing will happily de-instruct you down the line. If they de-instruct you, you can wave goodbye to all that time you spent initially canvassing for their instruction in the first place. And whilst you're doing that, wave goodbye to all that time and money you invested getting their property onto the market, too. You have been warned!

What if it simply isn't selling?

In this section, we're going to have a look at what you can do when a property isn't selling or even getting the amount of interest you think it might take to sell. The average property in the UK will statically have one price reduction on it before it sells, so I assure you that you are not the first estate agent to change a price, nor is this the first home going down this route.

On a personal level, please do not fall into a mental trap I like to call 'valuer's guilt'. This is the feeling you get when you go and meet with a homeowner, confidently say you should be able to sell their property at a certain price and timescale and then a few weeks later, call them up to say this is no longer the plan and that we need to look at the pricing. Pricing you obviously agreed with them on in the first place. It's the feeling of 'did I get it wrong?' or 'have I done a bad job on this one?' As long as you can hand on heart say you have done everything within your power to sell that home, then what else could you have done? I assure you from experience that sometimes you do everything you can, and a property simply won't sell at the price you set it at. Other times you will sell a property straight away by doing exactly the same thing. Sometimes it's just the right time and the right place and other times it's the complete opposite. Don't let this affect you.

If you have followed this book correctly, then you should have thrown everything at this listing when you first put it onto the market. So, by default, you shouldn't have any extra marketing avenues to add to the property as you'll have bolted these on from the very beginning. If you haven't, now might be the time to add these onto the property you are looking to sell.

Another quick win in these situations is to reorganise the photographs of the property that you are displaying online. Instead of having the front shot as the lead photo for the listing, change it up a bit so that the photograph of the kitchen is now the lead photo. The same rules apply as when we first added the photos to the instruction though; best photos toward the front of the list and make sure that you have one garden photo in the top four images. By swapping the order around on the photos, you will naturally increase the number of views the property gets as it'll stand out more than it may have done previously to any buyers who were used to seeing the old photos. The leading portals recommend that you go through this process with all your for-sale stock every 14 days to keep them fresh and interesting, no matter how much interest it is getting. I would advise adding this into your diary as a reminder to do every other week, otherwise it will be easily forgotten from one week to the next.

As we spoke about in earlier chapters, there is one big factor which will affect the selling of a property more than any other aspect. That is the price of the property. No matter how amazing you are at being an estate agent, if you are trying to sell a property which is overpriced compared to other properties currently on the market, you are going to struggle, as you're effectively pushing your property up a hill. In the following section, we are going to look at some of the key aspects of managing the price of a property and look at how and when we should consider dropping the price.

Let's focus on when you should look into changing the price of the property you have on the market. In my own personal experience, the timescale for this should be at around three weeks after first coming onto the market. In the first couple of weeks as a listing, you are fresh and new to the market and this is the most likely time to sell and for the highest price, statistically.

After this initial honeymoon period of a few weeks, interest in the property is going to start to die off and dwindle away, mainly because it's no longer the new listing on the block and most people who were potentially interested in buying the property have either viewed it already, or have ruled it out for one reason or another. This is where we start coming into price reduction territory, as if we don't change something with the listing, interest is just going to drop away week on week until it is a very stale piece of stock that no one wants to buy for no better reason than 'it's been on the market for ages.' As I'm sure you'll agree, we want to avoid this journey into this bleak future for the property we are trying to sell.

If we have been doing a solid job of our vendor care so far and updating our sellers about what we have been doing to try and sell their home, then the price change conversation can flow fairly organically. If your communication with the seller has been poor, don't expect to be welcomed back to their world with open arms when you first start the conversation with 'we need to change the price.' As we spoke about earlier, one of the core objectives of our vendor care is to get across how hard we are working and exactly what we are trying to do to sell the property, so if we speak to them on week three about the pricing of the home, they should know that we've been working hard with the initial price over the last couple of weeks.

Alongside this, if we priced the property in the correct style when we valued the home, we will have first put a price range on the property, rather than a definitive price. In the example we used, we priced the property between £240,000- £250,000 and decided to go on for £250,000 because the owners weren't in a hurry at the time. As you might imagine, this has left the door nicely open for us to line up a price reduction down to at least £240,000 if this property hasn't sold by week three.

Ultimately though, who decides what price any property is worth? That's right, it's not you, and it's certainly not the owners of the property. It's the people going around the home with a view to buy it. After all, it's their money being spent.

This is where price-sensitive feedback is going to be your best friend, as asking everyone who views a property what they think of the price will give you a good idea on where this sits compared to similar homes that are on the market. Imagine you have carried out 10 viewings on our example property at £250,000. The feedback from every viewer was that they felt the home was worth £240,000. What's the value of that home in the current market? £240,000. That's how much.

Now imagine that all of those 10 viewings came back to you with the feedback that they felt the property was too noisy as it's right on a noisy road. What's really the feedback here? The feedback is that for £250,000, the viewers would have expected a property that was quieter and not on a busy road, as another way of saying the price is too high at £250,000 compared to other properties they've viewed.

It's this style of wording that you should be using when you pass over any feedback to your homeowner. They can't move the road from outside their home, but they can adjust the price to accommodate the road being there. This applies for all negative feedback that might come back from viewings. Like if someone says the kitchen is too small, for £250,000 they would have expected a bigger kitchen. Or, the house needs too much work, for £250,000 they would have expected a property in better condition throughout. As you can see, everything we talk about is always about price as this is not only the biggest factor in a property selling or not selling, but it is also the easiest aspect of marketing to change. We can't expect our sellers to snap their fingers and extend their home, but we absolutely can snap our fingers and change the property's pricing.

Red, amber, green

To monitor our for-sale stock and to get an idea on not only how it's performing, but what the next stages for the instruction might be, we are going to start using a structure referred to as Red, Amber, Green with our for-sale stock. This is a simple process which will not only highlight which properties we think are going to sell but will highlight what needs to change to other listings to get them to the stage of getting some serious interest or offers in place.

To do this, we would need to make three lists, one called Red, one called Amber and finally, yes, you guessed it, one called Green. Pretty simple so far, right?

Let me highlight what the criteria is for going into one of those lists. We'll start with Green and work our way back from there. Green properties are any properties that you have on your books currently which are highly likely to sell in the short-term. These homes may have come onto the market recently, have lots of viewings or even second viewings lined up, and you're as confident as you can be that this home is going to go under offer in the not-too-distant future. If a property has been on the market for more than a couple of weeks and you can't see it selling very soon, then it isn't a green property.

Next up, we have the Amber list of properties. These are homes that are good properties we're confident will sell, but before this can happen, something has to change with the advertising of the property. This could be improving the marketing, or more often than not, it's based around the price changing on these homes, as this will carry the most weight.

Finally, we have the Red list. These are properties that, as you might think, you have no expectation in any way, shape, or form of them selling or even getting any interest any time soon. These are usually properties that are well overpriced or have some other issue holding them back from selling. You might have even spoken to the owners about changing the asking price of their property already and they simply aren't interested. It could also be properties for which there's very little demand in the local area.

Your next job is to divide your stock between these lists. Are they Red, Amber or Green? Most estate agency businesses that I work with are always surprised or shocked by how few properties are actually in the Green list when we go through this exercise. Some fall into Red, but the majority fall into the Amber list. Meaning they will sell but something has to change first, to speed up this process.

Our next task once we have done this, is to look at the properties on our Amber list and look at what needs to happen to get these properties sold. As we mentioned just now, this could be changing the marketing such as updating the photos or adding a premium listing. Most of the time though, this will involve the pricing of the property.

Next to each of the properties on this list, write down what needs to happen to help sell each of them. If you think it's a price issue, then write down next to the property what you think it will actually sell for. Notice we are not taking into consideration what the owner wants to accept on the pricing, we just want to know a baseline of what this property needs to go under offer. We'll look at the seller's expectation later on in this section and see if they align with our outline for the future pricing of the property. If you have been doing a good job at getting price-sensitive feedback from all your viewings, this part of the process should be really easy to do, as you just need to look at your feedback on the property and this should all point towards what price the home should actually be marketed at.

You should have this list running at all times in your estate agency office. When a new instruction comes onto the market, you should place it in the column you most think it fits into and when a property sells, you remove it from this list completely. Your goal over time is to move all the properties you have from Red over to Amber, and the Amber properties over to the Green. This will mean that your stock becomes more and more sellable rather than less attractive by simply sitting on the market, gathering dust.

When it comes to changing the price, there is no golden rule about how much you should adjust it by, as it will vary by how much the property is over the market value to start off with. One element we do need to keep in mind is the property portal and how much of the price we need to take off for the portals to count it as a reduction. Let me explain what I mean by this.

Estate agents are generally quite a canny lot, leave any kind of loophole and they will take full advantage of this. Remember when we spoke about when listing a property, how the main portals email their database of property hunters with an update including all new properties that have come onto the market? Well also included are properties that have had a price reduction. Meaning that if you change the price on a home, your instruction will be emailed out by the portals to tens, if not hundreds of thousands of potential buyers. Agents worked out pretty quickly that if once a week they changed their asking price by a small amount, say £50, they could be added to this email chain and benefit from this huge boost in exposure at no real cost to themselves.

As you might imagine, the portals weren't over the moon about agents abusing this system they had put in place, so they went about implementing a minimum reduction amount before a property would be included in this email round. That percentage was decided on being 2% of the listed price of the property. So, if you take our property from earlier on at £250,000 as an example, we could then reduce the price by £4,000 to £246,000. This would not be included in this mass mail out, but if we reduced it down to £245,000, it would just about make the cut. It's for this reason that if you are looking to get a price reduction on a property, you need to ensure wherever possible that it is at least 2% of the value of the property. If you're not great at percentages, work this out before you make the call, it'll save you a lot of panicking.

So, we now know the minimum we should be reducing a property by, but what's the maximum? Well, this is usually going to be determined by the seller's expectation on price. Because if they have a lot of wiggle room on the price they can accept on their home, then you may well set up a reduction in line with what you expect the property to sell for. Whereas if you speak to one of your sellers and they simply say they can't afford to take less than what we are on for currently, then this is a bit of a non-starter, and this property would move into your Red column.

Ultimately, what you should know with each of the properties you have up for sale at any one time, is what the homeowner can and can't afford to take for their home. Once you have a good idea about what someone will take for their property, you can make a far more structured process for not only initially pricing the property, but also structuring a price change on the property as well. There is a conversation I have used time and time again with sellers to find this figure. It's a technique where sellers want to correct an answer you have given that they know to be wrong or incorrect, and by doing this, they give you the answer you want. Sounds complicated, but it really isn't. I promise.

If you asked any homeowner on the market 'what will you take for your property?' or similar, you will get broad answers such as 'get me some offers and I'll let you know' or 'as close to the asking price as possible.' Both are fine I suppose, but we want a solid figure that we know they will accept or not accept.

Instead, ask the question this way, 'Tell me Mrs Jones, if a cash buyer walked through your door tomorrow with a bag full of money which meant you could move into your new property, what would you accept?' But don't stop there, the next bit is the most important section, because we are going to put forward a low figure which we are 99% that they won't accept as an example price. 'Would you take £230,000 for your property?' Then see what they come back with. More than likely, they will answer the question with 'No, I wouldn't take £230,000.' Over to you again, 'Okay, what would you accept?'

As you can see, we have low-balled the owner here, got the answer wrong (on purpose I might add!) and they now want to correct our £230,000 price with the actual price they would accept for their home – which is the information we wanted all along. With this information in hand, we can decide the next route to go down. If the owner has said they can't take below what the property is on for, then not much can change on this side, but if there is some flexibility then we can look at reducing the price by at least 2% as mentioned before.

Earlier in the book we spoke about the importance of hitting price points on the portals, these are the search ranges that potential property buyers use to look for properties online. Aligning with one of these price points boosts the amount of interest your property will receive online. We want to keep this information in mind when looking to adjust the price of any home. So where possible, try and get the price changed onto one of these.

In my experience, it is very hard to drop the price of a single property multiple times and still keep your sellers happy, no matter how good your communication levels are. Instead, what you are far better off doing is having a slightly harder conversation with your sellers initially and get the price down to where it actually needs to be to start with, rather than just where the owner wants it to be. If you have to drop the price multiple times, sellers can become frustrated that they are having to do it all over again and feel like they have wasted the time between price reductions, as really they should have had the actual correct price reduction the first time around.

Mastering applicant registration

If you've done your job correctly so far of pricing a property competitively and marketing it in the best possible way you can, then you should start to get people looking to view one or more of the properties that you have up for sale.

There is a viewpoint in the estate agency world which I fiercely disagree with; that someone who is looking to buy a property for themselves is somehow a second-class citizen in your business compared to someone who is thinking of selling their own property.

On the off chance you needed any convincing, here are a few key points to back up my argument. Firstly, in a fully functioning estate agency office, you should aim to have around one third of all your instructions come off the back of people who are looking to buy properties in your area. This is not only a massive amount of your annual listing goal from these people, but also the cost of acquisition on these clients and properties are next to nothing. This makes them a key part of any business growth in the future.

Secondly, without your buyers, you have no deals. It's as simple as that. If you provide such a poor service that alienates all of them, not only will you not sell any properties but also how long do you think it'll take before your sellers start jumping ship because no one wants to view a property with you?

Thirdly, there is a huge amount of income to be made from applicants flowing through your estate agency business. Sure, only one person can buy the property you have for sale. But off the back of this overflow of buyers, not only are there multiple options to get other properties on the market in the area you're selling in, but there is also a huge amount of potential income from third party suppliers. Something we'll get on to later.

Fourthly, in 10 years' time when you don't get called out for a market appraisal on that lovely property in the best part of your town, you'll know why. That's right, the applicants of today are your sellers of tomorrow. You really are shooting your future self in the foot here with the bad applicant customer service of today.

And finally, if you need any more reasons to treat your applicants well, their one-star reviews on Google carry as much weight as a seller's one-star review in the eyes of the general public. It goes without saying that this is obviously something we're looking to avoid at all costs.

Okay, so let's jump into looking at how to correctly register an applicant. This is something that if you do well, you can almost sell a property from your desk. But if you do it badly as you can see from the points we just covered, it doesn't play out very well.

Unless you have a high street office, and even if you do, most applicants you register are more than likely going to be over the phone. Either they're calling into your office, or they've emailed through to your office, and you are contacting them off the back of this email. There are generally two reasons why someone would call into an estate agency office. Either they're looking to register their details with your office so you can keep them posted of any upcoming properties that might suit them, or they have a property in mind already that they may have seen online, and they would like to book a viewing.

Either way, the process we follow is going to be fairly similar. For the sake of ease, we'll assume from here on that someone has seen a property they would like to view, because if a buyer is looking to only register their details, the registering process is fairly similar. The only difference with a viewing is that you bolt a bit more at the end to actually book the viewing in.

Similar to when we booked in the market appraisal, the first pieces of information we will want to get from anyone looking to view a property is basic personal information. This is going to include full names of everyone looking to buy, current address, phone numbers, email addresses and so on. Get as many contact details as you possibly can at this stage. Home numbers, partners mobiles, the whole lot. It'll make your life a lot easier when you are trying to get hold of them in the future. As we speak to potential viewers on the phone, we will want to use a method which is referred to as MAN. This is short for Motivation, Ability, and Need.

Let's start off with motivation as this is going to shape most of not only this call, but also the way you follow up with this client in the future. If you're speaking to an elderly couple who are looking to downsize but they mention they've been trying to do it for the last 10 years, how motivated do you think they are to move? Surely over 10 years of trying to buy, they must have found something they liked? Compare that to a married couple who are looking to move because they're getting a divorce and for one reason or another they absolutely can't stand each other, therefore, want to move as soon as they can. Are they motivated? Absolutely.

Clients with a high level of motivation should be a high priority as they could very well be your next sale. But for others with a more laid-back attitude to moving, we should be prepared for them to potentially be a slightly longer burn. However, we will still stay on top of them, nonetheless.

Ultimately, if someone doesn't have motivation to do something, then it usually won't happen. This doesn't mean that motivation can't change in almost an instant. That old couple we mentioned just now, their dream bungalow may suddenly come on the market, they might fear they'll lose it if they don't move quickly enough. Suddenly they've gone from zero to motivated very quickly. This is why we need to stay on top of all our clients in case something like this happens.

The A in MAN is for ability. This is where your money can really be earned. Sure, the viewer on the phone wants to move from a three-bedroom house to a four-bedroom house, but can they actually do it? Well, it sounds like they are going to need to sell their home first, get a mortgage sorted, get a solicitor lined up and find a four-bedroom house to move to. All of the above, not only can we help with, but we can get paid well to do so, too.

This stage can not only earn you a lot of money, but it can also work as a vetting process for whether a client is serious about or not. For example, I would love to buy a £5,000,000 house in Mayfair, but can I afford it? Absolutely not. I have the motivation, but the ability, which just so happens to be a fair few million short, is holding me back.

Finally, we look at Need. This is looking at what a person wants to buy versus what they actually need to buy. Talk to anyone when they first start looking for a property to buy and they'll give you a long list of things they want to have in their next home. Come back to them in a year's time once they have moved into their next property and you'll find a property which is very different from that list they gave you some 12 months ago. This is because we asked what they wanted rather than exactly what they needed. It's important to differentiate between these two aspects of the property search. If you don't, you may end up not contacting someone about a property that is perfect for them simply because it didn't have something they wanted. When in reality, they weren't really that fussed about it – it was just something that would have been nice to have.

Here's a story from personal experience which highlights this point well. I had an elderly client some years ago who was very specific that she wanted to buy a bungalow in the area I was working in. Now, bungalows were in very short supply and nearly never came onto the market, so I knew we were going to struggle to find somewhere that suited her.

But after talking to her and understanding exactly what she wanted. She mentioned that she didn't actually need a bungalow, she just wanted one. What she actually needed in her next property was a downstairs toilet, something that almost every house in her price range had. Needless to say, whilst the other agents in town were still waiting for that bungalow to come on the market, she was already packing her life up and getting ready to move into the new house that I had recently found her, with a downstairs toilet obviously! If we can understand all of the above with the applicants we talk to in our business, we'll have a greater understanding of what makes them tick and ultimately know what is going to work for them and what simply isn't.

All the details we capture at this stage should be added to our CRM system. Not only hard facts such as names and addresses, but soft facts as well, such as if they mention how many children they have, or if they have just got back from holiday. This will make great conversation starters the next time we catch up with them.

There's a selection of questions in the estate agency world referred to as the magnificent seven. I'm not too sure about the magnificent bit, but there are seven questions which if asked to anyone looking to register or view a property, will highlight key motivation, price range, any income opportunities for your business that you can explore further.

Those seven questions are:

- What's prompting you to consider moving?
- When do you need to have moved by?
- What's the situation regarding your current home?
- What budget do you have and what did you base it on?
- Who will be living in the home?
- Where do you currently work?
- If I found you the absolute perfect property, what's the very maximum you'd be prepared to pay for it?

As you might imagine, if you find out the answers to all of the above questions, you're going to have a pretty strong idea about not only what is motivating someone to buy a property, but also any timescales involved and budget, too. Again, all these details should be jotted down onto your CRM system for safe keeping.

Notice how so far in the conversation we have not spoken about the time or date that we're going to book the viewing for yet? This should be the last thing you do, in the same way that when we were booking the time and date on the market appraisal, this was also the last thing we did. As before, this comes down to 'wants' in the conversation. The applicant on the end of the phone simply wants a time and date to meet you at the property and that's it. You want a name, address, phone number, financial situation, search criteria, the list goes on and on. As soon as you give away a time and date, the person on the other end of the phone will lose interest in what you have to say very quickly because they got what they want from the conversation – a time and date. Once you have given this information up, they will more than likely just cut the conversation shorter than you want it to be, leaving information you wanted still on the table.

When registering and managing applicants, it's important to have a system in place to categorise them. This will make your life considerably easier when it comes to activities like calling out properties to try and get viewings or trying to find your next potential instruction.

In the estate agency world, applicants are typically divided up into three camps depending on their current situation, ability to move and motivation. Those three categories are hot, warm and cold. Let's talk through each of them so you can then categorise buyers as they come into your estate agency.

Let's kick off with hot buyers. The reason they're called 'hot' is because they buy really quickly. This means that they are going to buy a property in the next couple of weeks whether that is with you or with someone else. They'll have a really strong motivation to buy and will be in a position to move forward should the right property come up. This could be a cash buyer, someone who has sold, or could even be a first-time buyer that is being kicked out of their parents' house shortly, with a mortgage in place already. These buyers just need to find the right property for them, and they'll jump for it with both feet. When I used to manage a list of 100 applicants looking to buy in my town, at any one time I would have a maximum of around five really hot buyers who were going to buy in the coming days or weeks. Because these applicants are going to find a property so quickly, you need to stay in regular communication with them. If you leave it two weeks between calls, chances are they have found and instructed solicitors already by the time your call comes through. Not a good result.

Next let's have a look at warm buyers. Most buyers you deal with will fall into this category. These are applicants who want to purchase a property but something else needs to happen first to make this a reality. This is usually selling their own property, whether that be in or out of the area we cover. As you might imagine, you have a couple of really good reasons to stay in touch with these applicants. Firstly, they could become hot at any time. One good viewing on their own property with a solid follow-up offer, and they'll be under offer and keen not to waste the opportunity and find their next home. Secondly, they may well have a home in the local area that they're struggling to sell. I wonder if we could help them out with that? *Hint, hint.*

Finally, we have cold buyers, though don't be put off by the name. They should in no way be getting the cold shoulder from your business. These are applicants who have a property to sell which is currently not on the market. This could include in your area but also out of your area as well. As you might imagine, along with the warm buyers who are currently on the market, these can be a gold mine for your business for future listings. So, overlook them at your peril!

As you can see, there are many opportunities that present themselves with every applicant you speak to, but there are more opportunities on top of simply getting a market appraisal. We have a huge opportunity here to refer to mortgage partners and solicitors which can provide a healthy income into our business. You should be looking at each of these applicants as an opportunity. An opportunity not only to earn more money directly from them, which is obviously a good thing, but also how can you leverage these people to get more properties onto the market with you?

As we spoke about earlier in this book, if you are speaking to a buyer or a seller and they're struggling to find a property to buy, this is an easy win for you. Sure, you might not have any properties they want to go for currently on the market but that doesn't mean you can't deploy your agency skills to try and get properties on to your radar with some simple marketing in the area they want to live in.

Imagine now that you are talking to an applicant who is not yet on the market in your area and they want to register to buy a property through you. Most agents will purely focus on trying to get a market appraisal on their property as they see this as the biggest opportunity in front of them. It's easily done, but that is not the whole picture from the seller's perspective.

Their goal is to move to their next home, remember, not simply to sell their home. On top of this, when we get marketing materials out in the local area, this will present us as a proactive agent who has buyers looking in that area which is a positive regardless of whether or not it gets us any phone calls. Through this one small exercise, the applicant with the property to sell realises that we go above and beyond what any other agent will do and makes us a shoo-in for the listing. If we find them a property to buy as well, it's a formality – they are going to be selling with us.

In the same way that we covered in earlier chapters there should be a mental hierarchy in your mind when speaking to anyone looking to register to buy a property or book in a viewing. That should be, can I get a market appraisal from the conversation? Because this is the biggest ticket item. But as we just discussed, more than likely this is only half the conversation if we are doing our job correctly. We should then be exploring what properties we have that we might be able to sell them, and if we don't have any, what steps can we take to try and find them a property? Next, we should be looking at financial services referrals and solicitor referrals which we'll go into more detail on shortly. Finally, we should be asking them if they know anyone else looking to buy or sell in the local area that we could talk to. If we go through this list and get as much as we can from it, then it's sure to be a good result.

When it comes to how often you should speak to buyers you're dealing with, this will vary from person to person. As we covered just now, if someone is a really hot buyer, then we may well talk to them every day or even every couple of days to see how they are progressing. Whereas with someone looking to move to our area from the Shetland Islands and has been struggling to sell for the past five years, we may only speak to them every couple of months as chances are, they aren't going to be selling any time soon.

As you might imagine, our best route of communication with anyone looking to buy a property is to pick up the phone. This should be your go-to for onward communications for all the reasons we have spoken about previously, not only does this allow us to build better bonds and relationships with applicants who are looking to buy in the local area, but also it gives us further opportunities to again pitch services they may have initially declined. Sure, you can text and voice note applicants who are looking to buy, but only with very low-level communications such as confirming appointment times, for example. Nothing that requires any kind of influence in the conversation.

Getting that third-party income

We have mentioned third-party income a few times in this book already without going into any real detail on the subject. Well, now that time has come. In this following section, we are going to take a deeper dive into not only why this area is a crucial part of any estate agency business, but also how to include it into your everyday conversations to make it as easy as possible to earn from this.

Let's look at the two biggest potential third-party incomes for your estate agency business. They are referring to a mortgage broker and referring over to a solicitor or conveyancing partner.

Taking an overview of all the owned properties in the U K, just short of 40% of all these homes have some sort of mortgage on them. This is a huge number of properties as you might imagine when you have a population of nearly 70 million people. Meaning that lots of people you come into contact with on a daily basis either have a mortgage already or are looking to get a mortgage in place to enable them to buy their next home. This 40% split is not an even divide between all ages, either. There are certainly more cash buyers in the later years of their life than first-time buyers trying to get their first hand on the property ladder.

So why should we be looking to refer people across to a mortgage advisor? It comes down to two big reasons. First of all, let's talk about money, as apparently, it makes the world go round. Simply put, you can earn a huge amount of money from referring to a mortgage broker. I have had several clients in the past who have earned more on a monthly basis from referring to a mortgage broker than they have by selling properties. You've not read that incorrectly, as a business they brought in more income from referring financial services than they did from selling properties, which I assure you they were also no slouch at either.

This money they brought in was purely cash positive in their business, meaning that the third-party advisor they referred to, the company didn't pay their salary, electric bill or sick pay. The money was purely one way. When they had a client that they referred across then complete on a mortgage, they received a percentage of the fee due to the advisor. This is known as the procuration fee. That was it, purely income, nothing outgoing from their side. Also, as a bonus, the buyer they referred across didn't even need to buy through their estate agency business to get paid, they could buy a property through another agent in their town or anywhere else for that matter, and where they referred across to the advisor, their fee was due. A pretty sweet deal, you might agree.

The second reason it's paramount to refer across to a trusted mortgage advisor, is because it offers you control later down the line should the buyer in question buy a home through you. Imagine your frustration if you are trying to get a property to exchange and all you need to get is one piece of paperwork from a mortgage advisor that you don't know or have any kind of relationship with. Frustrating, to say the least. Whereas if you had referred them across to the mortgage advisor that you know and trust, firstly, you can be confident they're going to do a solid job for the client. And secondly, if you need to get hold of them you can simply pick up the phone and sort the issue quickly, leaving everyone in a better place.

The same goes when it comes to solicitors. Not only do they form a steady and consistent income stream into your business, but also referring to a trusted firm that you have a relationship with will pay dividends in future, because for issues that come up that need taking care of, you have a direct line of communication through to exactly the right person to speak to, sorting issues quickly and efficiently. No scenic route through the secretaries here, thank you.

To give you an idea of how much money you should be looking to earn, I have always worked on the figure of £1,000 worth of additional income off each property that you bring onto the market. Meaning if you brought five properties onto the market this month, great, our goal is to earn £5,000 in additional income from these properties. Anything below this number, I consider to be leaving money on the table. Anything above this number, feel free to take a short bow and keep doing what you're doing!

When looking for a referral partner, it's important to not only focus on who is going to pay you the biggest percentage or fixed fee, as tempting as this might be in the short term. Instead, you want to look for a company that pays you a competitive fee but also is a safe pair of hands to deal with. After all, it will negatively affect your business if you recommend your clients over to someone that doesn't offer a great service. It will reflect badly on you, who initially introduced them. Getting a good referral partner is also key to avoid hold-ups and headaches down the line. You want a firm that is proactive on getting properties across the line, it will match your desire to do this as well.

In this next section, we're going to look at how to effectively pitch for financial services and solicitor quotes in your business. This isn't an exhaustive list or guide as I could write another book on this subject alone. Instead, it's going to give you a solid starting point and some confidence and pointers to get you going in the right direction which you can refine over time.

"You miss 100% of the shots you don't take.' - Wayne Gretzky

Now I know that Mr Gretzky was talking about ice hockey when said this, but it falls into lots of areas in your estate agency business. Referring to financial services and solicitors are just one good example. Simply put, if you don't ask anyone if you can get them a quote for solicitors' or if you can try and save them some money on their mortgage, then the answer is always going to be no, because you'll simply never get that far.

I can remember only one time in my estate agency career when someone walked into my office and said, 'Excuse me, can I book an appointment with your mortgage advisor?' I can confirm I nearly fell off my chair. So, if I've had that once in 20 years, how many times do you think it will happen to you? Not a lot, I'll be willing to bet.

So, if you take nothing else from this chapter, just ask some kind of question on this topic, to your applicants, your sellers and pretty much everyone else you come into contact with, otherwise you'll just never know.

So that's rule number one. It doesn't matter how you ask the question, as long as you ask. Your results will be infinitely better through this one point alone. Now let's look at how we can refine this down to improve our conversion even further.

Let's look at when we are trying to refer over to a mortgage advisor. When we first register a buyer, or talk to anyone about their onward purchase, ask them how they arrived at the figure they're going to spend for the next property they want to buy.

For example, 'How much are you looking to spend on your next home?'

'£300,000'

'Brilliant, can I ask how you arrived at that figure?'

This question will give us a really good idea of what they have done so far with regard to their mortgage. Listen to what they say next as this is going to give you the ammo to go back to them shortly.

Notice how we haven't fallen into the trap that most estate agents fall into by asking 'Have you got your mortgage sorted?' Funnily enough, whenever you ask this question to people looking to buy a home through you, they always say yes!

Now, there are only certain answers we are going to get from this question, so it stands to reason that if we know what the answers are going to be, we can have a rebuttal in place for each of them that we can pick on as soon as we get the answer.

Those answers are going to be the below, or some combination of the below, more often than not.

- I'm buying the property in cash
- I've been to see my bank
- I've been to see multiple banks
- I've been to see a financial/mortgage advisor

As you can see, there isn't a huge range of answers here, so we can prepare for each of these replies in advance.

Let's take a look at the first one. 'I'm buying in cash.' Now you might think you're bang out of luck on the mortgage side, here. Most of the time you're right, except when you're speaking to a client who is looking to buy an investment property to rent out. Sometimes it can make more sense to buy multiple investment properties and share that £300,000 budget over three properties using buy-to-let mortgages for example, mitigating a lot of the risk of having all that cash tied up in one sole property. If they would like to explore how this looks, you've got a financial advisor who can quite happily help, and as a bonus, you've just turned a buyer who was looking to buy one property, into someone who wants to buy three. Pretty good result for you.

Next up, we have someone that says, 'I have been to see my bank' or 'I've been to see multiple banks.' This is probably the most common reply you will hear day-to-day as people still seem to believe that their bank will look after them in some way because they've had a current account with them for the last 40 years. Sorry to burst the bubble here, but we're just a number on a spreadsheet, these days.

To combat this reason, we need to lift the lid on banks and how they offer mortgages out. Most banks will only offer a very limited number of mortgages. This will be made up of their fixed rate deals, tracker deals, and buy-to-let deals, but usually you're looking at under 10 options available to anyone that walks through the front door of the branch.

So even if our client on the phone has been to three banks for example, the banks have probably looked at under 30 mortgage options for them. And in reality, it's often a lot less once you strip out options that simply won't work for them, such as buy-to-let mortgages. Compare this to a broker who can look at the best rates from hundreds and thousands of companies, with tens of thousands of mortgage options, who do you think has the better chance of getting a better deal? It's simply a numbers game.

On top of this, lots of high street banks offer introducer rates to financial advisors who pass across lots of business to them, which are better deals than you or I can get just by walking into a high street branch with your 40-year-old debit card. Crazy, right?

As you might imagine, our client who has told us they have been to see the bank, or even multiple banks, is about to be seriously outgunned by our reply.

'That's great news, can I ask, Mrs Jones, how many mortgage options did Halifax show you?'

'A couple'

'I see. We have an advisor here with access to thousands of mortgage products, who I'm confident could get you a better deal. Would you like to see if you could save some money?'

Find me someone that answers 'no' to the question 'would you like to save some money?' It's fair to say this one is in the bag. Also, you might have noticed that we complimented Mrs Jones on the work she has done so far, this is a good move as it shows you are on the same page as the client.

Now we have someone who has been to see a mortgage advisor already. Firstly, know your competition. If we know who all the advisors are locally and what they can and can't do, we'll have more ammo to go back with here. For example, some advisors will charge a separate fee to work with them along with the fee that the mortgage company pays them. If your advisor doesn't charge this upfront fee, then you've just made the following conversation a lot easier.

For the sake of the example, though, I'll keep it fairly broad, and you can add to it if you do have any information like this later on down the line.

'That's great Mrs Jones, out of interest though, who have you compared that advisor against to ensure you've got the best deal?'

Suddenly Mrs Jones is doubting whether she got the best deal with the first advisor she spoke to. The likely answer to this question is 'I haven't'. As you can see, you've left the door wide open for you to swoop in and offer her a conversation with your advisor 'if for nothing else just to give you peace of mind moving forward, Mrs Jones.'

So that's 99% of all conversations you are going to have with clients. Not all that complicated, I think you might agree. The key rule though, is no matter how you ask, the important bit is that you do ask! You'll be amazed how many options you get just from doing that alone.

Next, let's look at how we're going to get referral income and ultimately control of the sale progression process by referring to our solicitor or conveyancing partner.

Spoiler alert, if you can refer to your mortgage advisor, then getting a solicitors quote for your clients is an absolute walk in the park. The reason why is because most people don't prepare all that far in advance. They have enough going on in their lives already without proactively looking up local solicitors and finding out how much they cost or if they're actually any good.

So, when you ask the question 'Have you looked into how much a solicitor is going to cost you?' Usually, the answer is no which leaves you with a nice easy close of 'Would you like to find out how much it is going to cost?' Honestly, it is that easy for 80% of the public.

If the answer to this question is 'yes, they have looked up and found a solicitor already, then we can reply with,

'That's great, who have you compared them to, to make sure you're getting the best deal?'

Sound familiar? It should do. Chances are that the answer to this question will be 'no one.' This action will take care of the minority of people who have actually done anything about solicitors so far, leaving you free to send them over a quote or to get the solicitor to quote them directly, depending on how you have your referral process set up.

As you can see, this is easy money for your business for both financial services and solicitors as well. There is no cost to you, and for the sake of an extra minute or two of conversation with a client, you can earn thousands upon thousands of pounds in additional income. We should be asking these questions to everyone you come into contact with on a daily basis, no matter if they are registering to buy, having you out on a market appraisal or out on a viewing with you.

The earlier you can get these questions into the conversation with clients, the better. Because the longer you leave it, the more chance that another agent swoops in and does all the above for you. The great news is you also don't just get one crack of the whip with these conversations, either. If you can't overcome an objection whilst initially booking a viewing with an applicant, worry not, you're going to see them in a few days' time when you carry out the viewing, meaning you can think about how you can overcome their previous objections from the days before.

Are you looking at me?

Okay, let's have a little recap of where we're up to currently. Not only have we successfully generated leads into our estate agency business, but we have then converted them into a market appraisal, and then into a full-blown listing. Off the back of this listing, we have worked hard to boost our efforts with our excellent marketing. We have generated interest in the property we have up for sale and have booked people who are interested in buying the property. Great. Let's pick it up at the next stage, then. That being, carrying out the viewings on the property itself.

Firstly, let's look at what the job of a viewing is. As you might expect, the number one priority or goal of a viewing is to get an offer from the viewer on the property you're showing the applicant around. But there is a lot more we can get from a viewing outside of this core goal. Not only can we get an offer on the property we're selling, but we can requalify the potential buyer to ensure they're a good buyer for us to deal with in the first place. I've had multiple conversations with applicants in the past who have sounded like the best buyers in the world over the phone, but when you meet them in-person, they simply don't measure up to the optimism you had about them before you met them face-to-face, for one reason or another.

Outside of this requalification, we have an opportunity to re-pitch both financial services and solicitor referrals should we not have been successful on our first attempt. We can also get some valuable feedback from the appointment, ideally focused on the pricing of the property. Because the worst-case scenario is if all else fails, we can ask them if they enjoyed the viewing, and if so, could they please leave us a Google review.

As you can see, there is a lot to work through there. Especially keeping in mind most viewings tend to last under half an hour, as well. So, we need to have a structured plan in place to ensure we get as much value from a viewing as we possibly can.

One of the most important factors of this is that you know about the property before you even walk through the front door. If you are the person that has valued the property, and you know all about it then this is an easy part of the process for you. Whereas if you are a negotiator and you haven't visited the property before, you are going to want to not only have a conversation with the person who valued the home for any information you feel you might need to know. On top of this, you're going to want to study the property information form for the home so you know as much about it as you can.

This will also involve you getting to the property well before time to get yourself accustomed to the overall layout of the home and how to access certain areas of the property, such as getting into the garden or the garage, which might not initially seem that obvious. We also need to make sure that we have everything we need for the viewing to be a success, this includes keys to get into the property – which is a solid place to start – any alarm codes for the home, and also a set of property particulars that we can give to the buyer viewing the home as it will help them remember the property once they've left it.

When I talk to new estate agents up and down the country about viewings, one of the questions that regularly comes up is 'What should I talk about on a viewing?' I know it seems like a simple question to answer, but most people get it wrong.

I personally work on a 70/30 split, or at least aim for that when carrying out viewings on a property. 70% of the time we should be focusing on the person viewing the home, and 30% of the time you should be talking about the property that they're viewing. Yes, you read that correctly. You're spending more time talking to the person going around the property, about them and their property search, than you are the actual home they're looking around. We're going to be reconfirming motivation, search criteria, what they have been looking at recently and if the situation with their own property has changed. Effectively, we want to find out as much information as possible, because if they decide to offer on the home, we're going to have to know this information to ensure the owner can make an informed decision to move forward or not.

That's going to take up around 70% of our conversation with the person viewing the home. Now let's look at the 30%. The property itself.

A little play-along exercise here. Look around the room you're sitting in currently. Notice those see-through things that let light in? They're called windows. How about that weird bit of wall with a hinge on that lets people in and out of the room? Oh, that's a door.

As you can see from my slightly tongue-in-cheek example here, most people know everything that makes up a home already. You don't need to point out the kitchen sink, what a bath is, or even that 'this is the garden.' Thank you, Sherlock. The grass and plants were a giveaway.

The key here is to either link what you're looking at with something the buyer has previously mentioned when registering or tell them something that isn't completely obvious.

Imagine you're showing a potential buyer around a home with a big garden, and when you registered the buyer, they specifically mentioned they wanted a good-sized garden so their kids could have a trampoline. Instead of saying 'this is the garden' you'd be far better off saying 'I know when we first spoke on the phone, you mentioned that you wanted a big enough garden so that your kids could have a trampoline, is this one big enough for that?' Not only are we linking our question to an earlier conversation we had with them, showing the client that not only we remember but we actually care, but we're also mentally ticking off one of the needs they had highlighted as well. Something we'll come back to towards the end of the viewing when it comes to closing for an offer.

The other element we mentioned is highlighting what isn't immediately obvious to the person looking around the home. A few examples of this could be letting the viewer know what date the extension was added on and if it has any guarantee left on it at all. Even such nonobvious elements such as underfloor heating or which way the garden faces are good to highlight to them, but you need to know about the property to make these additions.

Let's now go over some basic rules of a viewing to ensure they're as high a standard as they possibly can be. Firstly, all homeowners should be out for viewings on their property. Studies have shown that properties that don't have the homeowners in whilst viewings take place actually achieve higher asking prices than properties that do. Sometimes you have certain property owners that would like to stay at home during the viewing. If this is the case, then ask them to be in the part of the house where they are tucked away. A conservatory for example or in the garden if it's a nice day. There are very few times in anyone's life when they can actually earn money by going to the local pub. This is one of them, so your sellers should take full advantage of this situation and vacate the property for appointments. The owner being present heavily restricts the open communication between you and your applicant viewing the home. As very few people are going to stand within earshot of a homeowner and say that a property 'needs a lot of work' or 'is on for too high a price currently.' It simply won't happen. They'll simply be polite, say they like it and never be heard from again.

Next, we should get to the property early. About 15 minutes should be plenty. In this time, we're going to go inside the property, take a lap around and ensure that the property is looking its best. This could involve turning some lights on, picking up the post and even opening some windows should it feel a bit stuffy.

Once we've done this, head out to the front of the property. That's right, outside the home. No sitting in the living room, waiting here. The reason we do this is twofold. Firstly, it makes it really easy for buyers to know we're there. And secondly, all the neighbours will see that you have a viewing on the property, which will show them that you're doing a good job at trying to sell the home.

Once the buyers turn up, meet and greet them and introduce yourself if you haven't met them before. Head towards the property and ask them to take their shoes off before they go inside. I don't care if they have Gucci sliders on, those things are coming off.

Remember earlier how we spoke about how 30% of all your listings in the future will come from people who view properties with you? Well, this is a test run for exactly that. Because the way you treat the property, you're all in today will reflect on how you're going to treat their property should they decide to come onto the market with you in future. This is why you must insist viewers take off their shoes and protect the property at all costs from any kind of damage or issues.

Next up, we are going to use our signposting technique that we used on our market appraisal. This is where we explain to the viewers what is going to happen next, so they have an idea about how the next 30 minutes or so are going to look. I would explain that the plan is to look at the downstairs of the property first, then the upstairs, then finally the garden. We'll be looking at the garden last of all 'to avoid bringing any mud in from the garden into the home'. Again, getting some brownie points here, to show how much we care about the properties we well.

Then I would have a quick chat with the viewers on the background of the property. This could include how long it's been on the market for, what the interest has been, and some information about how long the owners have been there and why they're looking to move.

I should put a caveat in here. Only disclose information which is going to be positive to the sale. I wouldn't expect your initial conversation to be, 'So this property has been on the market for ages, not many viewings and the homeowners are looking to move because they hate it around here.' Not exactly a strong start, I'm sure you'll agree. Instead, focus on the positives.

Once you have done this initial introduction to the property, you can then carry out the tour of the home as we have discussed – downstairs first, then upstairs, and finally the garden.

One thing you will get very good at, being an estate agent, is small talk. Meeting lots of strangers day in, day out, and talking to them for sometimes 30 minutes, sometimes a lot more, will have that effect on you. I used to always have what I called my 'fall-back questions' in my back pocket for any viewings. I would occasionally have to pull these out if I felt there was a lull in any conversation or some kind of awkward silence approaching. These are standalone questions that I could ask at any time which would boost the conversation again so we could get back on track and headed in the right direction. You can add your own here, but my list consists of:

- How many properties have you looked at so far?
- What's the best property you have seen?
- Have you got many other viewings booked in? (If yes) Which ones are you going to see?

I used to particularly like asking the last question, as once they showed me which properties they were going to see, I would purposely get the house number wrong. 'Oh right, I think I've seen that one. Number 6 New Road, isn't it?' 'No, that is number 2 New Road.' Well, guess which house is going to get a letter through their post-box very soon? Number 2 New Road! Even better, if we have that owner's contact details, call that owner at the end of the day today, ask them how their viewing went and what the feedback from the appointment was. Because I knew that they wouldn't have it yet.

As we go around carrying out the viewing, we should be looking to tick as many items as we possibly can from the applicant's 'needs' list and ideally a good amount of the 'wants' as well. The reason we are going to be aiming to do this is because when we get to the end of the viewing appointment, we are going to ask the viewer if this property is something they could see themselves buying. If, by the time we ask this question, we know that the property has ticked off a lot of the items on this list, then we know we stand a good chance of this being a positive answer.

It could look something like this, 'So, Mrs Jones, now we've had a look around, I feel you've ticked a lot of boxes from what I've seen. We've got the three good-sized bedrooms you wanted, along with the open-plan kitchen and the good-sized garden, as well. With all that in mind, is this a property you could see yourself moving into?'

As you can see, we have taken the information from the viewing and made it into a close. We'll get one of two answers here: yes, this is a property Mrs Jones can see herself living in, in which case let's start talking to her about making an offer on the home. Or no, this isn't the right property for her, in which case we want to start getting feedback from her for our seller on exactly why it's not the one for her. We should also be asking the viewer what they think of the price of the property and how this compares to other properties they're viewing at the moment. As we spoke about in earlier chapters, if we can get a good selection of price-sensitive feedback, it makes any price change conversations with owners a far easier process.

If you feel like the person you have met at this home is a good buyer and even though the property wasn't for them, they like the area you have shown them, you could also talk to them about looking for a new property for them. You could action this by sending out VIP letters to the local area, targeting withdrawn properties or even adding a post to your Facebook account stating that you have someone looking for a property in that area. Either way, it's all good marketing and advertising for your business to go alongside the advertising you 've been doing for the property you're selling.

By the time we leave an appointment, we should have a really good idea if this deal is going to come together or not, and if it isn't, we should know exactly why it wasn't the right property for the viewer.

The proof is in the feedback

As we have just mentioned, getting feedback from a viewing is key to the successful selling of a property. Not only could this include any small changes that we can make to the property to increase our chances of selling the home, it'll also prepare us for conversations with the homeowner about the price of the property and what we may need to do to get the home under offer.

Once you have finished a viewing of the property, or completed a batch of viewings, it's important that you communicate with the owner quickly and efficiently. Imagine you have spent the last four hours tidying up your home to an inch of its life, ready for viewings to take place. You would be keen to hear how the viewings went as soon as possible!

With this in mind as soon as you leave the property, you should call the owner and let them know you have finished viewing their home so they're all free to come back to the property. As you might imagine, their next question will be 'how did the viewings go?' You should then pass across some initial feedback on the viewing we hosted. Generally, this will be fairly high-level feedback of whether they liked it or they didn't. Make your homeowner aware that you're going to be in contact with all of today's viewers first thing tomorrow morning with some final feedback for them to digest.

If you can't speak to your owners over the phone, if they can't take calls at work for example, a good process to go through here is just to send the homeowner a one-minute-long video of you stating that you are just leaving the property now and locking up the home. You can then go on to explain how the viewings went and the process for further feedback tomorrow, as before. But if you are able to, make the phone call, it's the better customer service option.

All that's left to do now is exactly what we have already said we're going to do. That is, to call the viewers first thing the following day and ask them for their feedback on the viewing the day before. As a worst-case scenario if you can't get hold of the person who viewed the home, it is important to make sure you let your seller know you have tried to call them, you have left a message, and that you are going to try again later on today.

Remember that not only should we be recording this feedback on your CRM system, but also when we are passing across the feedback it should be done in a price-sensitive manner. This means that instead of saying for example 'the feedback from yesterday is that they don't want to go forward with your home because the felt the garden was a bit too small for them' we should be saying instead 'the feedback from yesterday is that they don't want to go forward with your home because they felt that compared to other properties in the price range the garden was smaller than they were expecting.' As we covered in the price reduction chapter, this is going to do you some solid favours if and when it comes to talking about potentially changing the price of the property in future.

You will sometimes find that when you want to get feedback from viewers, they suddenly become very hard to get hold of. This can prove very frustrating as you might imagine, but also goes to show how important it is to get feedback on the appointment when you can. Also, this reinforces why when registering a client, it's important to get as many contact details as you possibly can.

I would generally recommend you work on a three strikes layout with your feedback chasing. That is, that you'll try to contact the viewers from the day before for feedback on three different occasions before you finally admit that they're probably not going to come back to you.
Throughout this chasing process it is important that you keep the seller of the property in the loop, letting them know that you are indeed not giving up on getting the feedback from the viewer and that you're going

to keep trying. At least they will know you're doing everything you can and exploring every avenue as well.

Let's do a deal

We've been slightly negative in the last section and prepared you for viewers and applicants to not like the property they saw or even then not come back to you once after seeing it. Well, it's now time to turn that frown upside down and focus on what is going to happen next when someone wants to actually put an offer in on a property, what you need, and the processes to follow.

Dealing with offers is, in my opinion, one of the best parts of being an estate agent. It's the doing the deal part which I really love. You get to interact with many human emotions, and tactics and sales skills most definitely come into it. Though if I am 100% transparent here, and to give you some confidence if you need it at this stage, I still remember vividly not only receiving my first offer on a property, but then the feeling of dread as my boss said to me 'You can put that one forward to the owner, Chris.' Oh god. Ensue panic.

Like with anything you do, these things become easier over time. From that initial offer I put forward on a small house at £200,000, to now having dealt with house sales in excess of £4,000,000. Eventually it all just feels a bit like monopoly money and in no way hundreds of thousands or even millions of pounds going backwards and forwards. So, rest assured, if you feel slightly nervous when you not only get your first offer but then have to put it forward to the owner, it will get easier and more fun as you relax and deal with this situation more and more.

To start off with, let's look at what your legal obligations are as an estate agent in the UK. Sales in the estate agency world is still largely unregulated but there are some rules about putting offers forward on a property which we need to abide by to stay on the right side of the proceeding. Most of these are hugely obvious but we still should run through them, nonetheless.

To make sure we follow these rules, we need to have 100% clarity with a buyer about when they are making an offer on a property and when they aren't. Imagine you are talking to a viewer at a property, and you think that you're just having a conversation with them about the price of the property, but they think they're putting an offer forward in that same conversation. You can quickly see how there is a potential gap our compliance could fall short of simply due to a miscommunication. Imagine a viewer saying, 'Do you think the owners will take £240,000 for the house?' Is this an offer? Or is it just a conversational piece around the price? Either way, we will need to clarify if the viewer wants that £240,000 offer to be put forward to the owner or not, as it will affect what we do next. Offers can be put forward both verbally and in writing, there is currently no obligation for people who are looking to put offers forward to put this in writing to you, though in some situations it might prove a good idea. If you're ever in doubt, simply ask to save any later confusion down the line.

One of the key rules when selling a property is that you have a legal obligation to put all offers forward to the owner no matter how ridiculous or unacceptable they might be. I could walk into any estate agency office in the UK and offer £5 for a property they have up in the window and the poor agent would have a legal obligation to inform their sellers of my hugely embarrassing offer. A good way to make yourself very unpopular in the local area very quickly, as you might imagine.

There is an exception to this rule though, that is, if you have it in writing from the sellers of the property that they will not accept an offer below a certain price, you do not have to abide by the regulation and put any offers below this line forward to them. I have only had this happen a few times in my career, so it isn't exactly a regular occurrence. But even when I had an offer come forward, I would still make the owners aware and fulfil all legal obligations even if the conversation was about 30 seconds long in which I informed them of the offer and that I had rejected it. It's better to be safe than sorry.

The other big regulation we need to stay on top of, outside of putting all offers forward to the seller, is the manner and timescale in which we do this. This is made up of two parts, firstly what your legal obligations are, and secondly how you should communicate this offer to the homeowner to give yourself the best chance of it being accepted.

Initially, on the compliance side you have a legal obligation to put all offers forward to the homeowner as quickly as reasonably possible. As a worst-case scenario, you should confirm all offers to the sellers and buyers in writing within two working days.

Secondly, this letter to the homeowner that comes within two working days should absolutely in no way be the first time that a homeowner finds out about an offer on their property. I mean seriously, how busy or unorganised are you if it takes you more than a couple of days to pick up the phone to your sellers to put an offer forward?

As before, when it comes to putting offers forward, the phone is going to be your best friend for all the reasons we covered before. You may even consider going round to tell your sellers face to face, if you think the journey warrants it. After all, what's a 20-minute drive to get a house under offer?

So, those are your main obligations as an estate agent when it comes to dealing with offers. Don't withhold any, put them forward as quickly as you reasonably can, and ensure you send out offer letters to confirm this all within two working days. Pretty easy, right?

As a little bit of time saving advice for you, you don't need to write one letter per offer you receive on a property. In fact, you can just send one letter to the owner covering all the offers from all involved parties, and their increased offers as well. Just imagine the savings you'll make on stamps alone.

This means that if you hold a launch day on a home and you receive offers from four different parties, you can wrap this up into one letter to the owner. If they all decide to increase their offers the next day, you can do this all over again in another single letter. No need to post out eight different offer letters, you'll be thrilled to know.

Okay, so by now we should have a good idea about what our legal obligations are when it comes to offers being submitted on properties we're selling. We also know that the letters we send out should in no way be the way our sellers find out about offers on their home, as this carries very little information to go with the figure we have put forward to them.

So, what else goes into an offer being put forward correctly? Well quite a lot, in all honesty. I always think of putting offers forward a bit like being on a world-class bobsleigh run. Bear with me here, this will make sense I assure you! In a bobsleigh race, the most important part is the start, when everyone is pushing and piling into the sled first of all. They say that for every one second you can be quicker at the top of the course, you will be four seconds quicker by the end of the race. Well in my experience, dealing with estate agency offers is no different from this. Do a solid job when you first set up a sale and everything will glide through quickly and smoothly. On the other hand, throw the set-up process at the wall with the hopes that it will stick, and you've probably got a very long and bumpy run ahead of you. The choice is yours to make.

To start off, we obviously need to know how much the person looking to buy the property wants to offer on the home. This gives us a solid starting point. Once we have this figure, we need to find out whether they can actually afford to progress with this property at this price. After all, if we get to the end of the process and it turns out they don't actually have enough money to buy the property, this is not a great position to be in and you are going to look pretty stupid having this chat with your seller.

So how do we set about doing this? Well, it all depends on how they're looking to purchase the property. For someone that is looking to buy the home with cash from their bank account, the easiest and most direct way is to see a copy of their bank statement showing they have ample funds in the account. Most people are fine with this and will happily show you a statement proving they have the funds available. Don't think that people with lots of money are more hesitant to do this as well, the most I have ever seen in an account was just short of 60 million pounds and that man could not have been more happy to show me his bank statement, I can assure you. Some clients you deal with though, might be slightly more guarded about this subject. In these situations, you will need either a solicitor or an accountant to confirm that the client has ample funds in place to purchase the property and all the fees that go alongside this.

Notice how this is phrased: 'Does your client have enough funds in place to cover the purchase of £500,000 and all the fees involved? What I haven't asked is, 'How much money have they got in their account?' as this will result in a rather, beating-around-the-bush reply. The simple answer we are looking for here, in response to our correctly worded question is simply a 'Yes, I can confirm they do have ample funds in place for this transaction.' Great, let's get this email saved onto our CRM system as our proof of the funds being taken care of for our cash buyer.

As you might imagine with personal information such as bank statements, letters from accountants, agreement in principles from banks, these documents are confidential between you and the person offering on the property. At no time should they be passed or forwarded onto the owner of the home. The seller of the property will purely have to take your word for it that you have seen the relevant documents and that they are sufficient, as you are contractually obliged to work in their best interest. As we spoke about with our cash buyer, it's important that as you receive these documents that you upload everything to your CRM system. This means that all documents are not only stored securely but also if you ever had an audit of your business, you know exactly where to find the documents you should have in place.

Next, let's look at what is more than likely going to be the most common buyer you deal with on a day-to-day basis. That is going to be buyers who are buying a property using a mortgage. There will be two parts to this, one being us proving that they have a deposit in place to start off with and the second half will be confirming that they have an agreement in principle in place from a mortgage lender to make up the rest of the purchase price.

An example of this might be someone who is trying to buy a £200,000 house. They may have a £50,000 deposit to put down and the rest of the £150,000 is being made up of their mortgage. We need to prove both of these parts are there and are correct.

Starting with the £50,000 deposit, this will follow exactly the same process that we laid out with the cash buyer from. In some situations, though, buyers will be using the equity they have in their current property as this deposit amount for their next home. This means that in our example, we need to prove they have at least £50,000 worth of equity in their current home for this all to stack up. A simple way of seeing this is by viewing the buyer's mortgage statement. This will show exactly how much the person still owes on their home. We can then subtract this from the selling price of their property. The number we're left with is the equity in their home. As long as that figure is about the £50,000 mark in this example, then this box has been ticked off. You will get other situations, usually when people are looking to downsize later in life, where all of the money that they are going to use to purchase their next home is going to come from equity in their current property. For this, follow the same process as we have just laid out.

Next up, we need to make sure the potential buyer has their mortgage lined up. This can be done with either an agreement in principle, or a decision in principle from the lender they are planning on going with. This section of the process can be made even easier if you recommended this buyer across to your preferred mortgage broker as your broker will be able to confirm if this mortgage is likely given their current situation. Whereas if they have gone to an external broker that you don't have a relationship with, the most you'll probably get is a piece of paper stating that they have an agreement up to a certain amount. Once you're satisfied that these numbers all add up, upload any relevant documents to your CRM system and you can tick these buyers off as looking like they can afford the home.

A quick note from someone who has been around the estate agency block, here. Anyone who is very hesitant about coming forward and showing how they're going to buy a property should be treated as a red flag. Not only from a money laundering point of view but also acting in your seller's best interest. If I was keen to buy a property and a hoop that I had to jump through to give my offer the best chance of being accepted was to send over a copy of my bank statement, you would have that document in about a minute. A small price to pay to ensure I get the best chance of securing the property I want.

You might be wondering, what if someone puts an offer forward on a property I'm selling but won't provide me with any of the follow-up information that I need? Well, as we said before, you have a legal obligation to put that forward to the owner, but you also have a duty of care to the owner to inform them that you've asked for certain documents, why you asked for them, and that nothing has materialised as a result. I'm sure your sellers won't be biting their arm off to accept an offer from someone who refuses to show how they intend to pay for their home after your multiple attempts.

Now we're at the stage where we have an offer on the table and hopefully, we have proven that the buyer can afford to potentially move forward with the property at the price they want to offer.

The next section we are going to look at is buyer and seller timescale and the key factors that can affect this. Some clashes on this subject may be obvious straight away. Imagine you are selling a bungalow of a little old lady who may not have moved for the last 50 years and wants to find a small flat to move into. Contrast this against the potential buyer of her property, a developer who wants to get the sale to progress as soon as possible. Obviously, there would be a glaring difference in the upcoming speed of sale of the property, so it would be worth ensuring to the best of our ability that everyone is aware of this from day one.

In the UK property system, the biggest factor in the speed at which a sale moves, is mostly the position of not only the buyer of the property, but also the seller as well. As the sale progression process, which is the process after an offer has been agreed, is far from optimal. Something we'll come onto in later chapters. This means that when we look to put forward an offer to an owner, we firstly need to establish the position of the buyer and how proceedable they are.

If you have done a good job at registering the buyer to start off with, you should have a really good idea about their current situation. This could be living with family, renting a property, with their home under offer, being a cash buyer and so on. Effectively what we are doing here, is looking for potential issues that might affect us later down the line of the sale. This process is called chain-checking. Firstly, let's look at what a chain even is and why it is important to us.

A 'chain' simply refers to a situation where several property transactions are dependent on one another. This means that one person can't move into the property they are looking to buy until the owner of that property has found somewhere to move to and so this continues until finally a property is either vacant or the owners are moving into a different independent property, something that is known as 'breaking the chain'.

Chains have tops' and 'bottoms depending on where you are in the line of people looking to buy each other's properties. Usually, the top of the

263

chain would be a vacant property, therefore there is no one else to wait for, it's just sitting there ready to go. On the other end of the chain, we have the bottom. These are usually buyers that have nothing to sell, living in rented accommodation, investment buyers and so on. Effectively, they don't need to sell anything before they purchase the property they are looking to buy.

Top Of The Chain ———

Vacant Property

Sold Property

First Time Buyer

Bottom Of The Chain ———

Some chains are very short, in fact they can just be two people, perhaps if you had a buyer living with family and the property was vacant. Whilst others can be terribly long. I have no idea what the record is for the length of the chain in the UK property market, but I would imagine it would be pretty big. I've personally dealt with a chain of 15 properties before. I can assure you, it was pure stress from start to finish and I would not like to repeat it. That's one record you don't want to hold.

Now we'll look at how you find out what the chain information is with your buyer. For some, this might be a two-minute conversation. For example, for a potential buyer living with family, this could be a very quick exercise, even someone who is renting will be fairly quick. Though as a point to highlight here, when someone is renting a property, it's always worth finding out how long they have left on their rental agreement and what their notice period is. Because if they have just signed up for a whole year in their rental property, this could be an issue down the line when you're expecting everyone to complete in four months and they're going to have a vacant rental to pay on their hands for the next eight months. Either way, it's worth checking out from day one. Think bobsleigh.

The majority of time spent chain-checking occurs with potential buyers who have sold their current property. This is because we will need to establish the situation with this sale and check certain facts to ensure we highlight any factors which may become an issue later on down the road.

To give an example of this, with someone who wants to buy a home, we need to first establish further facts with regard to this potential buyer and the sale of their property which they need to complete to progress with our listing. To start this process, you will want to speak to the person offering on the property and find out some key facts about the sale of their home. Most of this is going to revolve around 'who is the estate agent selling your home?'

As an important rule here, never take your potential buyer's word for any information regarding the sale of their property, instead rely on the information that their agents provide to you. I have had many occurrences where potential buyers have looked me dead in the eye and told me that they have sold their property, only to speak to their agent who has told me they're still on the market and have been for some time!
Generally, estate agents in the UK don't get on all that well. We're a competitive bunch and don't like seeing other agents in our town doing better than us. You'll be pleased to know this is with one exception. When

it comes to checking chains, other agents will happily take your call and help you as much as they can, as it means that their seller has found a property and they're one step closer to getting their own sale through and getting paid.

Speak to the selling agent of your potential buyer and establish what is going on with their sale. Some questions you will want to ask them are:

- How long has this sale been agreed for?
- What's the position of the buyer?
- What are your buyers' names and their address?
- The buyer's buyer's estate agent (needed if they are also selling a property)
- Any timescales involved?
- Has there been a structural survey booked?
- Are the buyers getting a mortgage and has that survey been booked in?

As you can see here, there's a good amount of information we're trying to obtain. Now, some of these questions might be irrelevant when you speak to the agent below you in the chain. As you might imagine, if the buyer's sale was only agreed yesterday then I very much doubt surveys or mortgage valuations have been booked yet, a subject we'll come onto in following chapters.

What we are looking for here is, what could go wrong? Statistically, one in three sales fall through in the UK property market. One in three. That is massive. By doing this job correctly, we are highlighting any issues which might arise later on and looking for the path of least resistance.

Imagine you have two competing offers of a property. One is a cash buyer, and the other is sold to a first-time buyer with a mortgage. Ignoring the monetary amount of the offers on the property, which one would you choose?

I'd hope that given what we 've just spoken about, you went for the cash buyer as the issues that could go occur are far fewer in number. With the cash buyer, the biggest issues that could cause a problem down the line would include survey results or the buyer changing their mind.

Whereas with the person who is sold to a first-time buyer, we have to worry about the first-time buyer's mortgage, the first-time buyer's surveys, the first-time buyers changing their mind also our buyer's survey and their mortgage surveys, along with them changing their mind. As you can see, there are just simply more variables with the person who is sold to a first-time buyer and this just highlights more aspects of the sale that could go wrong.

Once we have established the facts from our buyer's estate agent, this may well be the research done, as long as this is the bottom of the chain. Meaning that our buyer's buyer has nothing to sell or is rented, for example. Though if we find out that our buyer's buyer has a buyer then this process starts all over again and we need to speak to that next estate agent down the chain and repeat the process until we get to the bottom of the chain. You can imagine how fun and exciting my day was when I carried out this exact task for my chain of 15 properties.

The mistake that many agents make is they will speak to the first agent in the chain and then simply take their word for the progress with the rest of the chain. This is a mistake, I promise you. You are relying on the agent you're speaking to being good at sales progression which many are simply not. Instead, speak to every agent down the chain to establish the facts.

I have had countless occasions in the past where the first agent I spoke to assured me that everything was progressing well with the downward chain. Only after speaking to every agent down the line, did I find out that actually one of the properties lost their buyer several weeks ago. Slightly embarrassing chat for that agent to have with their seller when another agent finds that one out!

When a chain of buyers has a missing link in it, it makes a buyer something that is known as 'unproceedable'. This simply means that a buyer is unable to buy the property they want to without something else happening first, which is usually the selling of a property.

Picture a person who wants to buy a property you're selling but they have their property on the market. They are an unproceedable buyer because they have to sell their home first. On the other side of the coin, a first-time buyer with a mortgage in place would be seen as proceedable as they are ready to go and nothing out of their control needs to happen before they are able to buy.

You will receive offers on properties you're trying to sell from both proceedable and unproceedable buyers. However, some unproceedable buyers will restrain from putting offers forward on properties until they are in a proceedable position, as it's all hypothetical unless they can actually proceed with the purchase.

So, let's take a breath and recap where we're up to with this offer. By now, we should know all elements that we need to present this information to the owner so they can make an informed decision on whether to accept or reject the offer. We should know how much the offer is for, any timescales involved, if they can afford to buy the property should the offer be accepted, and also their chain details. Phew! That's a lot of information.

We are now finally in a position to talk to the homeowner about the offer and the information we gathered alongside this to support it. As we covered already, this should be over the phone as a bare minimum, as we'll be able to gauge the reaction of the owners to the offer more successfully.

Personally, I have always found when putting offers forward, it is better if you can paint a picture of the buyer or tell a story to the owner about who they are and their situation first of all. After all, the owner has no idea who the people offering on the property are, they only know them as 'the viewing from last Tuesday' which isn't exactly endearing. We need to rectify this, so give the homeowner an idea of who they are and what is happening. This conversation could go something like this:

'Mrs Jones, I've got good news for you. I've heard back from the couple that viewed your home last Tuesday and they seem to really like the property. At the moment, they're living in rented accommodation where they have been for the last year, saving for their first home. Because of this, they can be flexible with timescales and are happy to wait for you to find your next property. I've also checked their finances and I can confirm they have a mortgage in place to proceed with. With this information in mind, they are looking to put forward an offer on your home of £240,000, so I wanted to give you a call to see how that sounds to you.'

As you can see, we have outlined not only who the buyers are, but their motivation as well. We've also thrown in a bit of bonus information into the equation by saying that they can be flexible with timescales. As you can imagine, this is very hard to get across well over text message or via letter, hence the call is preferred.

Your next step from this conversation is to just be quiet and listen to what the owner comes back with. Do they sound over the moon with the £240,000 or do they sound like they are about to jump out the window? This will affect how the conversation goes.

Generally, in my experience, when it comes to buyers offering on properties that are for sale, there are three stages that we will go through. The first stage is offer number one, this is usually a figure that the buyer would ideally like to buy the property for. The second stage of offering is an increase from offer number one and is generally the buyer starting to push themselves slightly more and hopefully this is getting closer to where the seller wants the price to be. Finally, we have stage three which is the best and final offer. This is usually the maximum the buyer is prepared to pay for the property, it's take it or leave it time.

This will give you a framework for most offers that you deal with on a daily basis, though this will vary from person to person. Some people will offer their best and final with their first offer, whilst others will inch up bit by bit over many more offers than this.

Let's assume for sake of argument that the owner comes back to us and asks if we can try and get some more money from the potential buyer. We can absolutely do this. Now there are many sales books out there that will spend hours talking through various techniques on leveraging more money from people in conversations just like this. What I'd like to give you, though, is a solid base to start with that will be fairly bullet-proof. I've used the below sentence many times in my career and it just works. It isn't fancy, it isn't clever, but it's a solid choice for any estate agent.

'Mr Taylor, I've spoken to the homeowner and put your initial offer forward in the best possible light. At the moment, though, due the amount of interest they have on the property, they are ideally looking for closer to the asking price. What flexibility do you have on your initial offer?'

Two clever bits from this sentence. One, we have highlighted that this is his initial offer, insinuating that there should be following offers from them. Secondly, we said that we've currently got a good amount of interest in the property he has offered on which directly translates to, 'Increase your offer before someone else does.
A small tip here. As you go backwards and forwards from buyers and sellers, you should not disclose what the homeowner will accept, but you can give guidance to the sort of ballpark you think it will be in. Firstly, take this figure and add a bit to it. If you think the owner will accept £245,000,

say you think they are looking for around £247,000 to £248,000. Two things will potentially happen here, the potential buyer will either try to low-ball this figure and offer £245,000 which we think the owner will accept already, or they will go along with our advice and pay £247,500 for the property. In which case, our owner now loves us because we just made them a few thousand more than they were expecting. A solid win. On the other hand, if you didn't add the extra amount to your prediction, you might end up with an offer below what the owner will accept, or an offer that just scrapes through either way – not great and more hard work for you.

Generally, offers are all about momentum, and where possible I would never try to leave an offer overnight with any party to decide. Instead, try to keep the backwards and forwards as consistent as you can, so that you have a better chance of getting the deal done.

Now, we are going to look at how you would handle this process when you have multiple offers on the same property in a short space of time. A very first-world estate agency problem to have, I think you'll agree. This usually happens when you have a lot of viewings on one property over a short period of time, such as a launch day, which we have spoken about in previous sections.

There are many ways that you could handle this process, but it's important to have a structure in place that is fair to all potential buyers involved, but at the same time, produces the best possible outcome for your client, the seller of the property. We are going to achieve this with a process known as 'best and final offers'. This is where we speak to all parties that have viewed the home and make them aware we have had multiple offers on the property already and if they wish to offer on the property themselves, then they should submit their best and final offer on the home by a certain date and time that we set.

Usually, this time is around 24 hours from the initial calls or offers, to give buyers enough time to get everything in place. We need to make buyers fully aware that this process is called 'best and final offers' for a reason. It means that they need to consider how much they're willing to pay for the property we're selling and put forward the best or highest offer they're willing to proceed with. As you might imagine, this is a confidential process and open conversations about what other parties have offered is a big no-no.

These offers can either be put forward in writing to you, via email for example, or can be from a phone call. No matter how the offers come through, though, we need to ensure we have all the information in place as with a normal lone offer, such as chain details, timescales, funding information and so on.

Once we have all this information collated, we can submit this to the homeowner in exactly the same way we did with the lone offer, telling a small background story for each of the offers we have on the table to go alongside the facts we have established already about the buyer's situation. It's then over to the owner to decide if they want to proceed with any of the offers.

Another tip here, when the owner has decided which offer they want to proceed with, do not call the person who has had the offer accepted first of all to pass on the good news. Instead, reject everyone else who hasn't had their offer accepted. You want to do it this way around to protect yourself, in case any of these rejected offers suddenly decides they would like to increase their offer. Now if they had understood the memo, they wouldn't be doing this. But it still happens, sometimes. Once you have rejected all the offers apart from the acceptable one, give the accepted party a call and pass on the good news. Once you've done this, call your owner back and confirm everyone has agreed to the offered amount.

Once a sale is agreed

We have now agreed an offer on the property we were looking to sell, this is good news! There are a couple of important steps we need to take, here, to not only make sure we are compliant but also to make sure the sale goes through as smoothly as it possibly can.

When confirming the offer has been agreed with the buyer, we should be asking not only to let us know which solicitors' firm they're going to be using for their conveyancing but also the individual solicitor at the company dealing with their case. We will also want to get this information from our sellers, as well, should we not have it already.

Most buyers and sellers should provide this within 24 hours of having an offer accepted. Again, if it's taking longer than this, this should be seen as a red flag against the slow-moving party, which will be worth keeping an eye on. If you haven't got it within a week, then you've got issues on the horizon.

A good way to ensure that you get this information quickly and efficiently is by telling the buyer that you won't be able to consider the property as 'under offer' until they not only provide this information, but also have their solicitor confirm they are acting on their behalf. Nothing shouts commitment like having to put your hands in your pocket and pay out some money.

As we spoke about earlier in this book, the UK government sees you as the first line of defence in the fight against money laundering in the British economy. Because of this, there is another step we need to undertake here. That is to perform customer due diligence on the people that are looking to buy this property. For most buyers, this is as simple as taking a scan of their passport and proof of address which will need to be uploaded to your CRM system. But for other 'higher risk' clients, you may need to undertake further due diligence to ensure they align with the current compliance regulations. There are multiple companies out there who specialise in this, so if in doubt, speak to one of those and they will point you in the right direction to make sure you are taking the correct steps and staying on the right side of the current regulations. Only once you are confident that this has been completed should you change the status of the property to 'sold subject to contract'.

By now, we have solicitor details for both sides of the transaction. The next task is to issue a document which is known as the 'memorandum of sale', also known as the 'memo of sale' or the 'MOS,' if you're feeling super cool.

This document acts as a summary of everything that has been agreed on the sale of the property, such as the price, and timescales, and items included as well. This document will also lay out the details of the buyers of the property and the sellers. Once you have all this information on there, a copy of this letter will go to the buyers, the sellers, and both of their solicitors acting on their behalf.

Most solicitors also request a set of the property's particulars to be included with this letter, so I would do this across the board to save time down the line. As a side note, the memorandum of sale does not negate the offer letter you need to send out to the buyer and seller for the final offer they've had accepted. All parties should receive an offer confirmation letter and a memorandum of sale.

Another aspect you will want to be aware of here, is that most memorandums of sale are created automatically by your CRM system and sometimes can include more information than we want to disclose to either the buyer or the seller. This could include phone numbers, email addresses and so on. It's important to remove these details from your document should they come through automatically, as not only is this potentially a GDPR issue, but also you might end up with a buyer and seller directly talking to each other about the sale of the property.

This may not sound all that bad, and to start with you might be right. But I promise that without you being between them, by the end of the sales progression process, they will have almost certainly fallen out, making everything much harder and more emotional than it needs to be.

Leveraging your sale

First of all, give yourself a pat on the back here. We've gone through quite a journey so far, from generating leads into your business, right the way through to listing a property and now having that property under offer. Phew! This also means that we can tick off one of our properties that we need to get under offer to set us on our way to having an £100,000 estate agency business in front of us.

We spoke in an earlier chapter about how we can leverage a home when it comes up for sale to get some more leads and potentially instructions off the back of it. In this section, we'll look at this all over again, but we now have the awesome marketing message that we have sold a property, too. This is all about getting further marketing touchpoints in the local area to get our phone ringing.

To start off with, let's look at what is probably the most obvious thing to do. That is, if you have a For Sale board on the property, to change it to Sold. If the owner of the property didn't want you to have a board up initially, this is a really good time to ask again, to see if they will allow it now that it's gone under offer.

A great thing to do when you are changing your board is to record a video of you next to the Sold board, saying not only what a great job you've done, but how happy the homeowners are, as well.

Don't forget to add a call to action here which could be something like 'If you'd also like me to sell your home, give me a call and I'll book in a time to come around and see you.' You could also talk about how many viewings or offers you had on the property, should this sound suitably impressive. But please don't go down this route if you only had one viewing in a month and were lucky to get one offer! Once you've prepared this video, add it onto your social media account for all to see.

Next up, we should be looking at getting 20/20 leaflets out in the local area. All the properties that will have received an initial For Sale 20/20 should now be getting the Sold version. As you can see, this is why it is important to get your time-sensitive marketing out as soon as you can. Because if you were a bit late or slow getting the For Sale leaflet out initially, then you may have to wait a few days before the next Sold leaflet goes out. If you have agreed a sale on exactly the right sort of property that you want to deal with in your business, and it's in your core area, the sky's the limit when it comes to Sold leaflet drops here. You could push the boat out and get 5,000 delivered throughout your core area, for example.

With regard to delivering leaflets near the property you have sold, local properties in the area should have already received a For Sale 20/20 leaflet, and then received a Sold 20/20 leaflet. We can build on top of these touchpoints if we have other buyers who missed out on the property we sold but would look to buy in the local area if another came up. For this, we could use the VIP letter template and adjust this slightly to include the fact that we have sold a property locally and now have multiple buyers who missed out due to its popularity. This is another marketing drop in itself and should be deployed no closer than a week to our other leaflets going out.

Next, we can write letters to anyone who used to be on the market but withdrew their property, to see if they would be interested in returning to the market considering our successful sale with one of their neighbours. We know already that one in three of these properties come back to the market within 12 months of withdrawing, so this could be a golden opportunity for our business because we also have buyers lined up, should they decide to come back on again.

This is another really good opportunity to ask your sellers for a review if you haven't got one from them already. They'll be over the moon and slightly relieved that their property has gone under offer, so it's worth striking whilst the iron is hot and asking them to leave you a Google review for your excellent work. Something you can make a big song and dance about on social media, yet again.

Remember that local Facebook group we posted in when we first listed the property for sale? Well, it's now time to post a friendly note in that group again, just informing the locals that the property has now gone under offer and to expect a new neighbour in the near future.

As you can see from these points, we are in no way being shy about the success we have had selling the property. We are getting out as much marketing collateral as we can in the immediate area. We're telling everyone that we've sold a home and if you want to sell your property, too, the choice of agent should be obvious.

If you would like a guide to show you how to best leverage a property once it goes under offer, simply scan the QR code below and download one I've already made for you.

Let's progress this further

I've got some bad news for you, I'm afraid. We are going to go from what many people, including myself, see as one of the best parts of an estate agency – agreeing deals on properties – straight into what is widely regarded as the most frustrating job in an estate agency business. Sales progression.

The reason it's frustrating is because there are many different cogs spinning at any one time, and to add to this, the UK post-sale system is in dire need of a digital transformation and upgrade. Many elements of information that you might expect take moments in today's digital world, instead take weeks and months to receive, due to it being a hugely manual process.

So, let's pick up where we left off. We have just issued the sales memorandum and all solicitors have confirmed they have been instructed to start the legal proceedings. This is a good start!

Now, let's look at each of the stages from here and what we need to be on the lookout for to make sure this process goes as smoothly as it possibly can. First of all, the seller's solicitor will issue something known as the 'draft contract pack' which will go to the buyer's solicitor. This is full of information about the property, such as a title plan, contract of sale, land registry details, fixture and fittings forms, property information forms, and any leasehold documents or any relevant planning documents for the property. We should look for this pack to be issued within the first couple of weeks of the offer being accepted. If it hasn't been issued by the seller's solicitor, this is something we should be chasing up to be sent out. The buyer's solicitor generally won't start doing any work until this comes through!

One of the first things the buyer's solicitor will ask for is 'money on account', which is a very posh solicitor's way of saying 'please send us some money.' They will use this money to pay for a search pack on the property their client is looking to buy. These are only valid for around three months, as over this time something could change, like a local planning application for example. These are also nonrefundable from the buyer's side, meaning that if we are at the stage where the buyer has put their hand into their pocket to fork out around £300 - £400, this is a good sign they are looking to proceed with the purchase. There are three areas of search a solicitor will send out for. They are:

- Water and drainage
- Local authority
- Environmental

Water and drainage will focus on, as you might have guessed, if the property is connected to a water supply and also information on the drainage on the property. This includes whether they are connected to the main drainage, or whether they have something like a septic tank in place.

The local authority search will focus on planning in the local area that couple affect the property down the line, such as a new housing development, for example. This will also include more local planning documents and even the history of the home.

Finally, we'll look at the environmental search, which will focus on the land around the property. For example, if there has been any subsidence in the local area, any kind of contamination and so on. As a person who has brought a property very close to a science park, I can confirm that these also include any nuclear materials in the vicinity, just in case you wanted to know!

Some of the above can take a long time to come back, so the earlier they are ordered the better. The slowest of the above, from personal experience, is the local authority search as this is still done manually.

This also means that some councils are quicker than others, it's just the luck of the draw.

Once the above has all been ordered and received, the buyer's solicitor will now be in a position to do something they call 'raise enquiries', which is solicitor talk for asking questions. This can be on a huge range of topics, from the information they have gathered during the searches, and the paperwork they have received so far. Anything from further information on planning applications on the property, right the way through to clarifying when the boiler was last serviced. By the end of this process, though, the solicitor should be in a position to report back to their client that they're happy with all of the information they've seen so far.

Only when both the seller's and the buyer's solicitors are happy with all of the above will they proceed to the next step, which is something called 'reporting to the client'. This stage involves the solicitor sending all the work they've done so far over to their client, with various bits of paperwork to sign off. Some of these are just the buyer's or seller's signatures, but sometimes these have to be witnessed, as well, to add another level of complication to this process.

Whilst all of this is happening, there are another two aspects of the sales process running in parallel. I did say there were many cogs, after all!

One aspect, for most buyers, is their mortgage application. Similar to the searches, these can take a fairly long time to come back and get set up, so getting this paperwork completed by the buyer as soon as we possibly can is going to pay dividends in the long run. Again, if the client is using your mortgage advisor here, this is where you have a direct line into what's happening and can potentially highlight some delays before they become too significant. Sometimes, mortgage lenders can ask for extra information from your buyer, such as additional pay slips for example, which could cause a delay if this process drags on longer than expected because it wasn't started quick enough.

Another aspect that comes along with a mortgage application is that most mortgage lenders will want to carry out a mortgage survey on the property they're lending on. This involves a surveyor going to visit the property to ensure that the money they're lending is a safe investment. This isn't purely a structural survey; they will also be looking at what the property has been agreed for and how that stacks up against other properties that have sold in the local area. What they're effectively looking for here is if the buyer were to stop paying their mortgage and the bank were to repossess the property, would they get their money back? Or is the buyer overpaying by so much that the bank is leaving themselves exposed in this situation? The other aspect the surveyor is looking for here is any structural issues which might affect the property down the line. After all, the banks don't want to lend out a couple of hundred thousand pounds on a property that is going to crack and fall over shortly. Not a great investment by them.

Alongside the mortgage valuation is a structural survey which some buyers may choose to have on the property they are buying. This isn't essential in most cases and comes down to the buyer's tolerance for risk. I used to work with a lot of developers who would buy run-down and tired properties and they would never worry about a survey, because the first day they bought the property, they would simply knock it down!

For example, a lot of buyers who buy newly built homes won't get a building survey, as they are usually covered by guarantees on the property they're buying from the builder. Whereas if I was buying a 16th century cottage for myself, I almost certainly would be getting a survey carried out before I committed to go any further.

These structural surveys usually fall under two categories, one being a homebuyer's survey and the other being a full structural survey. As the name might give away slightly, the homebuyer's survey is your fairly basic, run-of-the-mill survey on a property which will be ample, most of the time. Whereas the full structural survey will take a far more in-depth look at the property and will cover a far wider range of topics. Buyers of older properties usually gravitate towards this due to the conclusiveness of the report, as it gives them peace of mind in their purchase.

If a buyer finds something is amiss in their structural survey which wasn't immediately obvious, some buyers may come back to you and ask to renegotiate the asking price of the property. They feel they're overpaying for the property considering the amount of additional work needed which they weren't aware of when making their final agreed offer.

There is one key point to make here, whilst we're on the subject of surveys. A down valuation of the agreed price, or questionable structural survey can be the kiss of death on the property you're selling. One of the leading culprits in my experience is the owner of the property. Sometimes the seller doesn't know what to say to a surveyor who is visiting their home, so they just point out any issues they have or even had in the property. Or such golden nuggets as 'we couldn't believe the price it was agreed for, especially after being on the market for such a long time with so little interest.' I'm not joking.

In the same way that all owners should be out on viewing appointments, you should wherever possible ensure that sellers aren't at home for when surveyors visit their home. If they do need to be in the property for any reason, you will need to make them aware to just leave the surveyor alone to do their job. Lots of my clients choose to attend mortgage valuation appointments with surveyors if they are able to. The reason they do this is because they can add positive parts to the conversations that surveyors may not be aware of. For example, if you had lots of viewings on a launch day that prompted a load of offers to come through, make the surveyor aware of this. On the other hand, if you had it on the market for a while with seemingly little interest, then probably skip that chat for the best.

To support your conversation with the surveyor even further, you can even print off and take with you recently sold, local, comparable properties that further support the price of the property you have just agreed. Not only will this save the surveyor time, but also the comparables they have in their hand now are the ones that we have picked and that support our selling price, which can only help.

Only when all of the above has been agreed and all parties are happy to continue can solicitors go ahead and progress to the next and nearly final step of the process. This next stage is called the 'exchanging of contracts' and it's effectively the part of the process where the sale becomes legally binding. Before this can happen, though, the buyers must lodge a deposit with their solicitor which is usually 10% of the purchase price and everyone will have to agree on a completion date for this to happen. This is the date when everyone moves out of their old property and into their new one. Once these final points have all been settled with the solicitors, contracts can be exchanged on the property you're selling, and you can be almost certain that this sale is going to be through.

Well, I did promise you there would be a lot of moving parts in the sales progression process! As you can tell, sales progression can be a hugely complicated and time-consuming element of any estate agency business. It is important for you to understand the sale progression process and even progress a couple of sales yourself through from start to finish so you understand the nuances of this process. In my experience, from the moment a property goes under offer through to when you hand over the keys, this totals around 10-15 hours' worth of work. Which is a huge workload especially if you are a sole operator. It's for this reason that so many estate agents choose to outsource their sales progression, leaving them to focus on the core actions of the business.

If you do choose to do your own sales progression, personally I would just deal with the first few properties you sell so that you understand the overall process before you can quickly outsource.

Most importantly with sales progression, it's all about the set-up. Set a deal up correctly from day one and it will run smoothly, throw it together and you might have a fight on your hands later down the line to keep it all together. This means that everyone has a good understanding of what they're getting into and agreeing to down the line, preventing any big surprises coming out the woodwork.

As soon as we know a sale is agreed, solicitors have been instructed and paperwork has been issued, we need to start to chase. The number one reason for sales proceeding slowly is paperwork being sat on the kitchen counters of sellers and buyers. I have had countless conversations with clients over the years who have called me to ask why their buyer is taking so long. The answer? The owner who is on the phone to me, hasn't completed their paperwork yet and effectively everyone is waiting for them. Imagine my despair (albeit slightly smug), as I inform them of this later on in the day.

This means that you need to be on top of everyone and their paperwork as much as you can. Diary structure and your CRM system are going to really help you here. If a solicitor lets you know they are sending out some paperwork for the buyer to complete today, add a note to your diary to chase the buyer in a couple of days' time to confirm they've received it firstly, and if they have, to complete it as soon as they can. What you'll effectively end up being is everyone's sales progression accountability partner, making sure they have completed their paperwork for that week and sent it back where applicable.

With sales progression, I would always aim for at least one call per week to ensure everything is progressing smoothly and see what's waiting to come back. At the start of the sales progression journey, I'd suggest increasing this as we spoke about earlier. A good start will result in a quicker finish, meaning you get paid sooner. Also, towards the end of the progression timeline, you might find this call number needs to increase as the finer points need to be ironed out before anything else can happen.

Generally speaking, though, after a few weeks of progression and everything has been applied for and wheels have started turning, once a week should be fine for most properties. By this time, lots of the searches have been applied for and it can become a waiting game for these to come through and be addressed by the solicitor dealing with the case.

Personally, I would always chase the buyer's solicitor first to find out what they're waiting for and where the whole purchase is up to. How this conversation went would affect the following calls. If everything was up-to-date and we were just waiting for something out of our control to happen, then this feedback would go back to both the buyer and the seller as a general update.

If, however, the buyer's solicitor was waiting for specific paperwork from the seller's solicitor, my next call would be the seller's solicitor to see if they were in possession of that paperwork already or if they were waiting for the client to complete it. If they hadn't received those documents from their client, that would then form my next call to chase this all up. Once this has been done, I would do an update call with the buyer to inform them of where we're up to with the progression of their purchase.

As you can see, you effectively become the paperwork police, chasing up any gaps or inefficiencies from all parties in the chain. That is 90% of sales progression, I'm afraid.

There is one big golden rule in sales progression and please do not fall into this trap. Never ever (ever) talk about moving dates with a client until you absolutely have to. This means that I would leave this conversation as late as you possibly can in the entire sales progression process. Sometimes it would come out earlier, for example if someone offered a certain price on the condition that they're in by Christmas. Outside of these initial parts of the offer coming in, avoid the conversation for as long as possible.

Let me tell you why. As soon as you mention any date, or even a rough idea of potential dates, your buyers and sellers will catch on to this expectation and will be disappointed and usually frustrated should the property not go through at this time, even if it was just a rough pin on the calendar. Instead, only discuss dates when the property is due to exchange very soon, or you are just waiting on the last few pieces to fall into line. You'll need to have a completion date set up for the solicitors to exchange contracts anyway, so we know we'll need to have one by then, but I'd leave it as close to this as possible. Also, make your life easier, ask your sellers for three to five date options that work for them, then run past the buyers to pick the best one for them. Don't do it one by one, you'll be there forever!

Ensure that throughout the sales progression journey you add ample notes to your CRM system to back up not only what you are doing, but also the next steps, as well. This is especially important should you work within a team or when you are handling sales progression for multiple properties at once, as it can be very easy to confuse what's happening with each property when you have multiple sales going through.

The final straight

Now we are coming to the homestretch of getting the property that we have so lovingly nurtured from a lead into cold, hard money in your bank account. Once the property has exchanged contracts, you can be almost certain that the property is going to complete, so you can now take a breath and relax. Completion is the next part of the sales process where the property stops becoming the legal possession of the seller, instead becoming the legal possession of the buyer.

It's also at this stage of the process where the seller's solicitor will ask to be sent a copy of your invoice. This is because most fees to agents are paid out from the proceeds of the seller selling their property, meaning that a solicitor will need to allot all the monies needed before the completion day comes around. This will also include your share of the deal!

With regard to timing, completion is usually set around for a week after exchange of contracts has taken place, as it takes a certain amount of time for funds to come from the bank or building society lending the money to the buyer.

Although, there are situations where you have what is known as a 'simultaneous exchange and completion' which is exactly what it says on the tin. This is where the property exchanges and completes on the same day, meaning that as soon as the exchange goes through, you're able to release the keys to the new buyer and they can move into their new home. As you might imagine with the short timescale on this set-up, it can prove very stressful for all involved and won't be applicable for a lot of sales and purchases.

On the other side of the spectrum, you have open-ended completions. These are agreements for an open period of time to be announced in the future. These are very common when it comes to dealing with new-build homes when the builder wants to get an exchange of contracts confirming a buyer is going to be purchasing the property, but the property isn't finished yet and therefore cannot be moved into. Then when the property is ready, a completion date will be put forward and this will then be signed off from this point. These are fairly uncommon outside of the new-build world, as you might imagine. No one wants to be left hanging for three months about when they might be able to move.

With most sales though, a week between exchange and completion is the normal length of time you're looking for. Sometimes it may be slightly less, sometimes it's slightly more than this, but around a week is the average you'll come up against in your day-to-day business.

As we mentioned just now, on the day of completion the property becomes the legal ownership of the buyer. However, this is only once the seller's solicitor has confirmed this with you. What you absolutely cannot do here is hand the key out to the buyer on completion day before you have had this confirmation call come through. If you do, you have effectively just handed over a key to someone who doesn't yet own that property. As you might expect, this is frowned upon heavily. Instead, you'll need to wait for a phone call from the seller's solicitor to confirm that the sale has gone through and you're all okay to release the keys to the property to the new buyers. This can come as early as 10 am, though sometimes it can be as late in the day as 3-4 pm, it's just a waiting game up until that point.

When you do finally get the call through, though, the next job from here is to call your sellers and congratulate them on their property selling and going through the process. You will also want to ask them roughly how long they will need before they are clear of their old home with their removal firm. Sometimes the homeowners are already on the road and gone. Other times, they won't have even put a box in a van yet. It does vary! But usually, most people are more or less moving out by this stage.

Once you know how long they're going to remain at the property for, call your buyers and congratulate them on the sale going through, and let them know a rough timescale for the owners moving out of the property –if they're even still there at all. Once you know this information, arrange a time to visit the property that day and meet with the buyers to hand over the keys to their new home.

With most estate agents up and down the high street, this call would have gone slightly differently. They would have asked the buyer of the property to drive to their office so that they can hand over the keys to them, before wishing them the best of luck as they leave the office. Imagine doing all that in a hired van in a city centre! Instead, the better customer service here is to meet your buyers at the property where you can hand over the keys personally. Trust me, they'll love you for it.

How to get more

As we spoke about right at the start of this book, your estate agency business is one big sales funnel, and you are about to remove a unit from the very bottom of that system because the completion has gone through. As you might imagine, having this home come out of the bottom of our sales funnel leaves us in a situation where we need to find as many leads as it took initially to generate that singular completion or else our business is technically shrinking. We did this already when we first put the property onto the market, then we did it all over again when we marketed the property as sold subject to contract. Now we are going to go through this process all over again, giving us yet more marketing touchpoints in the area around the property we have recently completed.

To start, we're going to want to leaflet-drop all the properties we have leafleted twice already, with a final third message – that we have completed on a property in their local area. Similar to the For Sale and Sold 20/20 leaflet that went out, we should start off with delivering around 250-500, depending on how many you have disturbed on previous runs. You could look to increase this into the thousands if it's a property in the right part of your core area and in the right sort of price bracket you're looking to attract.

On the day of completion, when we are at the property handing keys over to the new buyers, we should aim to get at least a photo, or ideally a video to put onto our social media account. This can be anything from you handing over the keys to them, or just getting a selfie with them in the doorway of their new home. Either way, we will want to get a message out on our social media page, shouting about our victory and how happy everyone is in their new home. If you have a solid relationship, you may even ask the buyer if they are happy for you to tag them in your post. This will attract more attention as family and friends will be queuing up online to add their best wishes, all while improving engagement on your social media content.

At this stage, we should also be asking for a review from both the buyer and the old seller if we haven't already. This is one of the happiest moments of buying a home which makes it a good time to strike whilst the iron is hot and ask for a review of the service they received. Again, this will make the foundation of social media content once these reviews come back in.

Finally, you should be making your buyers aware that if you have a For Sale board at the property, that you'll have it collected in the coming days. Legally, you are allowed to have a Sold board outside a property for two weeks after the sale has completed, but in my experience, they're taken down by the new buyers long before this. This is why I'd make the buyers aware that you're taking care of this, otherwise, you'll find your board will disappear, never to be seen again. Well, until bonfire night anyway!

You might think this is where the journey ends for this client. Well, you would be wrong. In the UK, a shockingly low percentage of buyers can't even remember who sold them their current home, let alone use them again in the future. This is why it is important to put processes in place to make sure your past clients come back to your business and become your future clients. To do this, there are lots of details you can add to your business that don't take up much time. There are some really simple things you can do, such as giving out keyrings and other marketing materials that won't be thrown away by the new owners. You will also want to add your new buyers onto a moving in anniversary card list. This is a really simple process which keeps you front of mind with your buyers from year to year. Simply add the date the client moved into their brand-new home, and once a year, send them a card in the mail congratulating them for another year in their lovely home. Super easy to do but goes above and beyond what clients expect. You should also be looking to do exactly the same with Christmas cards, thanking everyone for their support over the last year and wishing them a fantastic new year ahead. As you can see, none of these are particularly complicated or taxing but they take a bit of organisation within your business to make them a reality.

Otherwise, they'll just end up on the list of jobs you know you should do, but don't.

Growing your business

As humans, we always strive for more, it's a blessing and a curse all in one go. I'm yet to meet anyone in the world who's completely at peace and satisfied about where they are in their life and doesn't want more for themselves or their loved ones.

I'm sure you can look back at times in your life where you felt that if you got to a certain level or ticked a certain box, you would feel differently. The reality is that once you tick one box, another one magically appears for you to chase after, and the system repeats itself forever more. In any business, though, I feel it's important to take a step back and acknowledge what you have achieved along the way, if only for a few moments. This will show how far you've travelled since then and the trajectory you're headed towards if you follow the right steps.

With this thought in mind, paramount to understanding what's possible within your business, is to look at what you're doing well and where you can make some strategic adjustments, moving forward. In my personal experience, a lone operating estate agent working for themselves can generally achieve 30 properties under their stewardship at any given time. This may be 15 of those properties for sale, and 15 homes under offer for example, but 30 in total, by using the best sales conversion you can set.

If you have less stock than this at the moment, and you feel like you're hitting the rev limiter in your business, chances are you have some optimisations and time efficiencies to make to give you more time to improve those numbers. On the other hand, if you are well in excess of those figures and provide excellent customer service, then I take my hat off to you. Keep up the amazing work.

Another important point is business aspirations and priorities. We are not all the same. I speak to clients up and down the country most days and the goals I hear day in, day out, vary from monetary amounts to achieve in a year, right through to being able to take a Wednesday off to pick up and drop off their children from school. I appreciate the title of this book is all about earning money, but for others, this might take a back seat to other priorities in their life, and that is absolutely fine. It's your life, after all.

If the figure of 30 units worried you at all, let's now focus on some changes that should help you and your business achieve that number comfortably. As you might imagine, this is all about time management and you focusing on the parts of the business which are crucial to it growing to the levels you want to hit.

In any estate agency business, there are three big cogs in the machine of the day-to-day running of the business as a whole. They are:

- Lead generation
- Listing & selling of properties
- Sales progression

As you can see, these are fairly high-level topics. As we spoke about in earlier chapters, lead generation is simply the part of the process that delivers warm leads into your business for you to then action into future listings. When launching your estate agency business, a lot of what you do will be generating leads manually such as going out leaflet-dropping, door-knocking and so on.

It's important to see where your sales funnel pinch points are in your own business, and for lots of estate agents, it is them and their time. Meaning that as soon as we find we're in a situation where the business is picking up, we need to invest further into the marketing avenues around us which are far less hands-on for ourselves and the day-to-day business. This could include diversifying into more digital marketing or outsourcing your physical marketing to a local provider, for example.

Outside of this, there are other day to day tasks which we can quickly look to outsource, not only to improve our time management but also to improve the quality of our listings that we bring onto the market. Outsourcing professional photography can be a big win for your estate agency. As we mentioned earlier, your portal pages and social media are effectively your business' online shop window in most situations. Therefore, the more attractive these sections can look, the better. There are multiple companies out there that will charge a very reasonable fee for photographing properties. Most also include a floorplan being produced as yet another win for both time saved and production quality. You could consider outsourcing this from day one or you might wait until your business has had a bit more traction. Either way, keep it in mind, it can be a fast way to find extra hours in the week and improve your listings in one go.

Finally, let's take a look at the third point. Sales progression in your business. I'm sure after reading the sales progression chapter of this book, it didn't exactly leave you licking your lips to jump into this aspect of the business. As we covered, it's worth seeing a few instructions through from start to finish so that you understand the processes and the stages that everything goes through. Once you have completed this task, though, I would be looking to outsource this. There are multiple companies out there who will not only carry out your sales progression for you, but as long as you refer to their solicitors for the property you are passing over, they will actually pay you for doing it. Sounds crazy, I know!

After you have outsourced efficiently in your business, you should only really be left with the middle point from the list. Listing and selling properties. This means that your day will be taken up with not only attending market appraisals, but also then carrying out viewings once you have taken them onto the market and negotiating any offers that come forward. Also, as most estate agents will confirm, this is the most fun part of the job as well.

If you have set up all these aspects of your business correctly, then the sky really is the limit.

I don't want to jump the gun and throw my future self under the bus too much here, but my plan for the future is to write another book all about this topic – how you can best expand your business from where it is today to where you want to be in the future. Keep your eyes peeled for that one when it comes out. I just need to get over writing this book, first of all!

Final thoughts

So here we are, at the end of the book. You should by now have a really solid plan for your estate agency business and what is going to make you have a business that you can look back on and be proud you started and produced.

If you are anything like me when I read books, it's more than likely that you have gone through this entire book from start to finish without yet having the chance to implement any of the systems or processes highlighted in the various chapters.

If this is the case, work your way back through this book, chapter by chapter, as you have your next or potentially your first ever property come onto the market. This way, you can make sure as the property moves through your sales pipeline that you get the most bang for your buck from your listing at every turn. If you can, try to be a chapter ahead of the stage the property is currently at. This way, you'll know what is coming next and how you can correctly leverage this stage of the property's journey for the ultimate success. Studies show that if you implement new techniques and processes as you learn them, you're far more likely to retain this knowledge for the long haul. You can then turn this into a habit that can help you for a lifetime.

As a final thought, estate agency is an up and down world where one minute you can feel like you're king or queen of the world, and the next you're recovering from a solid kick in the back. Most days, it's four seasons in one day on the job. So, for you to personally leap into this world with both hands open, ready to take that all on, takes a certain type of person, and my hat comes off to you for that. No matter what, as you go through your personal and business journey, look after yourself as this is the one part of the world that can never be replaced.

As Rocky Balboa once said: *'I didn't hear no bell.'*

Printed in Great Britain
by Amazon

50007261R00169